KT-416-648

Step-by-Step
Vegetable Cookbook

AUTHORS AND PHOTOGRAPHERS

AN INTRODUCTION TO VEGETABLES

– Friedrich W. Ehlert –
– Odette Teubner, Kerstin Mosny –

HEARTY HOME COOKING

– Rotraud Degner –
– Pete Eising –

DISHES FROM AROUND THE WORLD

– Rotraud Degner –
– Ulrich Kerth –

COOKING FOR SPECIAL OCCASIONS

– Marianne Kaltenbach –
– Rolf Feuz –

WHOLEFOOD RECIPES

– Doris Katharina Hessler –
– Ansgar Pudenz –

QUICK-AND-EASY RECIPES

– Cornelia Adam –
– Michael Brauner –

MICROWAVE RECIPES

– Monika Kellermann –
– Odette Teubner, Kerstin Mosny –

LEAN CUISINE

– Monika Kellermann –
– Anschlag & Goldmann –

Translated by UPS Translations, London
Edition edited by Josephine Bacon and Ros Cocks

4215
Published originally under the title "Das Neue Menu: Gemüse" by Mosaik
Verlag GmbH, Munich
© Mosaik Verlag, Munich
Project co-ordinator: Peter Schmoeckel
Editors: Ulla Jacobs, Cornelia Klaeger, Heidrun Schaaf, Dr Renate Zeltner
Layout: Peter Pleischl, Paul Wollweber

This edition published in 1997 by Colour Library Direct
English translation copyright © 1995 by CLB International, Godalming, Surrey
Typeset by Image Setting, Brighton, E. Sussex
Printed and bound in Singapore
All rights reserved
ISBN 1-85833-497-7

Step-by-Step
Vegetable Cookbook

Colour Library

Contents

INTRODUCTION TO VEGETABLES

HEARTY HOME COOKING

DISHES FROM AROUND THE WORLD

COOKING FOR SPECIAL OCCASIONS

An Introduction to Vegetables

*W*hether as a side dish, a main course or an ingredient in soups and stews, vegetables enhance the taste, appearance and nutritional value of any meal. Although the roots, stems, leaves and fruit of plants – which is precisely what vegetables are – used to be boiled to a soft pulp, we now know that the best way to cook vegetables is exactly the opposite. Vegetables that have been conservatively cooked – simmered in a minimum of water – so that they are still firm and crunchy, retain more vitamins and minerals, as well as tasting much better than vegetables which have been boiled until mushy. There are innumerable types of vegetable and just as many ways of preparing them – many of which are presented in this book.

VEGETABLES

Vegetables are low in calories, as well as being rich in valuable substances. All vegetables contain vitamins A (carotin), C and B2, minerals such as potassium, magnesium, calcium, iron and phosphorous, and roughage.

However, the amount and combination of minerals and vitamins varies from one vegetable to another, and they vary according to the amount of light, heat and oxygen to which it has been exposed. Vegetables lying in a bowl, exposed to the light and at room temperature gradually lose their nutritional value. For this reason, vegetables should always be kept cool and in the dark.

TYPES OF VEGETABLE

The almost unimaginable variety of vegetables can be divided into root vegetables, tuberous vegetables, fruit vegetables, leaf vegetables, shoot and stalk vegetables, bulb vegetables and pulses. Root and tuberous vegetables include potatoes, carrots, radishes, turnips and swedes. Courgettes, aubergines, tomatoes and peppers represent fruit vegetables, while all types of green salad and kale, spinach and spinach beet are examples of leaf vegetables. Asparagus, celery, kohlrabi and fennel, as well as other types of vegetables, belong to the group of shoot and stalk vegetables. All types of onion and garlic are combined in the group of bulbous vegetables. Finally, beans, peas and lentils are pulses. Mushrooms belong to a separate group of plants and are not technically vegetables because fungi, of which mushrooms are a species, are cryptogams or non-flowering plants.

The classification of vegetables according to the time of year when they are harvested is handy when buying vegetables. Spring vegetables are the first vegetables marketed in that year, for example spring onions, early carrots, turnips, asparagus and spinach. Artichokes, various fruit vegetables, beans, peas and spinach beet are harvested in summer and are therefore known as summer vegetables. Cauliflower and turnips are typical autumn vegetables. In winter, the vegetables available include kale, chicory, celeriac, Brussels sprouts, beetroot, carrots, leeks and scorzonera – these are known as winter vegetables. However, now that vegetables are marketed world wide, most are available all year round.

A – Z OF VEGETABLES

The following pages provide information such as the nutritional value of artichokes and many other vegetables, what to remember when preparing individual types of vegetable, plus other useful facts. The vegetables are arranged in alphabetical order. However, it is impossible to cover fully the enormous range of vegetables available, since about 40 to 50 types of vegetable are currently available in more than 1000 varieties. This huge range is constantly on the increase, both as regards what is commercially available and varieties that are home-grown.

Artichokes (globe artichokes) are a type of thistle. The green, still unripe flowering head is harvested as a vegetable and has long been an expensive delicacy. In France artichokes were originally seen as suitable vegetables for rich French noblemen.

Artichokes contain vitamins A and B and are rich in calcium and iron. They are very easy to digest and also stimulate the digestive system and the liver and gall bladder functions.

Two types of globe artichoke are generally available: large, round, green artichokes with a fleshy base, which are cultivated in Brittany; and small, purple ones with pointed leaves, from Italy and Spain.

Usually only the base and the fleshy part of the leaves are eaten. This is just 20% of the flower head! However, the tender, fresh stalks, when peeled and boiled, make excellent vegetables and are good in salads.

Artichokes should not be cooked in aluminium or iron saucepans, since they will colour them greyish-black.

Storage: about 3 days in the vegetable compartment of the refrigerator.

Asparagus is in season from mid-April to late June.

Green asparagus is favoured in Britain, but white (blanched) asparagus has long been known as the king of vegetables in central Europe, especially Germany and Austria. Large asparagus spears are expensive, but the thinner grades, especially the almost grass-like one known as sprue, are cheaper.

Asparagus is extremely low in calories (17 kcal per 100g) and contains protein, roughage, and various vitamins and minerals. Its characteristic flavour is derived from volatile oils, vanillin and other chemical compounds. Green asparagus takes its colour from the green pigment chlorophyll, and has a higher vitamin content than white asparagus. In contrast to white asparagus, it should not be peeled, though the lower ends may need scraping.

In addition to green and white asparagus, stronger-flavoured asparagus types with yellow or purple tips from France or the Mediterranean countries are also available. Good-quality fresh asparagus has straight stems of equal diameter. If the cut surfaces are scratched they should produce juice.

Storage: 2-3 days wrapped in a damp cloth in the vegetable compartment of the refrigerator. But whenever possible asparagus should be used fresh.

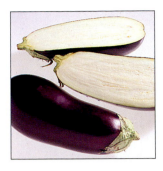

Aubergines, or egg plants, belong to the same family as tomatoes, peppers and potatoes. Originally they were white or yellow and about the size of a hen's egg, hence egg plant.

Now the elongated purple type is predominant. The flesh of aubergines contains calcium, iron and vitamins B and C. Aubergines stimulate the liver and gall bladder functions and have a favourable effect on rheumatism.

The flavour of these vegetables is only brought out by boiling, roasting or grilling. Eaten raw, they can cause diarrhoea, vomiting and stomach pains.

There is no need to peel them, especially as the dark colour of the skin is part of their attraction. Aubergine recipes often include instructions for 'degorging' them to remove bitterness, but this is not normally necessary nowadays as they should be nice and fresh when bought. However, if you are particularly sensitive to bitter flavours simply sprinkle the cut surfaces with salt and leave to drain for about 30 minutes. Salting draws the bitterness out of the fruit, but also the water-soluble vitamins and minerals.

Storage: about 5-6 days in the vegetable compartment of the refrigerator.

Broccoli is a member of the cabbage family and is an ancestor of cauliflower. The young flower heads are eaten while still in bud and, in contrast to cauliflower, some of the stalks as well. The delicate cabbage flavour is reminiscent of green asparagus. Compared with other types of cabbage broccoli is easy to digest and therefore suitable as a light food. It contains primarily vitamins A and C, and calcium.

In addition to green broccoli, there are also red, blue and purple types. Calabrese is a variety with extra-large tender greeny-blue heads, available in summer; sprouting broccoli is a winter vegetable producing lots of small spears. If broccoli is blanched before the actual cooking process, the taste is enhanced and the colour retained.

Broccoli should always be prepared fresh. Signs of freshness are a bright colour and tightly closed flowers.

Storage: about 2 days in the vegetable compartment of the refrigerator.

Brussels sprouts are one of the finest representatives of the cabbage family. They are typical winter vegetables, which were first grown more than 100 years ago near Brussels. If Brussels sprouts are to flourish, the autumn must be warm and the winter mild. Sprouts are rich in the minerals potassium, magnesium, iron and phosphorous, as well as vitamins B and C. Frost increases the sugar content of sprouts, which refines the flavour and makes them easier to digest, since the cellulose tissue (cell structure) is loosened.

Good-quality sprouts should be bright green and firm, with no discoloured outer leaves. Avoid small, pale ones: these are stale larger ones which have been trimmed by the greengrocer to make them look saleable.

The individual sprouts cook to a firm consistency in 15 minutes or less, according to their size. Cutting a cross in the base of the stalk is often recommended, but is not necessary unless some are larger than others, to ensure that they all cook at the same rate.

Storage: firmly closed sprouts, 2-3 days in the vegetable compartment of the refrigerator.

Cabbage, whether plain green, savoy or white, is always available and, like red cabbage, is a type of head cabbage.

Cabbage is a valuable foodstuff. In olden times, sailors protected themselves from scurvy, a disease caused by a lack of vitamin C, by eating pickled cabbage (sauerkraut) in addition to the more well-known ration of lime or lemon juice.

Cabbage is still a healthy component of our diets since it is rich in vitamins B1, B2 and C, and in important minerals (iron, magnesium, sodium and phosphorous).

Cabbage is difficult to digest, but can be made more digestible by blanching in hot salted water or by seasoning with caraway seeds. Cabbage heads should be firmly closed.

Spring greens or spring cabbage is a type of cabbage with a conical head. The large green leaves form a loose cone. It has a more delicate structure and flavour than other types, as well as a shorter storage life. Spring greens are small heads of a leafy green cabbage with no heart.

Storage: up to a fortnight in the vegetable compartment of the refrigerator. Always cover cut surfaces with cling film. Spring cabbage – a maximum of 2 days.

PULSES, FRESH AND DRIED

The mature seeds of members of the pea and bean family – pulses – are one of the oldest foodstuffs known. This group includes beans, peas, lentils and soya beans. Pulses contain plenty of roughage, biologically valuable protein, carbohydrates, minerals and B-vitamins. Combined with cereals (as in beans on toast) pulses provide a valuable replacement for meat in our diet.

Fresh peas and beans make the tastiest side dishes, after only a few minutes' cooking.

Beans come in a wide range of colours and sizes, particularly dried, but quite a few are also available canned. Popular ones include reddish flecked borlotti beans (12, 7), red kidney beans (15), reddish-black scarlet runner beans (13), olive green mung beans (17) and reddish-brown aduki beans (14). Both the latter types are suitable for germinating and eating as sprouts. In addition there are black beans, haricot beans, black-eyed beans (also known as black-eyed peas), the delicate pale green flageolets and the most valuable bean of all – the soya bean (16).

Most dried beans and peas require soaking to soften them and reduce the cooking time. Broadly speaking, the larger the bean the longer the soaking time; the exceptions are chick peas and soya beans, which are extremely tough. Lentils do not need soaking. Overnight soaking is often convenient for large or tough beans, but for smaller ones a few hours will suffice, especially if you use boiling water.

Boil the beans in fresh water, quite vigorously at first, then more gently. Do not add salt as this toughens the skins. Cook for as long as needed to make them really tender. Undercooked or improperly cooked beans cause digestive problems and some (red and black kidney beans) can be harmful.

French beans (8) are among the most widely used. Young, tender beans are suitable for use in salads, while the medium-sized ones are used as a vegetable.

Runner beans (6) are climbing plants grown up poles or strings, and so also known as pole beans or string beans. They are usually flat-podded, with quite rough skins, but can also be round-podded. When young they are tender, with good flavour and texture, and can be treated like French beans. But they are commonly sold far too big, when they are coarse and stringy. Such beans must be de-stringed and finely sliced to be edible. Runner beans are mainly used as a vegetable and in soups.

Wax beans (9) or yellow beans are the yellow variety of the French bean. They are very tender and best suited for salads.

Dwarf French beans (10) are very tender, early beans, with a delicate flavour and fine texture. They are divided into three grades – extra, very fine and fine.

Broad beans are not really beans, but are eaten as such; they are also known as fava beans. When dried, the beans are light to dark brown (11).

Unless they are very young, beans should not be eaten raw. In this state, they contain the poisonous substance phasin, which can lead to inflammation and stomach complaints. During cooking this heat-sensitive substance is destroyed. So cooking them requires careful timing to ensure that they are tender but still crisp.

Fresh beans are juicy and evenly green or yellow in colour. They make a sharp cracking sound when broken in the fingers, which is why they are also known as snap beans.

Storage: about 3 days in the vegetable compartment of the refrigerator, in a plastic bag.

Peas are not only delicious in stews and soups, but can also be made into tasty purées. Yellow (3) and green peas (4, 5) and chick peas (2) are the best-known types. Dried peas can be obtained either whole or split. Discoveries in various parts of the world indicate that people ate peas as early as 7000 BC. Until well into the Middle Ages only peas from mature pods were eaten; they were a basic foodstuff as well as a medicine. Then Italian cooks discovered that peas can also be cooked and eaten when green and unripe. Fresh peas in the pod are unfortunately not frequently found in shops, since most are processed for canning or freezing.

Peas are classified according to type and pea size:

Wrinkled peas are sweet and tender, contain mainly carbohydrate as sugar and are almost square.

Round-seeded peas are also known as garden or shelled peas, and are rounded and smooth, with a high starch content, giving them a floury taste.

Mange-tout peas, snow peas or sugar snaps (1) are a special variety of pea, eaten whole when the seeds inside have scarcely developed and the pod is paper-thin and extremely tender. Mange-tout have almost completely flat pods, while the sugar snaps are more rounded. They are increasingly popular, and are very quick to cook.

Peas in the pod. The peas inside are not tough, and although time-consuming to prepare, are well worth the effort, for the flavour of truly fresh peas is unsurpassed. They can be eaten hot or cold.

The high protein, carbohydrate, vitamin and mineral content of peas makes them a nutritious food. Small, fresh, crisp peas are always the best. The same applies to mange-tout peas. Dried peas, by contrast, should be large.

Storage: 1-2 days in the vegetable compartment of the refrigerator. The boiling time should be doubled after one day's storage!

Lentils have been grown in Asia for millennia and today are grown mainly in India and Turkey. The greenish-brown or Puy lentils (20), black (18) and orange or Egyptian lentils (19) are only available dried, either whole or split. As with all pulses, the cross-section determines the price. The smaller and therefore better-value types are of course the most tasty. Red or Egyptian lentils have the best flavour of all, and these are usually sold split. They do not take as long to cook as brown lentils.

Soya beans (16) are extremely high in protein and have far and away the highest fat content of all pulses – 100 grams of soya beans contain 18 grams of fat. The whole beans are always eaten dried; they have little flavour and take a long time to cook. However, they can be used in many other ways, and as a result of their versatility the area cultivated for soya beans is increasing all over the world. Soya beans are used to make soya oil, lecithin, soya meal and soya flour, protein concentrate, soya milk, tofu (bean curd) and soy sauce.

Carrots come in two types – short, rounded ones and long, pointed ones. Carrots are an extremely old variety of vegetable, which have been eaten for a good 5000 to 6000 years in central Europe.

They are one of the most popular and frequently used vegetables and contain the most carotin (provitamin A) of all. Carotin is only absorbed by the body in combination with fat. Minerals, vitamins C and E, few calories and easy digestibility make carrots a much-loved ingredient in our diet. They have a sweetish, nutty flavour, as a result of their high fructose content. Young carrots do not require peeling, only scraping or scrubbing, as preferred.

Early carrots are smaller varieties which have not overwintered. They are about the length and thickness of a finger and are usually sold in bunches with the leaves. They have a sweet, delicate flavour.

Summer carrots are sold from about June to September. They are larger than early carrots.

Late carrots are suitable for storing. They are available from November to March.

Storage: about 3-4 weeks, ventilated and kept cool in a dark place or in the vegetable compartment of the refrigerator.

Cauliflower is one of the few types of vegetable from which the flower head or inflorescence is eaten. It has a delicately pronounced cabbage flavour which is easily lost through over-cooking, and is best steamed or boiled whole rather than cut into florets.

Its delicate cell structure and relatively high vitamin C and calcium contents endow the cauliflower with its nutritional value. The Romans and Greeks prized cauliflower, not only for its taste. Various healing powers were also attributed to it.

Cauliflower is available in various types. In addition to the well-known white cauliflower, there are also green (romanesco) and purple types. Firm, closed heads are the mark of freshness of this vegetable.

Storage: 3-5 days in the vegetable compartment of the refrigerator.

Celeriac looks like a large, misshapen turnip root but tastes strongly of celery. It is actually a swollen stem that grows above ground. Although not as popular in Britain as it is in central Europe it can be found during the winter months. It is used in a similar way to celery, makes a flavoursome addition to soups and stews, and can also be eaten raw in salads. To prepare celeriac, which is often very knobbly, cut it into thick slices, then peel each slice. Stack the slices and cut them into strips, then into dice. Using plenty of celeriac means using less salt. If lemon juice is added to the water it remains white when boiled.

Storage: about 8 days in the vegetable compartment of the refrigerator.

Celery is available all year round in two basic varieties, white and green. The fleshy stalks are rich in Vitamin C and also contain an extremely large amount of potassium. Fresh celery has crisp stalks and green leaves. Because of its crunchiness celery is very good raw, especially with cheese; when cooked the flavour intensifies and it is eaten as a vegetable or added to stews and soups.

Storage: 1-2 weeks in the vegetable compartment of the refrigerator, kept in its plastic sleeve.

Chard (also known as Swiss Chard or Silverbeet) is an unusual vegetable, a member of the beet family, grown mainly for the large thick stems or ribs, ending in rather coarse green leaves. The common variety has creamy white stems, but there is also one with red stems, known as ruby or rhubarb chard.

Chard is rich in protein and is made up of a combination of substances similar to those of spinach. It contains primarily the minerals phosphorous, potassium, calcium, magnesium, iron, iodine and vitamins B1, B2 and C. Chard is recognised as a medicinal plant as a result of its laxative properties and its sedative effects. The stems and leaves are cooked separately. The chopped or cut stems are steamed, braised or boiled, and best served on their own as they have a delicate flavour reminiscent of asparagus. The leaves are cooked in the same way as spinach.

Storage: in the vegetable compartment of the refrigerator. In a plastic bag, the leaves keep for 2-3 days. Wrapped in damp paper, the stems keep for about 8 days.

Chicory is a close relative of witloof chicory, or Belgian endive. It was discovered accidentally at the end of the 19th century by Belgian farmers, who found that when grown in the dark it develops strong, pale shoots – chicory. Today, Belgium is still the main source of chicory, and Brussels witloof is synonymous with quality. Chicory is grown underground or under black polythene so that it stays tender and pale.

Chicory has a bittersweet flavour which not everyone appreciates, but it is rich in vitamins and minerals. In addition, it is considered good for diabetics and people suffering from rheumatism. Radicchio is the Italian name given to the red variety of chicory.

When buying chicory make sure that it is tightly closed and pale.

Storage: about 4-5 days in the vegetable compartment of the refrigerator, wrapped in damp paper. If kept out too long the leaves turn light green and the bitter taste becomes stronger.

Corn on the cob is not a vegetable, but a cereal grain (maize), which originally comes from America and was introduced to Europe by Christopher Columbus. The tender, pale golden niblets of sweetcorn are used as a vegetable. Corn contains valuable protein, little fat and a lot of carbohydrate, in the form of starch. In addition, it also contains vitamins from the B group (particularly niacin) and potassium.

Sweetcorn is the term used to refer to corn off the cob, almost always canned or frozen. It is one of America's favourite vegetables and is also increasing in popularity in Europe.

Corn cobs are harvested when unripe, as soon as the niblets have developed and are juicy. The cob is broken from the stem during harvesting and sold in its leafy shell. Look for cobs with pale gold niblets – if they are dark, the corn was too old when picked and will be tough. Baby sweetcorn, harvested when immature, is a popular ingredient in Oriental cooking, but has little flavour.

Corn cobs should be boiled for 5-8 minutes in slightly sweetened water, without salt, which stops them from hardening.

Storage: fresh corn keeps for a few days in the vegetable compartment of the refrigerator.

Courgettes or zucchini belong to the gourd or squash family and are a type of baby marrow. They come originally from America where they have been grown for over 6000 years. Courgettes, together with avocados and chillies, are among the oldest cultivated plants.

'Zucchino' is the diminutive form of the Italian word 'zucca', meaning gourd. Courgettes are harvested when unripe and only 15-20 cm (6-8 in) long; at this stage they have no seeds in the centre. They are usually dark green but there are also types which are flecked or striped white, entirely white, yellow and golden. Young, tender courgettes do not have to be peeled, but some people find the skin of larger ones slightly bitter. They are boiled or fried in vegetable dishes, and can also be added raw to salads. Even the yellow courgette flowers are enjoying increasing popularity in our kitchens.

Like all gourd vegetables, courgettes contain a great deal of water, are low in calories, rich in vitamins and easy to digest.

Storage: 3-4 days in the vegetable compartment of the refrigerator or other cool place.

Cucumber is one of the oldest cultivated plants. It is said to have been grown in India in 4000 BC. In the Middle Ages it became known in southern, central and northern Europe.

Long, thin salad cucumbers and fatter, cylindrical ridge cucumbers are suitable in salads and as a vegetable. After sorting according to size, immature, smaller pickling cucumbers are industrially processed into fine-quality gherkins and pickled gherkins. The smallest are known as cornichons. Both outdoor and greenhouse cucumbers are available on the market. Outdoor cucumbers have a stronger flavour. Cucumbers are extremely low in calories as they consist almost entirely of water, and are rich in vitamins and minerals. Look for cucumbers that are firm, especially at the stalk end. Do not peel unless it is essential to the recipe, as most of the food value lies in the skin.

Storage: 6-7 days in the vegetable compartment of the refrigerator.

Fennel should really be called bulb fennel, to distinguish it from the green leafy tops. While fennel bulbs have been valued for a long time in southern Europe, particularly in Italy, both as a vegetable and in salads, they have been slow to catch on over here. They have a distinct taste of aniseed and go particularly well with fish.

There are two types of bulb fennel – Florence fennel, which has a narrow, elongated bulb and a delicate flavour, and Italian fennel, which has a firm, thick bulb and a more pronounced flavour. Fennel contains essential oils which are responsible for its typical flavour, as well as minerals and vitamins C and E. Once sliced, fennel should be sprinkled immediately with lemon juice to maintain its whiteness. It can be eaten raw or cooked and goes well with tomatoes, courgettes and aubergines.

Storage: at least 14 days in the vegetable compartment of the refrigerator.

Kale is a member of the cabbage family with loose curly green leaves, which was enjoyed as a vegetable in the winter months even before Roman times. It actually comes from the countries around the Mediterranean Sea. Kale is very hardy and only develops its full flavour after the first frosts. For this reason freezing actually improves the quality of this vegetable, both in terms of taste and nutritional value. Frost breaks down its starch content into sugar, which makes it easier to digest. It contains a great deal of calcium, vitamin A (carotin) and vitamin C. A kilogram of freshly cut kale contains one gram of vitamin C – a vitamin content surpassed only by Brussels sprouts. Kale matches spinach in terms of its mineral content. Fresh kale can be recognised by its stiff green leaves.

Kale can be made into an especially hearty dish if braised together with loin of pork, pork sausage and smoked bacon.

Storage: 2-3 days in the vegetable compartment of the refrigerator.

Kohlrabi is probably descended from the cabbage eaten in Pompeii by the Romans and was first grown in Europe as early as the 16th century. It is a member of the cabbage family, and is sometimes called turnip-cabbage but differs from other types in that the round root is eaten and the leaves are usually cut away. Kohlrabi comes in various shapes and colours: rounded or flattened, from almost white, through greenish-white to purple. The colour reveals the origin of the kohlrabi. The white variety is usually grown in greenhouses, while the red is grown outdoors. Both varieties have white flesh. Greenhouse kohlrabi has a more delicate structure and taste, while outdoor kohlrabi has a stronger flavour.

Kohlrabi is rich in vitamin C and minerals such as calcium, potassium, phosphorous, magnesium, iron and sodium. Young kohlrabi are particularly suitable for vegetable dishes and salads. The leaves, if present, contain a great deal of carotin (provitamin A) and should be used chopped in vegetable dishes or salads.

Storage: 2 days if kept cool and moist. Kohlrabi becomes woody if stored longer than this.

Leeks form part of the extensive onion family and are used as vegetables, for flavouring and in soups and salads. They are extremely rich in valuable substances, particularly iron, carotin (provitamin A) and vitamins B1, B2, C and E, and contain the appetite-stimulating sulphurous leek oil, which is responsible for the typical leek smell.

Leeks can be divided into three groups:

Early leeks are tender and mild, with pale green foliage and a white stalk. They are highly suitable for use as vegetables, in soups and as a flavouring. They are also suitable for eating raw with mixed raw vegetables and in salads.

Summer leeks have thin skins and a long white, fairly strong stalk, with green foliage. They are delicious eaten as a cooked vegetable.

Winter leeks have green/blue foliage and a strong, short stalk. The foliage has a strong flavour, while the stalk is mild and delicate. In winter, blanched leeks are also available. Their white colour is caused by the lack of light. The soil is heaped up around the stalks, which also makes them hard.

Storage: 10-12 days in the vegetable compartment of the refrigerator.

Onions are indispensable in cooking, both as a flavouring and a vegetable. In addition to vitamins A and C, they also contain minerals such as potassium and magnesium, and they have an antibacterial effect.

The following types of onion are sold:

The brown onion, which has the strongest flavour, is the most common; the colour of the flesh ranges from white to yellow.

The Spanish onion is the largest and mildest. Its flesh is juicy and is suitable for eating raw in salads or with bread and cheese, roasting, baking, stuffing and boiling.

The spring onion is a miniature variety picked when the bulbs are barely developed. It is eaten raw in salads and is an important component of Chinese cooking. The green tops are a good substitute for chives.

The red or salad onion has a spicy but mild flavour compared with the common brown onion. It is good in salads, and can be used in cooked dishes.

Shallots, the smallest and finest representatives of the onion family, are very popular in French cuisine. They have a very delicate flavour and are used in classic sauces, regional dishes and salads.
Storage: several weeks if kept cool and dry.

Peas: see Pulses

Peppers should actually be referred to as sweet peppers, bell peppers or capsicums to distinguish them from their much hotter relative the chilli pepper. The most commonly available are bell shaped and green, red, yellow or black. In addition to carbohydrate and protein, they contain important minerals and vitamins, including ten times more vitamin C than lemons. The white cores and membranes contain capsaicin, which gives peppers their spicy flavour.

Hot peppers or chillies are also members of the capsicum family, but are much smaller and slimmer. They originate in Mexico, where endless different varieties are used, with varying degrees of hotness. Green chillies are generally hotter than red (ripe) ones. They are used whenever a hot taste is required in a dish, notably in chilli con carne, and to make cayenne pepper and paprika. When preparing chillies, wash hands and equipment thoroughly afterwards, and be very careful not to get the juice in your eyes via your fingers; it stings. If fresh chillies are not available dried ones are a good substitute.
Storage: 3-5 days in the vegetable compartment of the refrigerator.

Red cabbage is a type of head cabbage and has been enjoyed as a vegetable since the 8th century. It differs from other head cabbages in that it has a higher vitamin C content. In addition, it is easier to digest, contains more roughage and is – naturally – red. Its reddish blue leaves turn a deeper red with the addition of acid, which is why most recipes for cooking it include a little vinegar, wine, lemon juice or cooking apple. It associates especially well with pork and game. Red cabbage should never be boiled in an aluminium saucepan, because the red dye reacts with aluminium and loses its strength and the cabbage turns a blueish colour. Red cabbage is available almost all year round, as early cabbage, semi-early cabbage and autumn cabbage.
Storage: up to 14 days in the vegetable compartment of the refrigerator. Always cover a cut cabbage with foil.

Savoy cabbage is another major type of cabbage, in addition to the green and red varieties. It comes from the northern Mediterranean area and was cooked as long ago as the Middle Ages.

Savoy cabbage is not as tightly closed as red and green cabbage types. Its leaves are wrinkled and curly. It comes in many types and colours, from dark green to yellow. The dark green early Savoy cabbage is the most valued variety. In addition to the early variety, Savoy cabbage is also available in autumn and winter varieties. Savoy cabbage keeps the least well of all cabbage types. It is cooked in the same way as the other types and goes well with game and lamb.

Dark green Savoy cabbage contains more valuable nutrients than white cabbage and is also easier to digest.
Storage: about 14 days in the vegetable compartment of the refrigerator.

Scorzonera (black salsify or oyster plant) is relatively uncommon in Britain, although very popular in Europe. It is a winter root vegetable which has been cultivated since the 17th century. Its wild form, which is native in southern Europe, had already been in use as a medicinal plant for a long time. Scorzonera is highly nutritious, mainly as a result of its carbohydrate, mineral (potassium, calcium, phosphorous and iron) and vitamin contents. Its inulin content is particularly noteworthy. This is a carbohydrate made from fructose which is suitable for diabetics. When peeled, scorzonera produces a milky juice that darkens the skin, so wear gloves. It also discolours rapidly after peeling, but this can be prevented by immediately putting each root into water with a little vinegar added. When buying scorzonera make sure the surface is smooth and the flesh pale and juicy.
Storage: 14 days in the vegetable compartment of the refrigerator, wrapped in paper.

Spinach is notable for its relatively high iron content in comparison with other vegetables. Many vegetable types contain between 1 and 3 milligrams of iron per 100 grams, but spinach contains over 4 milligrams per 100 grams.
By contrast, it should be noted that spinach is high in nitrates, which are further increased by the use of chemical fertilisers. Oxygen (air) and heat convert nitrates into poisonous nitrites, which are particularly harmful to children. For this reason, spinach should only be used fresh (without being stored) and should not be reheated. The nitrate level can also be reduced by thorough washing. Cook while still wet without adding any extra water; cover the pan and shake it from time to time. Spinach cooks down tremendously, so buy at least 250g/8oz per person. Fresh spinach should be crisp and dark green.
Spinach beet looks very similar to spinach and is often sold as such, but it is actually a completely different plant, related to beetroot but grown for the leaves rather than the root. The leaves are larger and the stems coarser; remove these when washing. Otherwise treat exactly like spinach.
Storage: not recommended.

Tomatoes were first grown in Italy and in the south-eastern Mediterranean area. Tomatoes are rich in minerals and vitamins, especially vitamin C. Round tomatoes account for the largest market share. They are suitable for both cooking and salads Their sweet-and-sour flavour can be enhanced by adding a pinch of sugar. Green parts, which should always be removed before eating, indicate the presence of the toxic substance solanine.
Beefsteak tomatoes are large, with a very fruity flavour and a high proportion of meaty flesh. They are best enjoyed raw but can also be used in hot dishes.
Plum tomatoes are named for their shape, and are the ones peeled and canned in great quantities. They have an excellent flavour but this only develops with cooking, so they are not at their best in salads, although very firm and with a deep red colour. The canned ones are excellent for use in made-up dishes.
Cherry tomatoes are a relative novelty. These mini-tomatoes have a fruity flavour and are ideal for garnishing and salads.
Storage: several days at room temperature, longer in the refrigerator.

Turnips come in various shapes and sizes and used to be extremely widespread, but have now been displaced by the potato. During periods of crisis and in wartime they have always experienced an upswing in consumption. Most turnips do not contain any substance of note, but all types are low in calories.
Baby or white turnips are the first of the year, with a white skin, white flesh and a sweetish flavour. They taste best when they are about the size of a hen's egg, and do not need peeling.
Navets or french turnips are a small variety, rather flattened, with pale purple and white skins which should be left on. The flavour is delicate, rather like that of kohlrabi.
Late turnips are larger than baby turnips, with white flesh and a sharp flavour. They are good with lamb and pork.
Swedes or rutabaga are larger than turnips, greenish-yellow or purplish-yellow on the outside, and with pale orange flesh on the inside. They are a good winter vegetable, suitable for use in stews and soups. They are also delicious cooked and mashed with plenty of butter and pepper. In northern parts of Britain they are known as turnips or neeps.
Storage: about 1 week in the vegetable compartment of the refrigerator.

POTATOES

Potatoes are one of our major basic foodstuffs. They originated in the central highlands and coastal area of the Andes. In the 16th century, sailors brought this nondescript tuber to Europe, via a circuitous route. Today, nutritious and vitamin-rich potatoes are indispensable in our cuisine. The starchy tubers contain a relatively large amount of calcium, iron, potassium, sodium and phosphorous, vitamins A, B1, B2 and C. Green potatoes contain the toxin solanine and for this reason should not be eaten.

The range of possibilities for using potatoes is enormous. Whether boiled or steamed, roasted or baked, fried or chipped, made into gratins, soups or stews, they always taste good!

TYPES

There are currently between 100 and 120 types of potato, only a few of which are marketed. They are subdivided as follows:
Earlies: available May-July. Usually sold as new potatoes for immediate use.
Second earlies: available August-March. Can be stored for a short time.
Maincrop: available from September-May. Suitable for storing in a frost-free dark place.

TEXTURE

Potatoes are not only classified according to type, but also according to their texture once cooked, which is determined by their starch content. The earlier the potatoes ripen, the less starch they contain and the firmer they are when cooked. Only the older types accumulate so much starch during the

SUMMARY OF COOKING TYPE AND STORAGE LIFE OF SOME POPULAR TYPES OF POTATO

Types	Cooking characteristics	Storage
earlies (scrapers)		
Maris Bard	soft waxy texture	intended for immediate
Pentland Javelin	soft waxy texture	use after harversting
Rocket	firm waxy texture	
second earlies		
Estima	firm, moist texture	can be stored for a few
Wilja	firm, slightly dry texture	weeks if kept cool and dark
maincrop		
Desirée	firm texture	suitable for long storage
Maris Piper	floury texture	suitable for long storage
King Edward	floury texture	suitable for long storage
Romano	soft dry texture	suitable for long storage

sunny summer months that they become light and floury when cooked. All the available types of potato fall into one of three cooking categories (see table). Buy from good shops where the varieties are properly labelled, so that you can be sure they will be suitable for your purpose.

Waxy potatoes have a low starch content and do not fall apart when cooked. They are firm and should be used for potato salads, unpeeled boiled potatoes and plain boiled potatoes. Examples are Jersey Royal, Maris Bard, Pink Fir Apple, Pentland Javelin, Rocket.

All-purpose potatoes have an average starch content. They remain firm when cooked and are slightly floury. During boiling, the skins split open. Some are mainly waxy and suitable for potato salads and for unpeeled boiled potatoes, but most are good all-rounders, used for roasting, boiling, chipping and baking. Examples are Cara, Desirée, Estima, Maris Piper, Pentland Dell, Wilja.

Floury potatoes have a high starch content. After cooking, they are floury, dry and light. They also tend to be large, and are ideal for mashing and baking. Examples are King Edward, Pentland Squire, Romano.

STORAGE

Smaller quantities of potatoes should be kept cool, if possible in the dark and ventilated (preferably in a cardboard box). Carefully remove all plastic packaging. Do not put potatoes in the refrigerator, where they will quickly go off. If storing larger quantities for a longer period, or putting them in a cellar or outhouse, bear in mind the following:

Potatoes for storing must be fully ripe with a firm, undamaged skin; if possible they should be clean. On no account should the potatoes be washed before storing. A thin layer of dry soil on the skin does no harm and even provides protection against rotting. The ideal storage temperature is around 4°C/40°F. Cool, dry, dark cellars

or store-rooms make good storage places, but they must always be frost-free and well ventilated. Frost eventually converts the starch into sugar and gives the potatoes a slightly sweet taste. Adequate ventilation, particularly from below, is important. Paper sacks or plastic mesh bags are suitable, but they should not be piled higher than 40cm/16 inches. Never store in polythene bags. If the potatoes are not in paper sacks it is worth loosely covering them with newspaper since light can cause green patches to form, which contain toxic solanine (all patches must be cut out before cooking). Sprouting potatoes should be used quickly; remove the sprouts before cooking.

MUSHROOMS

Mushrooms may well be used as vegetables, but they are fungi. They form an individual, large botanical group.

In terms of nutritional value, edible mushrooms are similar to vegetables. In terms of minerals, they contain primarily potassium and phosphorous. They also contain vitamin D, which only occurs very rarely in vegetables. Since the cell walls of mushrooms contain chitin and cellulose, they are difficult to digest. Even mushroom protein is relatively difficult to digest and is poorly absorbed by the body.

Ordinary closed cup or button mushrooms are often the only type available. But other types are slowly coming onto the market, and the following are the most likely to be found:

Birch boletus (4) are closely related to the cep and are associated mainly with birch trees. They have white flesh which quickly discolours and yellow pores. As soon as the cap and stalk have been cut, it becomes deep red to violet in colour. These wild fungi have an aromatic flavour and go well with game dishes.

Boletus luteus (8) is a close relative of the cep (Boletus edulis), but is not often offered for sale in Britain. It has white, butter-soft flesh. The slimy brown skin of the cap can easily be removed.

Storage: this mushroom goes off quickly and should be used immediately.

Ceps or penny buns (10) grow in deciduous and coniferous forests. The cap of young mushrooms is light brown and semi-spherical. Older ones have red to dark brown, parasol-like caps. Thanks to their nutty flavour, ceps have a wide variety of uses; they are widely used in the production of canned and packeted soups. They are also suitable for use raw in salads.

Storage: use immediately. Dried mushrooms should be soaked in cold water for a little while before use.

Chanterelles (9). These bright yellow edible mushrooms with funnel-shaped caps grow in deciduous and coniferous forests. They can be prepared almost without waste and are suitable as an accompaniment to game dishes, egg dishes or as a flavouring for sauces.

Storage: fresh mushrooms can be kept for one or two days in the vegetable compartment of the refrigerator or in a cool, dark place. Chanterelles become very hard if allowed to dry out and are less suitable for deep-frying, since this gives them a bitter taste.

Closed cup (1, 3) or brown mushrooms (2) are the best known and most widely used edible mushrooms. They are always available. The caps of young mushrooms are still firmly closed and have grown with the stalk. The cap gradually opens as the mushroom ages and the colour of the originally pale gills changes to dark brown, via dark pink. The progressive stages are known as button, closed cup, open cup and flat. Fresh button or closed cup mushrooms should be firm and crisp. If the stalk ends are dark, this indicates that the mushrooms have been stored for some time. Button mushrooms are ideal for cooking whole, or for use in creamy sauces, as the pale gills cause no discolouration. Closed cup mushrooms are extremely versatile and can be fried, braised, stewed or grilled and are especially tasty used raw in salads. Open cup mushrooms are good for frying, stuffing and baking; flat mushrooms are only suitable for use in stews and mushroom soup as they impart a dark colour; but they have the best flavour. Brown mushrooms, sometimes labelled chestnut mushrooms, have a stronger flavour than the white types, but are not so widely available.

These mushrooms are grown in clean conditions and do not need peeling or washing, just wiping with absorbent paper.

Storage: mushrooms pre-packaged in film should be removed from the packaging after purchase. If the mushrooms are fresh, firm and not too damp, they will stay fresh in the vegetable compartment of the refrigerator for a few days. Closed cup mushrooms which have dried during storage can still be used if soaked in milk for a little while before cooking.

Morels (6) are some of the most strongly flavoured edible mushrooms of the genus Morchella. The stalk is wrinkled and hollow, the cap is pitted and honeycomb-like. Depending on the shape of the cap, a distinction is made between round and pointed morels. Since fresh morels are very sandy, they must be thoroughly washed before use. Dried morels need to be soaked for 2 hours, after which they still have to be washed. Morels are used more as flavouring than as an edible mushroom.

Storage: use as fresh as possible. These mushrooms should not be stored.

Oyster mushrooms (5) or oyster fungus. The cap ranges from 5cm/¼ inch to 15cm/6 inches across, is rounded or semi-circular and varying in colour from grey/mauve and blueish-grey to olive/black. There are also yellow to brownish types. Oyster mushrooms are mildly aromatic with a delicate flavour. When bought they should feel firm and robust, and small to medium ones are preferable to larger ones. In addition to their many uses as a side dish or flavouring, the caps can also be breaded and fried like escalopes of meat. They are often used in Oriental cuisine.

Storage: if not used immediately, they are best stored in the refrigerator, preferably in the vegetable compartment, or in a cool, dark place for a further 2 to 3 days. Dried ones should be soaked briefly in hot water.

Shiitake mushrooms (7) came originally from Japan, where they have been cultivated for many centuries. They have been commercially available for only a short time but are gaining in popularity due to their strong spicy flavour and pronounced aroma. The mushrooms have a slightly ribbed, pale to dark brown cap, covered in pale scales. If it is fresh, the cap should be cupped. Shiitake mushrooms are mainly suitable in Oriental cuisine, particularly stews.

Storage: will stay fresh for a few days if stored loosely in a cool, dark place.

Truffles (11, 12) are bulbous fungi, covered in a rough skin. They have firm flesh. Specially trained dogs or pigs are sometimes used to find these fungi, which grow underground. The best black truffles come from southern France (Périgord truffles). They are best when cooked in champagne or Madeira. The best white truffles come from northern Italy (Piedmont truffles) and are usually sliced wafer-thin, raw, over food, as they are incredibly expensive.

TIPS FOR BUYING VEGETABLES

Healthy eating means buying vegetables which are in season at a given time of year, because artificial after-ripening and long transportation reduce the levels of valuable ingredients in vegetables. In addition, greenhouse vegetables contain a higher level of harmful chemicals (fertiliser residues and nitrates) than vegetables grown outdoors.

Organically grown vegetables may not be entirely free of harmful substances, but they do contain considerably fewer undesirable substances than conventionally cultivated vegetables.

Although most vegetables are available all year round, some vegetables are most definitely seasonal. Since vegetable growing is dependent on the weather, changes in the times shown on the vegetable calendar cannot be ruled out. When buying vegetables, fresh ones are not always available. In this case, frozen vegetables are recommended as an alternative. Vegetables can be more gently frozen in bulk than in one's own freezer.

STORING VEGETABLES CORRECTLY

It goes without saying that vegetables should always be eaten when they are as fresh as possible, but often stocking up on vegetables cannot be avoided. Almost all vegetables can be stored in the vegetable compartment of the refrigerator, loosely packed and at the correct temperature. However, each vegetable type has its own individual storage time (see THE A-Z OF VEGETABLES).

Vegetables can be stored for several months at -18°C /0.4°F in a freezer compartment or chest freezer. It is important only to freeze fresh, undamaged, blanched vegetables. Some types of vegetable should be cooked before freezing, for example aubergines, chicory and some types of bean.

Storage times vary from 3 months (aubergines) to 10 months (types of cabbage, pulses).

Industrially frozen vegetables provide another storage possibility, where small portions can be sold. Prepared frozen vegetables can be stored for several weeks in a home. freezer compartment or chest freezer. When buying these products, make sure that the packaging is not damaged. The time which elapses between buying them and putting them back into storage should be short, so that the vegetables do not thaw. Thawed or defrosted vegetables must be used immediately.

Yet another way of storing vegetables is to bottle or pickle them in liquid made from vinegar, salt, sugar and spices. Vinegar prevents the development of mould and putrifying or fermenting bacteria. The correct mixture of vinegar and other ingredients gives vegetables a spicy, sweet-and-sour flavour. Pickled vegetables go well with meat dishes.

TRIMMING, WASHING AND CHOPPING VEGETABLES

Before cooking, vegetables have to be trimmed, washed and cut into slices or diced. Whether to peel or not is largely a matter of personal taste, but in the interests of healthy eating one should remember that a lot of vitamins and minerals are concentrated in the skin. Onions and garlic are always peeled. Trimmed vegetables should never be washed after chopping or slicing, to prevent water-soluble vitamins and minerals from leaching out. If chopped vegetables are not to be used immediately, they should be covered with a damp cloth. This protects the vegetables from reacting with oxygen (oxidation), which often turns vegetables brown. Sprinkling vegetables with lemon juice or vinegar also prevents this discolouration.

VEGETABLE CALENDAR

The months shown on the calendar indicate the main harvesting period. Almost all types are available as imports and from greenhouses outside these months.

Vegetable	J	F	M	A	M	J	J	A	S	O	N	D
Artichoke						▬	▬	▬	▬	▬		
Asparagus				▬	▬	▬						
Aubergine						▬	▬	▬	▬	▬		
Broccoli				▬	▬	▬	▬	▬	▬	▬	▬	
Brussels sprouts	▬	▬	▬									
Carrots					▬	▬	▬	▬	▬	▬	▬	▬
Cauliflower			▬	▬	▬	▬	▬	▬	▬	▬	▬	
Celeriac			▬	▬	▬	▬	▬	▬	▬	▬	▬	▬
Celery						▬	▬	▬	▬	▬	▬	
Chicory	▬	▬	▬							▬	▬	▬
Common cabbage			▬	▬	▬							
Corn on the cob							▬	▬	▬	▬		
Courgettes						▬	▬	▬	▬	▬		
Cucumber					▬	▬	▬	▬	▬	▬		
Fennel						▬	▬	▬	▬	▬	▬	
Green beans						▬	▬	▬	▬	▬		
Kohlrabi			▬	▬	▬	▬	▬	▬	▬	▬		
Leeks						▬	▬	▬	▬	▬	▬	▬
Onions						▬	▬	▬	▬	▬		
Peas					▬	▬	▬	▬				
Peppers						▬	▬	▬	▬	▬		
Red cabbage						▬	▬	▬	▬	▬	▬	▬
Savoy cabbage			▬	▬	▬	▬	▬	▬	▬	▬	▬	▬
Scorzonera	▬	▬	▬							▬	▬	▬
Spinach			▬	▬	▬				▬	▬	▬	
Swiss Chard						▬	▬	▬	▬	▬		
Tomatoes						▬	▬	▬	▬	▬		
Turnips	▬	▬	▬									
White cabbage						▬	▬	▬	▬	▬	▬	▬

COOKING VEGETABLES

Regardless of how vegetables are cooked, the process should be quick so that the vegetables stay firm, with as little vitamins lost in the water as possible.

It is not necessary to arrange the following cooking methods per type of vegetable, since in general all vegetables can be cooked in any of these ways. Green beans, for example, can be blanched, boiled, steamed or braised.

Blanching means boiling vegetables in water and then cooling them in cold water. To prevent the vitamins leaching out excessively, a little salt should be added to the water. If vinegar or lemon juice is added to the water the vegetables will retain more colour.

Blanching makes vegetables more pleasurable to eat or work with, particularly spinach and some types of cabbage. It takes the bitterness out of chicory, prepares vegetables for freezing, makes the skin easier to remove (tomatoes, for example) and makes leaf vegetables easier to shape.

Blanching times vary between a few seconds for delicate vegetables (young spinach, tomatoes) and 2-4 minutes for more sturdy types (cabbage). Except for spinach, the blanching water should be saved because it contains many nutrients and can be used in sauces and soups.

Steaming without pressure is a fat-free, extremely gentle cooking method, which involves cooking the vegetables in water vapour. The vegetables do not come into contact with water. All you need is a saucepan with

Fresh vegetables in great variety are available all year round.

a tightly fitting lid and a steamer. Cover the base of the saucepan with about 4cm/1½ inches of water. Season and bring to the boil. Then place the vegetables in the steamer over the saucepan and steam gently, depending on type. Using this method, many vegetables take between 15 and 20 minutes to cook.

Steaming with pressure has its advantages and disadvantages. Although the shorter cooking time does retain the nutrients better, the flavours cannot develop properly during this time. The vegetables therefore have less flavour than when cooked without pressure. A pressure-cooker should only be used when time is genuinely of the essence. The cooking times given in recipes must be observed carefully to prevent over-cooking the vegetables.

Sweating is another gentle way of cooking vegetables. This involves cooking chopped or sliced vegetables with a little fat and/or liquid, at just below boiling point. Use a large frying-pan so that the vegetables can lie flat next to each other. First heat the fat, then add the vegetables and seasoning,

including salt, cover and sweat for 1-2 minutes. This allows the typical smells and flavours of the vegetables to develop. Only then should a little water be added and the vegetables cooked over a low heat until firm. When the cooking process is complete only a little liquid should be left. Cooking times may be a little longer than for steaming without pressure.

Glazing is a version of sweating. As well as fat and/or liquid, sugar is also added to the saucepan, so that the vegetables are given a shiny coating. It is important to remove the lid when two-thirds of the cooking time has elapsed so that most of the liquid can evaporate. In addition, the vegetables should be tossed frequently during cooking. Pearl onions, turnips, carrots and chestnuts are especially suitable for cooking in this way.

Boiling means cooking in bubbling, slightly salted liquid in a fully covered saucepan. This cooking method causes the most leaching from vegetables which is why it is best for cooking whole vegetables, such as cauliflower. There should be sufficient water in the saucepan just to cover the

vegetables. In addition, the vegetables should be placed straight into the vigorously boiling water, then cooked until firm in water which is just boiling gently.

Braising is usually only used for stuffed vegetable dishes (such as for aubergines, cucumber, courgettes and cabbage). The stuffed vegetable should be placed on a bed of finely chopped vegetables, such as carrot slices and onion rings. First, brown all the vegetables and then just cover in liquid (vegetable stock) and cook in the oven. Braising juices from which the fat has been skimmed make a good base for vegetable stock.

Frying is good for sliced vegetables such as aubergines, courgettes, artichoke hearts, potatoes and mushrooms. Season the vegetable slices and fry them in oil or butter. Place on absorbent paper after frying to remove excess fat.

COOKING FROZEN VEGETABLES

Frozen vegetables can be sweated or boiled. To sweat, place a little butter, the frozen vegetables, a little liquid and seasoning in a saucepan. Cover and sweat. To boil, place the frozen vegetables in vigorously boiling salted water and cook, covered. Cooking times for frozen vegetables are much shorter than for fresh vegetables because they have been blanched before freezing and because the cell structure of the vegetables loosens with freezing.

COOKING WHOLE ARTICHOKES

1. Always break off the stalk right next to the base so that the fibres in the heart come away with the stalk.

2. Cut about 3-4cm/1½-2 inches from the leaf tips using a carving knife.

3. Remove the small lower leaves and cut away the remaining leaves from the base using a sharp knife.

4. Remove the tips from the remaining leaves using scissors. If the prepared artichoke is not to be cooked immediately, soak it in slightly salted, acidulated water.

5. Put the artichoke in salted, boiling water to which a few drops of lemon juice have been added, cover and simmer for 20 minutes.

6. Twist out the inner leaves; set aside.

7. Using a sharp spoon, scoop out the choke from the heart. Replace the inner leaves, upside-down.

3.

4.

5.

1.

6.

2.

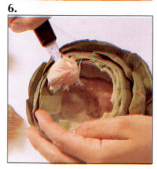

7.

COOKING ARTICHOKE HEARTS

1. Pull off the stalk right next to the base so that the fibres come away with the stalk. Remove the outer leaves by hand.

2. Carefully cut off the medium-sized leaves immediately above the base, using a large sharp knife.

3. Now carefully remove any remaining leaves from the base, using a small sharp knife.

4. Using a sharp spoon, remove all the inedible choke.

5. Either rub the prepared artichoke heart with lemon or place in slightly salted acidulated water before boiling, so that it does not discolour.

6. Boil the hearts in salted water to which a few drops of lemon juice have been added until just tender.

3.

4.

5.

1.

2.

6.

Artichoke heart

STUFFING AUBERGINES

1. Halve the aubergines lengthways. Make several criss-cross incisions in the flesh, using a sharp knife.

2. Place the halves, with the cut surfaces face down, on a lightly oiled baking sheet and brown in the oven.

3. When the aubergine flesh is soft, remove it using a sharp spoon or a melon baller.

4. Mix the chopped flesh with 250g/8oz minced raw meat, a finely diced red pepper, 3 tablespoons of cooked rice and 2 crushed garlic cloves. Season with salt, pepper and paprika and use the mixture to fill the aubergine halves.

5. Place the stuffed aubergines in a buttered ovenproof dish. Cover with sliced tomato, sprinkle with grated cheese and drizzle with oil.

6. Cook in the oven until browned.

3.

4.

5.

STUFFING CUCUMBERS

1. Thinly peel the cucumbers, removing each end.

2. Cut the cucumbers in half crossways. Using a thin wooden spoon handle, loosen the core, then carefully push it out using a thicker handle.

3. For the stuffing, mix together 200g/7oz minced raw meat, 4 tablespoons of finely diced red and green pepper and 1 tablespoon of chopped dill.

4. Put the stuffing into a piping bag fitted with a large nozzle and pipe into the cucumbers.

5. Butter a flat, ovenproof dish and cover the base with slices of carrot and onion. Place the cucumbers on top.

6. Season the cucumbers with salt, pepper and a pinch of sugar. Just cover with stock and cover the container with a lid or with aluminium foil.

7. Bring to the boil, then cook in a moderate oven for about 25 minutes.

3.

4.

5.

1.

6.

1.

2.

Stuffed aubergine

2.

7.

SLICING ONIONS

1. Cut the onion in half lengthways, then cut off the root end and the tip.

2. Cut the prepared onion lengthways into slices.

3. For onion rings, first cut the tip from the whole onion. Then cut the onion across into thin, even slices.

CHOPPING ONIONS

1. Halve the onions lengthways and make a vertical cut to just above the root.

2. Make several fine horizontal incisions in each onion half.

3. Finally, hold the onion firmly and slice thinly; it will fall into fine dice.

PREPARING TOMATOES

1. Remove the stalks. Using a small sharp knife, make a shallow crossed incision in the base of each tomato.

2. Briefly plunge into boiling water or pour boiling water over the tomatoes.

3. Cool immediately in cold water, peel and at the same time cut out the flower end, which contains solanine, and any green parts.

4. To remove the seeds, halve the tomato and scoop them out with a small sharp spoon, without damaging the outer wall of the fruit.

5. For salads, wash thoroughly, cut out the stalk end by making a cone-shaped incision in the fruit, and cut into thin slices using a very sharp knife.

COOKING ASPARAGUS

1. If using white asparagus, peel before cooking. Peel the stalk from tip to base using a swivel-action vegetable peeler.

2. Wash the asparagus and divide into bundles. Loosely tie each portion together with kitchen string, so that the tips are all at the same level.

3. Trim the base of the asparagus spears to the same length.

4. Add 1 tablespoon of salt and 1 teaspoon of sugar to 1 litre/1¾ pints of water. Cook the asparagus in the water for about 15-18 minutes.

2.

3.

1.

4.

Boiled white asparagus

BLANCHING BROCCOLI

1. Remove any leaves from the broccoli. Divide the head into florets and wash them under cold running water.
2. Peel any large coarse stalks and cut them into slices.
3. To blanch, put the broccoli florets and the stalks into boiling, salted water for 2-3 minutes.
4. Remove the broccoli from the boiling water and cool in cold water (do not use ice).
5. Place the broccoli in a colander to drain.

3.

4.

1.

5.

2.

Broccoli ready to serve

Hearty Home Cooking

There was a time when no courgettes, aubergines, peppers, fennel or okra were available to us. Vegetable dishes consisted of cabbage and sprouts, beans and leeks, turnips – and of course potatoes, potatoes and more potatoes! But housewives really knew how to transform them into tasty everyday meals and feasts for special occasions! We still like broad beans, stuffed cabbage, potato pancakes and Brussels sprouts. So in this chapter we have brought together the best vegetable recipes using the kind of vegetables that used to be available in abundance from every kitchen garden. If some of the quantities seem large (as in the broad bean recipe on page 36) or the vegetables hard to find (as with fresh grated horseradish on page 39) this is because we know that people like to grow these traditional crops in their own gardens or on their allotments.

Beetroot with Bacon
(see recipe on page 39)

MUSHROOMS IN CREAM SAUCE

SERVES 4 ■

Preparation and cooking time: 30 minutes
Kcal per portion: 450
P = 9g, F = 41g, C = 6g

1kg/2¼lbs button mushrooms
2 shallots
100g/4oz butter
juice of ½ lemon
250ml/8 fl oz single cream
salt and pepper
2 tbsps brandy
1 tbsp chopped chervil

Cut off the stalk ends, then wipe the mushrooms.

1. Cut off the stalks (use these in soup) and wipe the mushrooms with absorbent paper. Slice the mushrooms evenly. Finely chop the shallots.
2. Heat the butter in a large frying-pan and sweat the shallots until transparent. Add the mushrooms and continue cooking until all the liquid has evaporated and the mushrooms begin to change colour. Pour in the lemon juice.

Braise the thinly sliced mushrooms in butter with the diced shallots.

3. Put the cream in a small saucepan and bring to the boil. Add almost all of it to the mushrooms and cook over medium heat until reduced. Season with salt and pepper to taste.
4. Combine the brandy with the remaining cream and pour over the mushrooms. Bring back to the boil , then remove from the heat. Serve immediately, sprinkled with chervil.
Accompaniment: new potatoes; or arrange on four slices of toast and serve as a starter.

Heat most of the cream, pour over the vegetables and reduce.

BROAD BEANS

SERVES 4 ■

Preparation and cooking time: 1 hour
Kcal per portion: 1425
P = 88g, F = 37g, C = 184g

2.5kg/5lbs 6oz fresh broad beans
150g/5½oz smoked rindless bacon
20 spring onions (white parts only)
1 large onion
1 bunch parsley
1 tbsp oil
475ml/15 fl oz vegetable stock
1 tsp dried savory
salt and pepper
2 tbsps crème fraîche

1. Remove the beans from their pods and wash them. Finely dice the bacon.
2. Wash and trim the spring onions. Finely chop the onion and parsley.
3. Melt the oil in a casserole and sweat the bacon until the fat is transparent. Add the onion and parsley (reserve some parsley for garnishing) and sweat briefly. Add the beans and fry for a few minutes.
4. Pour the stock over the vegetables. Add the savory, salt and pepper. Cook the beans over a medium heat for about 40 minutes.
5. 10 minutes before the end of the cooking time, remove the lid so that the liquid can reduce completely.
6. Add the crème fraîche to the vegetables and bring to the boil. Serve sprinkled with the reserved parsley.
Accompaniment: new potatoes.

KOHLRABI

SERVES 4 ■

Preparation and cooking time: 25 minutes
Kcal per portion: 115
P = 4g, F = 6g, C = 10g

6 young kohlrabi
250ml/8 fl oz water
salt
30g/1oz butter
1 tbsp flour
freshly grated nutmeg

First remove any green leaves from the kohlrabi, then peel. Reserve young tender leaves, chop finely and add to the kohlrabi just before the end of the cooking time.

1. Peel the kohlrabi and cut into thin slices or matchsticks. If there are any leaves, wash them, roll up and cut into strips.
2. Put the kohlrabi slices and the water into a saucepan with a little salt. Cook, covered, over a medium heat for about 15 minutes. Add the leaves just before the end of the cooking time.
3. In the meantime, thoroughly mash together the butter and flour with a fork to make beurre manié. Stir this into the kohlrabi in small lumps to thicken the liquid and bring to the boil. Season with nutmeg to taste.
An accompaniment to fried meat.

RED CABBAGE

SERVES 4 ■

*Preparation and cooking
time: 1 hour 10 minutes
Kcal per portion: 235
P = 3g, F = 13g, C = 20g*

1kg/2¼lbs red cabbage
2 cooking apples
50g/2oz pork dripping or
   butter
1 small onion
2 cloves
250ml/8 fl oz water
125ml/4 fl oz red wine
3 sugar lumps
2 tbsps vinegar
2 tbsps cranberries

1. Remove the hard outer leaves from the cabbage. Halve the cabbage and cut out the stalk. Slice the cabbage or cut into thin strips.
2. Quarter, core, peel and chop the apples.

TIP

Red cabbage is almost always available fresh because there are early and late types. Red cabbage contains a great deal of vitamin C and is rich in iron.

3. Heat the fat in a large saucepan and gently fry the apple pieces. Add the cabbage and the onion. Pour in the water and red wine.
4. Heat the sugar lumps in a small frying-pan until they caramelise. Add the vinegar and bring to the boil. Add to the cabbage mixture.
5. Tightly cover the saucepan and cook over a low heat for about 45 minutes. Finally, add the cranberries.
An accompaniment to roast pork, goose and duck or to game dishes.

BEETROOT WITH BACON

(see photo on page 34)

SERVES 4 ■

*Preparation and cooking
time: 1 hour
Kcal per portion: 555
P = 8g, F = 51g, C = 17g*

750g/1½lbs raw beetroot
salt
200g/7oz rindless streaky
   bacon
¼ stick horseradish
45g/1½oz butter
125ml/5 fl oz single cream
1 tbsp red wine vinegar
1 tsp sugar
2 tbsps crème fraîche or
   soured cream (optional)

1. Scrub the beetroot thoroughly under running water; do not break the skins. Parboil in plenty of salted water for 30 minutes. Cool in cold water and remove the skins.
2. Chop the beetroot, not too finely, preferably in a food processor. Finely dice the bacon. and finely grate the horseradish.
3. Melt the butter in a large saucepan and brown the bacon. Add the beetroot and cook over a medium heat, stirring occasionally.
4. Add the horseradish, cream and salt to taste; bring back to the boil. Season with the vinegar and sugar. If desired, garnish with a dollop of crème fraîche or soured cream.
An accompaniment to boiled ham, roast pork or fish.

Peel the cooked beetroot.

Chop the beetroot, preferably in a food processor.

Add the horseradish, cream and salt to the cooked vegetables and bring to the boil.

LEEKS WITH HAM

SERVES 4 ■

*Preparation and cooking
time: 40 minutes
Kcal per portion: 280
P = 13g, F = 16g, C = 22g*

12 small leeks
salt and white pepper
4 slices cooked ham

FOR THE BECHAMEL SAUCE:
30g/1oz butter
30g/1oz flour
500ml/16 fl oz milk
1 egg yolk
freshly grated nutmeg

1. Cut the roots and tough green parts from the leeks, so that only the white and pale green parts remain. Wash them very thoroughly.
2. Put enough salted water to cover the leeks into a large saucepan and bring to the boil. Put in the leeks and boil for 10 minutes until almost cooked. Drain in a sieve.
3. Melt the butter for the béchamel sauce in a saucepan. Add the flour and cook gently until pale yellow. Gradually add the milk, stirring constantly with a whisk. Bring to the boil, then remove from the heat. Stir in the egg yolk. Season with salt, white pepper and nutmeg.
4. Heat the oven to 200°C/400°F/Gas Mark 6.
5. Butter a large shallow ovenproof dish. Wrap three leeks in each slice of ham and arrange side by side in the dish. Pour over the sauce.
6. Put the leeks in the centre of the oven for about 15 minutes, until the top is golden brown.
Accompaniment: mashed potato

TASTY POTATO CAKES

SERVES 4 ■

Preparation and cooking time: 45 minutes
Kcal per portion: 240
P = 7g, F = 13g, C = 25g

500g/1lb2oz floury potatoes
salt
50g/2oz flour
2 eggs, separated
2 tbsps single cream
freshly grated nutmeg
oil and butter for frying

1. Peel and quarter the potatoes. Cook, just covered in salted water. Discard the boiling water and shake the potatoes in the saucepan until completely dry.
2. Press the potatoes through a potato ricer or vegetable mill into a bowl. Add the flour, egg yolks,

Press the boiled potatoes through a potato ricer.

Fold the beaten egg white into the seasoned potato mixture.

> **TIP**
>
> *For a change, add finely chopped herbs or finely diced onion, fried in butter until transparent, to the potato dough.*

Fry the potato cakes on both sides until golden.

cream, salt to taste and nutmeg. Beat the egg whites until stiff and fold into the mixture.
3. Heat 1 tablespoon of oil and 15g/½oz butter in a large frying-pan. Using a spoon, place small balls of potato dough in the pan and press flat. Fry until pale brown, turn carefully and fry the other side until golden.
An accompaniment to meat and game dishes, or vegetable dishes without meat, e.g. served with French beans as a main meal.

CREAMED POTATO WITH CRESS

SERVES 4 ■

Preparation and cooking time: 30 minutes
Kcal per portion: 240
P = 6g, F = 9g, C = 34

1kg/2¼lbs floury potatoes
salt
250ml/8 fl oz milk
30g/1oz butter
1 carton mustard and cress
freshly grated nutmeg

1. Peel and finely dice the potatoes. Place in a saucepan, just covered with water. Add salt and boil for 15 minutes until soft. Pour away the water. Dry the potatoes by shaking the saucepan.
2. Heat the milk in a large saucepan. Press the potatoes through a potato ricer

> **TIP**
>
> *Instead of cress, chopped herbs such as parsley or dill, or finely grated raw carrot can be added to the creamed potato.*

or vegetable mill into the milk. Whisk until the mixture is creamy.
3. Season with salt to taste, then stir in the butter in small knobs. Finely chop the mustard and cress with scissors and add to the creamed potato. Season with nutmeg. An accompaniment to baked fish or meat.

CREAMED POTATO AU GRATIN

SERVES 4 ■■

Preparation and cooking time: 50 minutes
Kcal per portion: 685
P = 35g, F = 45g, C = 34g

1kg/2¼lbs floury potatoes
salt
250ml/8 fl oz milk
60g/2oz butter
freshly grated nutmeg
3 eggs, beaten
2 tbsps creamed horseradish
300g/10oz Cheddar cheese

1. Peel and finely dice the potatoes. Put into a saucepan, just cover with water, add salt and boil for 15 minutes until soft.
2. Pour away the water. Keep the saucepan over the heat and shake until the potatoes are completely dry.
3. Heat the milk in a large saucepan. Press the diced potato through a potato ricer or vegetable mill into the hot milk. Whisk until the mixture becomes creamy. Stir in the butter in small knobs. Season with salt and nutmeg.
4. Add the eggs, horseradish and 250g/8oz of cheese to the creamed potato.
5. Butter a baking dish. Heat the oven to 200°C/400°F/Gas Mark 6.
6. Transfer the potato mixture into a piping bag. Pipe the mixture into the baking dish. Sprinkle with the remaining cheese.
7. Bake in the centre of the oven for 20 minutes, until golden.
An accompaniment to fried fish or meat dishes; can also be served with salad as a vegetarian meal.

Dishes from Around the World

*O*ur foreign neighbours – both close at hand and further afield – have always known how to prepare vegetables, particularly in countries around the Mediterranean and in the Orient. The selection of wonderful vegetables always available cheaply in the markets *inspired* culinary imagination and produced a wealth of recipes. Even in our own country, aubergines, courgettes, artichokes, avocados and chicory are no longer just occasional guests. We can now choose all year round from an enormous range of vegetables and make dishes that bring aromas and flavours from all over the world into our kitchens.

Savoy Cabbage Indian Style
(see recipe on page 52)

VALAIS-STYLE CHARD ROLLS

SERVES 4 ■■
*Preparation and cooking
time: 1½ hours
Kcal per portion: 920
P = 32g, F = 75g, C = 30g*

24 large chard leaves
2 tbsps oil
600ml/18 fl oz milk
300ml/12 fl oz stock
½ Continental pork sausage
100g/4oz grated cheese
45g/1½oz butter

FOR THE FILLING:
150g/5½oz wholemeal flour
2 eggs
salt and pepper
freshly grated nutmeg
100ml/3 fl oz water
50g/2oz rindless streaky
    bacon
30g/1oz cooked ham
100g/4oz onion, finely diced
3 small smoked sausages
1 kabanos sausage (200g/7oz)
1 bunch parsley
45g/1½oz chard leaves
1 sprig thyme
1 sprig rosemary
½ bunch chives
30g/1oz butter

1. First prepare the filling. Put the flour into a bowl. Make a well in the centre and put in the eggs, salt, pepper and nutmeg. Using a fork, mix the eggs with some of the flour.
2. Add the water, stirring with a wooden spoon. Continue beating until the mixture becomes smooth and creamy. Leave to stand for 30 minutes.
3. Meanwhile finely dice the bacon, ham and sausages. finely chop the parsley, chard leaves and remaining herbs.
4. Melt the butter in a frying-pan and brown the diced meat and onion. Add the herbs and stir briefly. Thoroughly mix this mixture, while hot, into the egg and flour mixture. Cool.

5. Wash the chard leaves and blanch in salted water. Drain well and spread out on a board. Place 1 tablespoon of filling on each leaf. Fold the sides of the leaves over the filling and roll up lengthways.
6. Heat the oil in a frying-pan and carefully brown the rolls all over.
7. Heat the oven to 220°C/425°F/Gas Mark 7.
8. Bring the milk and stock to the boil in a flameproof dish. Place the rolls side by side in the liquid and simmer for 15 minutes over a low heat.
9. Skin and chop the pork sausage and sprinkle over the chard rolls. Top with the cheese and dot with butter. Brown in the centre of the oven until the cheese melts. If you cannot obtain chard leaves, large spinach beet leaves will do.
Accompaniment:
noodles or rice.
Recommended drink:
strong, young red wine from Valais

The filling for the rolls is made from a seasoned dough of eggs and flour, flavoured with chopped herbs, onions, ham, bacon and chard leaves.

Place 1 tablespoon of the cooled filing mixture on each leaf.

Place the spinach beet rolls in the milk and stock mixture. Sprinkle with chopped pork sausage and grated cheese. Dot with butter and bake.

BAKED POTATOES WITH CREAMY ROQUEFORT

SERVES 4 ■
*Preparation and cooking
time: 1 hour
Kcal per portion: 540
P = 14g, F = 38g, C = 34g*

8 baking potatoes
2 ripe avocados
4 tbsps crème fraîche
100g/4 oz quark or curd
    cheese
60g/2oz Roquefort cheese
juice of ½ lemon
45g/1½oz red caviar

1. Heat the oven to 220°C/425°F/Gas Mark 7.
2. Wash the potatoes and dry with absorbent paper. Put each one on a square piece of aluminium foil. Fold the corners upward and squeeze together to enclose the potatoes.
3. Place the parcels directly on a shelf in the centre of the oven for 50-60 minutes or until cooked.
4. Meanwhile halve the avocados lengthways, stone and peel. Chop the flesh and purée in a liquidiser.
5. Mix the crème Fraîche with the quark or curd cheese. Mash the Roquefort with a fork and stir into the quark mixture. Stir the avocado purée into the mixture and season with the lemon juice.
6. Take the cooked potatoes out of the oven and remove the Foil. Cut a cross in each potato and open out slightly. Divide the Roquefort cream between the potatoes and garnish with the caviar.
Accompaniment:
mixed salad.
Recommended drink:
crisp, dry white wine, e.g. Chablis.

SERBIAN-STYLE PEPPERS

SERVES 4 ■

Preparation and cooking time: 30 minutes
Kcal per portion: 335
P = 6g, F = 29g, C = 13g

1kg/2¼lbs yellow peppers
750g/1½lbs tomatoes
50g/2oz rindless smoked bacon
90g/3½oz pork dripping or lard
2 large onions
1 tbsp paprika
salt

1. Halve, core, de-seed and wash the peppers. Slice into strips. Blanch the tomatoes in boiling water. Peel and quarter.
2. Dice the bacon. Heat the fat in a frying-pan and sweat

> ### TIP
>
> *A complete main course dish can be made by adding slices of smoked dried sausage to the peppers.*

the bacon until the fat is transparent. Dice the onion, add to the pan and brown.
3. Add the strips of pepper and tomato quarters to the frying-pan. Sprinkle with paprika and fry the vegetables over a low heat for 20 minutes, stirring from time to time. Season with salt to taste.
Accompaniment: rice or un-peeled boiled potatoes.
Recommended drink: red vin de pays.

HUNGARIAN STUFFED PEPPERS

SERVES 4 ■ ■

Preparation and cooking time: 1¾ hours
Kcal per portion: 465
P = 33g, F = 23g, C = 31g

8 large green peppers
100g/4oz rice
salt and pepper
500g/1lb2oz boneless lamb
2 small onions
1 garlic clove
1 tbsp finely chopped mint
1 tbsp finely chopped dill
250ml/8 fl oz stock
15g/½oz butter
150g/5½oz crème fraîche

1. Cut small lids from the peppers. Carefully remove the cores and seeds and wash the inside and outside of the peppers.
2. Pre-cook the rice in a little salted water for 5 minutes. Drain in a sieve.

> ### TIP
>
> *Tomato sauce, made from fresh tomatoes, can be poured over the peppers instead of crème fraîche.*

3. Put the meat, onion and garlic through a mincer or chop, not too finely, in a food processor. Mix with the rice and herbs. Season well with salt and pepper. Stuff the peppers with the meat. Place upright in an oven-proof dish and cover with the lids removed earlier.
4. Heat the oven to 200°C/400°F/Gas Mark 6.
5. Heat the butter and stock in a saucepan until the butter has melted. Pour over the peppers. Cover the dish with a lid or foil.

Chop the meat, onions and garlic in a food processor. Mix with the rice and herbs, and season.

Put the lids back on the stuffed peppers. Place the peppers upright in an ovenproof dish or pan, close together so that they cannot fall over. Pour over the butter and stock and bake in the oven.

6. Cook the peppers on the bottom shelf of the oven For 60-70 minutes. Place on a serving plate and keep warm. Stir the crème fraîche into the pan juices and cook until reduced to a creamy sauce. Serve with the peppers.
Accompaniment: rice.
Recommended drink: full-bodied, aromatic red wine.

MORELS WITH CREAM

SERVES 4 ■

Preparation and cooking time: 45 minutes
Soaking time for dried morels: 1 hour
Kcal per portion: 365
P = 4g, F = 33g, C = 10g

500g/1lb2oz fresh or 50g/2oz dried morels
60g/2oz butter
salt and pepper
juice of ½ lemon
200g/7oz crème fraîche
2 tbsps brandy

1. Soak dried morels For 1 hour; place fresh morels in cold water for 5 minutes. Wash the mushrooms thoroughly under running water to remove sand from under the wrinkled cap.
2. Halve or quarter large mushrooms. Dry carefully with absorbent paper. Pour the soaking water from dried morels through a fine sieve into a bowl.
3. Melt the butter in a flame-proof casserole. Add the mushrooms and season with salt, pepper and lemon juice. Cook for 10 minutes over a low heat, stirring from time to time.
4. Add a little cream and, if using dried morels, the soaking water. Cook for a few minutes to reduce the liquid.
5. Add the brandy and the remaining cream. Simmer to make a thick creamy sauce. An accompaniment to fillet steak, veal cutlets or lamb chops (use half quantities). Can also be used as a vol-au-vent filling.

MOUSSAKA

SERVES 4 ■ ■
*Preparation and cooking
time: 2 hours
Kcal per portion: 605
P = 36g, F = 45g, C = 14g*

*6 aubergines (about
    1kg/2¼lbs)
salt and pepper
flour
125ml/4 fl oz olive oil
500g/1lb2oz minced lamb
2 small onions
500g/1lb2oz tomatoes
200g/7oz yoghurt
3 eggs
butter for the dish*

While the salted aubergine slices
are soaking, brown the minced
meat in hot oil, add the diced
onion and fry until transparent.

Arrange two layers each of
aubergines, tomatoes and minced
meat in a baking dish. Before
browning, pour over the yoghurt
and egg sauce.

1. Cut the aubergines into thin slices lengthways. Sprinkle salt over the cut surfaces and leave for 30 minutes to draw out the bitter juice.

2. Pour away the juice and wash the slices. Dry them on absorbent paper and toss in flour. Heat half the olive oil in a large frying-pan and fry the aubergine slices in batches until pale brown.

3. Break up the minced lamb and dice the onions. Heat the remaining oil. First brown the meat, then add the diced onion and fry until transparent. Season with salt and pepper.

4. Blanch the tomatoes in boiling water. Peel and slice thinly.

5. Heat the oven to 200°C/400°F/Gas Mark 6.

6. Butter a baking dish and cover the base with a third of the aubergine slices. Cover with sliced tomato and half the minced meat mixture. Then add another layer of aubergines, tomatoes, minced meat and the remaining aubergine slices. Bake in the centre of the oven for about 30 minutes.

7. Mix together the yoghurt, eggs, 1 tablespoon of flour and salt and pour over the aubergines. Bake for a further 15 minutes, until the crust is golden brown.

Recommended drink:
full-bodied red wine, such as a Corbières, Côtes de Provence or Chianti.

RATATOUILLE

SERVES 10 ■ ■ ■
*Preparation and cooking
time: 3 hours
Kcal per portion: 575
P = 6g, F = 51g, C = 18g*

*3 large Spanish onions
3 garlic cloves
250ml/8 fl oz olive oil
1kg/2¼lbs beefsteak tomatoes
125ml/4 fl oz tomato juice
125ml/4 fl oz dry white wine
1 bouquet garni (2 bay
    leaves, rosemary and
    thyme sprigs, 3 parsley
    sprigs)
salt and pepper
2 red and 2 yellow peppers
    (about 750g/1½lbs)
1.5kg/3lbs 6oz aubergines
1.5kg/3lbs 6oz courgettes*

1. Slice the onions and crush the garlic cloves with the back of a knife. Blanch the tomatoes in boiling water. Peel and chop, removing the hard yellow cores.

2. Heat 4 tbsps of the oil in a large heavy pan. Fry the onions until transparent, then add the tomatoes and garlic cloves. Pour in the tomato juice and half the white wine. Add the bouquet garni, salt and pepper and stew over a low heat for 10 minutes.

3. Meanwhile halve, core and de-seed the peppers. Slice into strips.

4. Wash the aubergines and courgettes, then slice thickly. Heat another 4 tbsps of oil in a saucepan. Cook these vegetables over a high heat, stirring from time to time, until golden.

5. Heat the oven to 190°C/375°F/Gas Mark 5.

6. Heat the remaining oil in another saucepan and brown the sliced peppers.

7. Put all the vegetables in the saucepan with the onion and tomato mixture. Add the remaining wine and cover the pan.

8. Place in the centre of the oven and stew for 2 hours.

Remove the vegetables using a slotted spoon. Drain briefly (the vegetables should still be soaked in olive oil) and place in a serving dish.

This dish tastes even better the following day, whether served hot or cold.

Accompaniment:
fresh French bread.

Recommended drink:
red vin de pays or a light French rosé.

TIP

Preparing this ratatouille is really only worthwhile if you are catering for a large group of people. Since each vegetable must be pre-cooked individually, it takes a lot of time and effort. Ensure that you have a big enough pot to hold the entire mixture.

GRATIN DAUPHINOIS

SERVES 4 ■

*Preparation and cooking
time: 1 hour
Kcal per portion: 430
P = 10g, F = 28g, C = 34g*

*1kg/2¼lbs floury potatoes
250ml/8 fl oz single cream
1 garlic clove
60g/2oz butter
salt and pepper
freshly grated nutmeg
50g/2oz Gruyère cheese*

1. Peel and wash the potatoes. Slice very thinly (preferably in a food processor). Put the slices into cold water for a couple of minutes, then drain in a sieve and dry with absorbent paper.
2. Bring the cream to the boil in a small saucepan. Cut the garlic clove in half and rub the inside of a large shallow baking dish with the cut surfaces. Grease with a third of the butter.
3. Heat the oven to 200°C/400°F/Gas Mark 6.
4. Arrange a third of the sliced potato in the dish and season generously with salt,

> **TIP**
>
> *If you are serving
> the gratin with a
> particularly
> tender meat dish,
> omit the cheese so
> that it does not
> overpower its
> delicate flavour.*

pepper and nutmeg. Grate the cheese and sprinkle half over the potato. Arrange half the remaining potatoes on top, season again and sprinkle with the remaining cheese.
5. Make a third layer from the remaining potato, arranging them carefully. Season with salt and pepper and pour over the cream.

Thinly slice the potatoes in a food processor.

Arrange potatoes, seasoning and cheese in alternate layers in an ovenproof dish. Pour the cream over the top.

6. Dot the remaining butter over the gratin. Bake the potatoes on the bottom shelf of the oven for 45 minutes until golden. Test to see if the potatoes are done. If not cook for a little longer.
An accompaniment to grilled and roast lamb or other meat dishes. Can also be served as a main dish with vegetables or a colourful, mixed salad.

SAVOY CABBAGE INDIAN STYLE

(see photo on page 44)

SERVES 4 ■

*Preparation and cooking
time: 30 minutes
Kcal per portion: 170
P = 7g, F = 12g, C = 9g*

*1 Savoy cabbage (about
1kg/2¼lbs)
2-3 dried red chillies
salt
3 tbsps oil
1 tsp mustard seeds
1 tbsp chick-pea flour
2 tbsps finely chopped fresh
ginger root
1 tsp turmeric
3 tbsps desiccated coconut*

1. Pull any limp leaves from the cabbage. Separate the remaining leaves, wash and slice into fine strips. Wash, halve, de-seed and finely chop the chillies.
2. Bring a little salted water to the boil in a saucepan. Blanch the strips of cabbage quickly in the water, then drain in a sieve.
3. Heat the oil in a deep non-stick frying-pan and fry the mustard seeds briefly. Add the chick-pea flour, chillies, ginger, turmeric, coconut and cabbage.
4. Fry vigorously over a high heat for a few minutes. Then cook over a low heat for 10 minutes until soft, stirring occasionally. Season with salt.
Accompaniment:
boiled brown rice.
Recommended drink:
mineral water or beer.

COURGETTE OMELETTES

SERVES 4 ■

*Preparation and cooking
time: 40 minutes
Kcal per portion: 475
P = 27g, F = 33g, C = 19g*

*6 small courgettes (about
750g/1½lbs)
1 tsp salt
4 eggs
4 garlic cloves
1 bunch parsley
200g/7oz mature Cheddar
cheese
6-8 tbsps self-raising flour
oil for frying*

1. Wash and trim the courgettes; grate coarsely. Put into a bowl and stir in the salt and eggs.
2. Finely chop the garlic cloves and parsley and grate the cheese. Add to the courgette mixture and sift in enough flour to make a firm dough. Mix together thoroughly.

> **TIP**
>
> *These delicate
> courgette
> omelettes with
> cheese make a
> satisfying
> vegetarian main
> dish.*

3. Heat a generous amount of oil in a large frying-pan. Using a spoon, put small balls of courgette dough into the oil and press flat. Fry on both sides until brown and crispy. Serve immediately.
Accompaniment:
tomato salad or mixed salad. Serves 6-8 as a side dish.
Recommended drink:
crisp, white vin de pays.

STUFFED ARTICHOKES

SERVES 4 ■ ■ ■
Preparation and cooking time: 70 minutes
Kcal per portion: 410
P = 12g, F = 35g, C = 9g

4 large artichokes
½ lemon
salt and pepper
90g/3½oz butter
150g/5½oz smoked salmon
2 tbsps cream
½ tsp lemon pepper
4 tbsps dry white wine
1 tbsp finely chopped shallot
3 egg yolks
a little lemon juice

1. Cut off the top third of the artichoke and snap off the stem. Rub the cut surfaces and bases immediately with lemon.
2. Boil the artichokes in very lightly salted water for 30-40 minutes (depending on size). Remove with a slotted spoon and cool. Loosen the outer leaves; remove the soft inner leaves and discard the bristly choke.
3. Generously butter four small ovenproof dishes (use about 15g/½oz).
4. Finely chop the smoked salmon. Using the back of a spoon, squeeze the artichoke flesh out of the inner leaves and mix it with the salmon, cream and lemon pepper.
5. Put the wine, shallot and a pinch of pepper into a small saucepan. Boil until only about 1 teaspoon of liquid remains.
6. Put the egg yolks into a heatproof bowl set over a pan of gently simmering water. Press the reduced wine and shallot mixture through a sieve into the egg yolks. Add a small knob of butter and beat over a medium heat until the sauce is creamy and sticks to the whisk.

7. Remove the bowl from the heat. Stir in the remaining butter, in small knobs. From time to time, return the bowl very briefly to the hot

TIP

When buying artichokes, make sure that the heads are tightly closed and have no black spots. An artichoke should feel heavy for its size and should not look dry.

water so that the sauce does not cool and the butter melts completely. As soon as all the butter has been used up season the sauce with salt and lemon juice.
8. Place the prepared salmon mixture in the artichokes. Pour over the sauce and brown for 1-2 minutes under a hot grill. Serve as a starter.
Recommended drink:
white Bordeaux.

SPINACH-STUFFED MUSHROOMS

SERVES 4 ■ ■
Preparation and cooking time: 50 minutes
Kcal per portion: 210
P = 6g, F = 17g, C = 4g

25 open-cup mushrooms
30g/1oz butter
100g/4oz button mushrooms
100g/4oz young spinach
1 bunch parsley
2 shallots
1 tsp oregano
salt and pepper
125ml/5 fl oz single cream
1 egg
6 tbsps white wine

1. Clean the open-cup mushrooms; remove and reserve the stalks. Grease a large ovenproof dish with half the butter and arrange the mushrooms in it, gills upward.
2. Wipe the button mushrooms. Wash the spinach and the parsley.
3. Chop the button mushrooms, reserved stalks, spinach and parsley.
4. Heat the oven to 220°C/425°F/Gas Mark 7.
5. Put the remaining butter in a saucepan. Finely chop the shallots and sweat until transparent. Add the mushrooms, spinach, parsley, oregano, salt and pepper. Cook briefly, then remove from the heat.
6. Mix the egg with the cream and stir into the mixture. Spoon into the mushrooms.
7. Sprinkle with the wine and cover the dish with aluminium foil. Cook in the oven for about 20 minutes. Serve as a starter.
Recommended drink:
spicy Müller-Thurgau from Baden or the Palatinate.

Clean the mushrooms with a brush.

Carefully separate the stalks from the caps.

Place the mushrooms in a buttered ovenproof dish.

Using a teaspoon, fill the mushrooms with the spinach mixture.

SCORZONERA IN PUFF PASTRY

SERVES 6 ■ ■ ■
*Preparation and cooking
time: 1 hour 20 minutes
Kcal per portion: 500
P = 13g, F = 35g, C = 32g*

*500g/1lb2oz frozen puff
pastry, thawed
butter and flour for the tin
1kg/2¼lbs scorzonera
1 tbsp lemon juice
150g/5½oz cooked ham
150g/5½oz broccoli
salt and pepper
1 egg yolk
4 tbsps dry white wine
125g/5oz crème fraîche*

1. Roll out about two-thirds
of the pastry 3mm/⅛ inch

> **TIP**
>
> *Clean scorzonera
> with a brush
> under running
> water and peel
> using a swivel
> vegetable peeler.
> Always wear
> plastic or rubber
> gloves when
> peeling
> scorzonera,
> because the juice
> stains the skin.*

thick. Butter and flour a 23-
cm/9 inch springform cake
tin. Line with the pastry and
put in the refrigerator.
2. Peel the scorzonera and
place immediately in water
containing a squeeze of
lemon juice, to keep it white.
3. Dice the ham. Divide the
broccoli into small florets.
Heat the oven to
220°C/425°F/Gas Mark 7.
4. Cut the scorzonera into
5cm/2 inch pieces. Cook in
salted water For 15-20 minutes until just soft. Drain,
reserving the stock and set
aside.

5. Prick the pastry base with
a fork and cover with greaseproof paper. Fill the tin with
dried beans and place in the
centre of the oven. After 10
minutes, reduce the heat to
190°C/375°F/Gas Mark 5.
After a further 5 minutes,
remove the beans and the
baking paper and put the tin
back into the oven.
6. Roll out a lid from the
remaining pastry (5mm/
¼ inch larger than the tin).
Decorate with left-over pastry and brush with egg yolk.
Slide the lid over the tin, in
the oven, and bake until it
changes colour. The pastry
should not darken.
7. Boil the broccoli florets in
a little salted water for a few
minutes. Remove from the
water and cool in ice-cold
water, so that they retain
their colour.
8. For the sauce, reduce
500ml/16 fl oz of the scorzonera stock by half. Blend
in a liquidiser with the wine
and a few pieces of scorzonera. Heat in a saucepan with
the crème fraîche, but do
not boil. Season with salt
and pepper.
9. Add the well-drained scorzonera and broccoli florets,
together with the ham, to
the sauce. Reheat and pour
into the rough puff pastry
casing. Cover with the lid
and serve immediately.
Recommended drink:
Johannisberg Riesling or a
medium dry Müller-Thurgau.

*Butter and flour a springform
cake tin.*

*Roll out the puff pastry and use it
to line the cake tin.*

*Cover the pastry case with a layer
of greaseproof paper, then fill the
tin with dried beans.*

*Roll out a lid from the remaining
pastry and decorate with pastry
leftovers.*

SCORZONERA FRITTERS

SERVES 6 ■ ■ ■
*Preparation and cooking
time: 1 hour 10 minutes
Kcal per portion: 330
P = 9g, F = 19g, C = 25g*

*1kg/2¼lbs scorzonera
salt and pepper
1 tbsp lemon juice
oil for deep frying
lemon wedges to garnish*
FOR THE BATTER:
*150g/5½oz wholemeal flour
200ml/6 fl oz dry cider
2 egg whites*
FOR THE SAUCE:
*2 egg yolks
2 tbsps lemon juice
½ tsp Dijon mustard
1 tbsp oil
4 tbsps chopped herbs
100g/4oz quark or curd
cheese
Worcestershire sauce*

1. First make the batter. Sift
the flour, mix with the cider
until smooth and leave to
stand for 1 hour.
2. Wash and peel the scorzonera. Cut into 5cm/2 inch
pieces and boil in salted
water with 1 tbsp of lemon
juice for 15 minutes, until
soft. Cool in the liquid.
3. Make the sauce. Mix the
egg yolks with the lemon
juice and mustard, preferably in a liquidiser. Gradually
add the oil. Add the herbs
and quark or curd cheese.
Season.
4. Whisk the egg whites with
a pinch of salt until stiff, then
fold into the batter.
5. Heat the oil in a deep-fat
fryer or large saucepan to
180°C/350°F.
6. Drain the scorzonera. Dip
into the batter and deep-fry
in the oil until golden brown.
Drain on absorbent paper.
7. Arrange the fritters on a
serving platter, garnish with
lemon wedges and serve
with the sauce.
Recommended drink:
Pinot Noir.

KOHLRABI WITH CHANTERELLES AND MASCARPONE

SERVES 4 ■■
Preparation and cooking time: 1 hour
Kcal per portion: 315
P = 10g, F = 24g, C = 14g

750g/1½lbs young kohlrabi
salt and white pepper
300ml/12 fl oz milk
2 shallots
15g/½oz butter
200g/7oz chanterelle
*   mushrooms*
1 tsp chopped marjoram
150ml/5½ fl oz single cream
2 egg yolks
1 tsp cornflour
75g/3oz mascarpone cheese
pinch of nutmeg

1. Peel the kohlrabi and cut into slices about 5mm/ ¼ inch thick. Lightly salt the milk, bring to the boil and add the kohlrabi. Boil over a low heat for 10 minutes until half cooked.
2. Heat the butter in a small pan. Chop the shallots and sweat until transparent.
3. Clean and trim the chanterelles; if large, halve lengthways. Add to the kohlrabi and cook gently for 10 minutes.
4. Butter a gratin dish. Drain the kohlrabi and chanterelles; arrange in the dish in layers, finishing with kohlrabi.
5. Heat the oven to 190°C/375°F/Gas Mark 5.
6. Mix together the marjoram, cream, egg yolks, shallots, cornflour and mascarpone; season with salt, pepper and nutmeg. Spread the mixture over the kohlrabi and bake for 30 minutes.
Accompaniment:
fresh crusty bread.
Recommended drink:
Valpolicella.

KOHLRABI STUFFED WITH SAUSAGE

SERVES 4 ■■
Preparation and cooking time: 1 hour
Kcal per portion: 300
P = 11g, F = 27g, C = 4g

4 young kohlrabi
200g/7oz pork sausagemeat
2 tbsps finely chopped
*   parsley*
salt and pepper
butter for the dish
250ml/8 fl oz stock
2 tbsps finely grated Cheddar
*   cheese*
30g/1oz butter

1. Heat the oven to 180°C/350°F/Gas Mark 4.
2. Peel and carefully hollow out the kohlrabi. Finely chop the flesh and mix with the sausagemeat and half the parsley. Season with salt and pepper.
3. Stuff the kohlrabi with this mixture. Butter a gratin dish generously. Put in the kohlrabi, pour over the stock and cover with a lid or aluminium foil.
4. Bake the kohlrabi for about 35 minutes. At the end of the cooking time remove the lid from the dish, sprinkle the kohlrabi with the cheese and dot with the butter. Return briefly to the oven, then brown under the grill until golden.
Just before serving, sprinkle with the remaining parsley.
Accompaniment:
fresh wholemeal bread.
Recommended drink:
Burgundy or good vin de pays.

CREAMED CARROTS

SERVES 4 ■
Preparation and cooking time: 35-45 minutes
Kcal per portion: 220
P = 3g, F = 18g, C = 13g

1kg/2¼lbs carrots
1 tsp sugar
75g/3oz butter
500ml/16 fl oz stock
2-4 tbsps single cream
salt and pepper
pinch of thyme
2 tbsps finely chopped parsley

1. Scrub young carrots; peel older ones with a swivel peeler. Slice thinly.
2. Melt the sugar and one-third of the butter in a large saucepan. Add the carrots,

> **TIP**
> *The purée can be seasoned with chopped chervil. If you are using winter carrots, add a pinch of sugar.*

turn in the butter and cook gently for 3 minutes. Pour in the stock and cook for 20 minutes or until very tender.
3. Drain the carrots. (Reserve the stock, which can be used to make soup.) Purée the carrots in a liquidiser, food processor or vegetable mill.
4. Put the carrot purée in a saucepan, add the cream and season with salt, pepper and thyme.
5. Dice the remaining butter and stir into the hot creamed carrot. Serve sprinkled with the parsley, as a side dish with roasts or grilled meat.

CARROTS IN VERMOUTH SAUCE

SERVES 4 ■
Preparation and cooking time: 30-40 minutes
Kcal per portion: 240
P = 3g, F = 19g, C = 14g

1kg/2¼lbs carrots
45g/1½oz butter
1 tsp sugar
500ml/16 fl oz stock
2 tbsps dry vermouth
125ml/5 fl oz single cream
salt and pepper
pinch of nutmeg

1. Scrub or peel the carrots and slice thinly. Heat the butter in a large saucepan, add the carrots and cook gently for a few minutes, stirring frequently. Pour in the stock, cover and cook slowly for about 15 minutes until slightly soft.
2. Uncover the pan and cook until all the liquid has evaporated.
3. Add the vermouth and the cream. Season with salt and

> **TIP**
> *Vermouth gives the sauce a distinctive touch. Serve the carrots sprinkled with chopped parsley, chives or chervil.*

pepper and heat gently until the sauce is creamy.
Serve as a side dish with roast meat or as part of a mixed vegetable dish.

VEGETABLE FLAN

SERVES 6 ■ ■

Preparation and cooking time: 1 hour 5 minutes
Kcal per portion: 360
P = 8g, F = 27g, C = 22g

300g/10oz carrots
1 head calabrese
2-3 large mushrooms
1 small red pepper
3 small courgettes
salt and pepper
1 tbsp lemon juice
300g/10oz frozen puff pastry, thawed
butter for the tin
2 eggs
200ml/7 fl oz single cream
freshly grated nutmeg

Finely slice the individual vegetables, preferably in a food processor.

1. Scrub or peel the carrots; slice thinly. Divide the calabrese into florets and wipe

TIP

Hard vegetables should always be pre-cooked so that they take the same time to cook as other, softer vegetables.

Arrange the finely sliced vegetables in concentric rings on the puff pastry.

the mushrooms. Wash and quarter the pepper; remove the core and seeds. Slice the flesh into strips. Thinly slice the courgettes.
2. Blanch the vegetables, excluding the mushrooms, in salted water for 3-4 minutes. They should still be firm.
3. Put the lemon juice in a saucepan with a little salted water and blanch the mushrooms briefly. Drain and slice thinly.
4. Butter a springform tin or quiche dish about 30cm/12 inches in diameter. Roll out the pastry and use it to line the tin. Prick all over with a fork.
5. For the glaze, beat the eggs, cream, salt, pepper and nutmeg.

6. Heat the oven to 200°C/400°F/Gas Mark 6.
7. Arrange the carrot slices, overlapping, around the edge of the pastry case. Arrange the courgettes in the same way inside the ring of carrots. Then arrange the remaining vegetables (calabrese florets, strips of pepper and, in the centre, the mushrooms) similarly on the pastry.
8. Bake for 10 minutes. Then pour half the glaze over the flan, bake for 15 minutes, then add the rest. After another 15 minutes remove the flan from the oven. Slide onto a round plate and serve immediately as a hot starter.
Recommended drink:
Beaujolais, mature Burgundy.

STUFFED AUBERGINES AU GRATIN

(see photo on page 31)

SERVES 4 ■ ■

Preparation and cooking time: 20 minutes
Kcal per portion: 260
P = 11g, F = 17g, C = 15g

4 medium aubergines
salt and pepper
2-3 tbsps oil
150g/5½oz Cheddar cheese
2 large tomatoes
16 basil leaves
8 slices Parma ham

1. Halve the aubergines lengthways. Sprinkle the cut surfaces with a little salt to draw out any bitterness. Leave for about 15 minutes.
2. Meanwhile cut the cheese into 3mm/⅛ inch thick slices. Blanch the tomatoes in boiling water, then peel and slice. Chop eight of the basil leaves into strips.
3. Heat the oven to 220°C/425°F/Gas Mark 7.
4. Line a large baking sheet with aluminium foil and brush with a little oil.
5. Pat the aubergines dry thoroughly with absorbent paper and place, cut sides down, on the sheet. Bake for 20 minutes.
6. Turn the aubergines over and brush the flesh with oil. Cover each half with a slice of ham and 2 slices of tomato. Sprinkle with the basil strips and a little salt. Cover with the cheese slices and return to the oven until the cheese has melted. It should not change colour.

Halve the aubergines lengthways and sprinkle with salt.

After 15 minutes, pat the cut surfaces dry with absorbent paper.

Place the aubergines on a baking sheet, cut surfaces downwards.

7. Arrange the aubergines on warmed plates. Garnish each half with a basil leaf, sprinkle generously with pepper and serve as a starter.
Recommended drink:
red Côtes de Provence or Côtes-du-Rhône.

RED CABBAGE WITH RED WINE

SERVES 6-8 ■

Preparation and cooking time: 2¼ hours
Kcal per portion (8 portions): 150
P = 3g, F = 10g, C = 7g

1 red cabbage (about
  1kg/2¼lbs)
1 large onion
50g/2oz lean rindless bacon
5 tbsps olive oil
200ml/6 fl oz red wine
250ml/8 fl oz stock
1 cooking apple
1 small potato
1 tsp caraway or dill seeds
pinch of sugar
salt and pepper
2 tbsps wine vinegar

1. Finely chop the red cabbage, removing the stalk. Finely dice the onion and bacon.
2. Heat the oil in a large flameproof casserole. Add the onion and bacon and sweat until the onion is transparent. Gradually add the cabbage, stirring frequently. Cook for about 15 minutes, until it collapses.
3. Pour in the red wine. Then add just enough stock to cover the cabbage.
4. Coarsely grate the apple and potato into the cabbage. (The apple can also be cooked whole and added to the finished dish by pressing through a sieve.) Add the caraway or dill seeds, sugar, vinegar, salt and pepper. Cover tightly and simmer gently for about 1½ hours. At the end of the cooking time the liquid should have reduced considerably.
4. Ten minutes before serving, add the vinegar.
5. Serve as an accompaniment to chestnuts, game, poultry or pork.

SAUERKRAUT WITH SPARKLING WINE

(see photo on page 54)

SERVES 4-6 ■

Preparation and cooking time: 1 hour 20 minutes
Kcal per portion (6 portions): 315
P = 5g, F = 27g, C = 6g

1 onion
30g/1oz butter
500g/1lb 2oz bottled
  sauerkraut
200ml/6 fl oz stock
1 apple
200g/7oz rindless smoked
  bacon
10 juniper berries
½ tbsp brandy (optional)
250ml/8 fl oz dry sparkling
  white wine

1. Finely chop the onion. Heat the butter in a large saucepan and sweat the onion until transparent. Add the sauerkraut, fry briefly and pour in the stock.
2. Peel and slice the apple. Chop the bacon and crush the juniper berries lightly.

> **TIP**
>
> *Leftover sauerkraut can be layered with minced roast chicken and cheese sauce and baked.*

Add all to the sauerkraut, cover and cook for at least 1 hour.
3. Thirty minutes before serving turn the sauerkraut mixture into a sieve and drain. Return to the pan with the brandy and sparkling wine; cook until ready.
4. Serve as an accompaniment to roast game.

CHINESE-STYLE CABBAGE

SERVES 4 ■ ■

Preparation and cooking time: 30 minutes
Kcal per portion: 615
P = 30g, F = 47g, C = 14g

500g/1lb2oz pork
2 tbsps peanut oil
½ tsp ground ginger
salt
100ml/3 fl oz strong chicken
  stock
2 tbsps sake or dry sherry
2 leeks
750g/1½lbs Chinese leaves
1 tsp sugar
3 tbsps soy sauce
1 garlic clove
pinch of cayenne

1. Slice the meat into thin strips. Heat 1 tablespoon of oil in a wok or deep frying-pan and stir-fry the meat briefly over a high heat. Season with ginger and salt. Add 2 tablespoons of chicken stock and the sake or sherry. Reduce the heat and stir-fry for a further 15 minutes.
2. Meanwhile trim and wash the leeks; slice into rings.
3. Heat 1 tablespoon of oil in another frying-pan and sweat the leeks for a few minutes.
4. Wash and drain the Chinese leaves. Cut into 2cm/¾ inch strips and add to the leeks. Stir-fry until tender-crisp and remove from the pan.
5. Add the sugar, soy sauce, crushed garlic and remaining chicken stock to the frying-pan and quickly bring to the boil.
6. Add the vegetables and sauce to the meat and season with cayenne.
Accompaniment:
rice.
Recommended drink:
rosé wine.

PEAS WITH HAM AND PEPPER

SERVES 4 ■

Preparation and cooking time: 30 minutes
Kcal per portion: 175
P = 12g, F = 8g, C = 15g

100g/4oz cooked ham
1 small onion
1 green pepper
1 tbsp olive oil
400g/14oz frozen peas,
  thawed
4 canned tomatoes
1 garlic clove
salt and pepper

1. Dice the ham and finely chop the onion. Halve, core and de-seed the pepper; cut into small squares.
2. Heat the olive oil in a frying-pan and gently cook the ham, onion, pepper and peas for 10 minutes.

> **TIP**
>
> *These vegetables can be transformed into an excellent pasta dish when mixed with 125ml/5 fl oz single cream and 2 tbsps grated Parmesan. Bring to the boil and serve mixed with freshly cooked ribbon pasta.*

3. Chop the tomatoes. Add to the braised vegetables, together with the crushed garlic, and cook for 5 minutes.
4. Season with salt and pepper and serve immediately as a side dish.

Wholefood Recipes

*W*holefood cuisine revels in making the most of each season's vegetables, using the right herbs and spices with each dish so that delicious aromas issue from every pot and pan. Fresh, crisp vegetables are essential, perfectly prepared so that every dish brings out each unmistakable flavour.
Why not try for yourself the Celeriac Pancakes with Tomatoes, Chard Strudel Stuffed with Vegetables and Cracked Wheat, or Mushroom Patties with Chervil Sauce. You will soon realise why wholefood cooking is becoming so popular.

Courgette and Mushroom Terrine
(see recipe on page 75)

CRACKED WHEAT AND COURGETTE RISSOLES

SERVES 4 ■■
*Preparation and cooking
time: 50 minutes
Kcal per portion: 580
P = 19g, F = 22g, C = 77g*

*600g/1¼lbs small courgettes
salt and pepper
200g/7oz cracked wheat
4 slices wholemeal bread
bunch of spring onions
2 garlic cloves
½ tsp rosemary
1 tsp thyme
2 eggs
breadcrumbs
4-5 tbsps oil*

1. Cut the ends off the courgettes, wash and coarsely grate. Sprinkle with salt and leave to stand for 30 minutes.
2. Cook the cracked wheat in the pressure-cooker, covered in water, for 15 minutes. Soak the slices of bread in lukewarm water.

TIP

If you do not have a pressure-cooker, it is better to soak the cracked wheat in cold water for a few hours, then boil them in a saucepan for 25-30 minutes until tender but still firm.

3. Trim and wash the spring onions. Slice finely, including some of the green parts. Finely chop the garlic.
4. Squeeze out the courgettes and slices of bread thoroughly. Put into a bowl. Thoroughly drain the cracked wheat in a sieve. Add to the courgettes and bread, together with the spring onion, garlic and herbs. Gradually add the eggs. Season with salt and pepper and work into a soft dough. If it is too wet, bind with breadcrumbs.
5. Heat the oil in a non-stick frying-pan. Fry the rissoles over a medium heat for 3-4 minutes on each side.
Accompaniment:
cheese sauce.

The best way to grate courgettes is in a food processor.

Finely slice the spring onions, including some of the green parts.

Fry the rissoles in oil on both sides for 3-4 minutes.

SPANISH ONIONS WITH SOUFFLE STUFFING

SERVES 2 ■■
*Preparation and cooking
time: 1½ hours
Kcal per portion: 730
P = 47g, F = 48g, C = 28g*

*4 Spanish onions
butter for the dish*

FOR THE STUFFING:
*125ml/5 fl oz single cream
200g/7oz curd cheese
100g/4oz grated Parmesan
    cheese
3 eggs, separated
salt and white pepper
freshly grated nutmeg*

1. Heat the oven to 200°C/400°F/Gas Mark 6. Bake the onions, un-peeled, for 1 hour.
2. Cool and peel the onions. Cut a lid from the top and hollow out the centre, leaving three layers of onion intact. Butter an ovenproof dish and put the onions in it.
3. For the stuffing, finely blend the onion flesh and the cream in a liquidiser. Press through a sieve and mix with the curd cheese, Parmesan and egg yolks. Season with salt and pepper. Whisk the egg whites stiffly and fold into the mixture. Stuff the onions and bake in the centre of the oven for 15 minutes.
An accompaniment to any meat dish. Also makes a good starter.

COURGETTE AND MUSHROOM TERRINE

(see photo on page 68)

SERVES 4 ■■
*Preparation and cooking
time: 1 hour 20 minutes
Kcal per portion: 460
P = 14g, F = 40g, C = 13g*

*500g/1lb2oz small courgettes
200g/7oz mushrooms
2 small shallots
45g/1½oz butter
250ml/8 fl oz single cream
250ml/8 fl oz milk
4 eggs
bunch of parsley
salt and white pepper
freshly grated nutmeg*

1. Wash the courgettes, trim and slice thinly. Wipe the mushrooms and slice thinly. Finely dice the shallots.
2. Heat the butter in a flameproof casserole and lightly brown the vegetables.
3. Heat the oven to 200°C/400°F/Gas Mark 6.
4. Thoroughly whisk together the cream, milk and eggs. Finely chop the parsley, add to the mixture and season with salt, pepper and nutmeg. Add the vegetables. Butter a 1.5-litre/2½-pint terrine (or line with greaseproof paper) and fill with the mixture. Bake in the centre of the oven for about 45 minutes.
The terrine looks very attractive if it is made in a round, dome-shaped dish and covered with slices of lightly cooked courgette after turning out.
Excellent hot or cold.
Recommended drink:
strong, full-bodied white wine, e.g. Pinot Bianco from Friuli.

CHARD STRUDEL STUFFED WITH VEGETABLES AND CRACKED WHEAT

SERVES 4 ■■
*Preparation and cooking
time: 1 hour 10 minutes
Kcal per portion: 420
P = 21g, F = 20g, C = 39g*

*200g/7oz cracked wheat
400g/14oz mixed vegetables
   (leeks, carrots, courgettes,
   kohlrabi)
10 large chard leaves
salt and white pepper
2 shallots
30g/1oz butter
freshly grated nutmeg
200g/7oz quark or curd
   cheese
4 eggs*

1. Cook the cracked wheat, covered in water, in a pressure-cooker for 15 minutes. Discard the water and drain.
2. Trim and wash the vegetables and cut into fine strips. Separate the chard stalks from the leaves. Finely slice the stalks and add to the other vegetables.
3. Bring a generous amount of salted water to the boil. First blanch the mixed vegetables for 2 minutes, then the chard leaves for 30 seconds. Drain the leaves. Spread them out next to each other, slightly overlapping, on a large piece of greased aluminium foil.
4. Dice the shallots finely. Heat the butter in a large frying-pan, add the onion and sweat until transparent. Add the drained vegetables. Cook for a few minutes, then season with salt, pepper and nutmeg.
5. In a bowl, mix the quark or curd cheese with the eggs. Add the cracked wheat and the vegetables. Mix well and season generously.
6. Spread the mixture over the chard leaves and roll the

Spread the chard out on a large piece of aluminium foil, with the leaves just overlapping.

Spread the quark mixture evenly over the chard leaves.

Wrap the chard leaf strudel tightly in aluminium foil.

leaves up into a strudel. Wrap tightly in the aluminium foil and cook in lightly simmering salted water for 15 minutes. Serve hot cut into thick slices.
Accompaniment:
sherry or port sauce.

BRUSSELS SPROUT LEAVES IN CREAMY SAUCE

SERVES 4 ■
*Preparation and cooking
time: 30 minutes
Kcal per portion: 340
P = 6g, F = 31g, C = 8g*

*500g/1lb2oz Brussels sprouts
salt and white pepper
250ml/8 fl oz single cream
3 tbsps white port
50g/2oz butter
freshly grated nutmeg*

1. Trim and wash the Brussels sprouts. Separate the individual leaves. Bring a large amount of salted water to the boil and blanch the leaves for about 1 minute. Drain in a sieve.
2. Bring the cream, port and butter to the boil in a high-sided frying-pan or shallow flameproof casserole. Season with salt, pepper and nutmeg and cook until reduced a little.
3. Put the Brussels sprout leaves into the cream sauce and toss gently. Serve immediately.
An accompaniment to white meat, rabbit and poultry, as well as game dishes in a white sauce.

> **TIP**
>
> *Use fairly large sprouts for this dish. The firmer and more tightly closed the sprouts, the better they are.*

CHARD TOPPED WITH PARMESAN

SERVES 4 ■
*Preparation and cooking
time: 30 minutes
Kcal per portion: 310
P = 14g, F = 27g, C = 3g*

*12 large chard leaves
125ml/4 fl oz beef stock
200ml/7 fl oz single cream
salt and pepper
freshly grated nutmeg
125g/5oz grated Parmesan
   cheese
2 egg yolks*

1. Wash the chard leaves. Cut out the stalks and slice both the stalks and the leaves into thin strips, keeping them separate.
2. Bring the stock to the boil in a flameproof casserole and briefly poach the chard stalks. Pour in just under half

> **TIP**
>
> *Chard stalks and leaves take widely varying times to cook, so always cook the stalks first, then just heat the leaves.*

the cream and simmer until reduced by a third. Add the leaf strips and cook for about 1 minute. Season with salt, pepper and nutmeg.
3. Heat the grill to high.
4. Put the chard mixture into an ovenproof dish and sprinkle over a thick layer of Parmesan. Whisk the egg yolks with the remaining cream and pour evenly over the cheese. Brown quickly under the grill.
An accompaniment to poultry and game.

MUSHROOM PATTIES WITH CHERVIL SAUCE

SERVES 4 ■■
*Preparation and cooking
time: 45 minutes
Kcal per portion: 640
P = 13g, F = 56g, C = 21g*

FOR THE PATTIES:
*1 Spanish onion
300g/10oz mushrooms
oil for frying
100g/4oz cooked whole oats
2 tbsps chopped flat-leaved
   parsley
3 eggs
salt and white pepper
wholemeal flour if needed*

FOR THE SAUCE:
*250ml/8 fl oz stock
   (vegetable, beef or chicken)
125ml/5 fl oz single cream
50g/2oz butter
salt and white pepper
2 tbsps whipped cream
50g/2oz fresh chervil*

*If liked, peel the mushrooms with
a pointed knife.*

*Just before serving, mix the
whipped cream and chervil into
the sauce.*

1. Finely dice the onion.
Wipe or peel the mush-
rooms and finely dice.
2. Heat 2 tablespoons of oil
in a frying-pan. Gently sweat
the onion without allowing it
to change colour.
3. Combine the onions,
mushrooms, oats and pars-
ley in a bowl. Gradually add
the eggs. Season with salt
and pepper and work into a
soft dough If it is too soft add
a little flour.
4. For the sauce, heat the
stock, cream and butter in a
saucepan. Season with salt
and pepper and cook until
reduced by a third.
5. Make small patties from
the mushroom mixture.
Heat 4-6 tablespoons oil in a
non-stick frying-pan. Fry the
patties for 3-4 minutes on
each side.
6. Meanwhile finely chop
the chervil, reserving a few
springs to garnish. Beat the
reduced sauce with a hand-
held mixer, adding the
whipped cream and
chopped chervil. Pour the
sauce over the patties and
garnish with chervil.
Accompaniment:
glazed carrots or broccoli
florets.

ASPARAGUS AND WHOLE-WHEAT GRAINS TOPPED WITH PARMESAN

SERVES 4 ■■
*Preparation and cooking
time: 45 minutes
Kcal per portion: 455
P = 23g, F = 28g, C = 36g*

*2kg/4½lbs asparagus
salt and white pepper
1 tsp sugar
30g/1oz butter
1 tbsp chopped shallot
125g/5oz cooked wholewheat
   grains
100g/4oz grated Parmesan
   cheese
125ml/5 fl oz single cream
2 egg yolks*

1. Scrape the asparagus
stalks and cut off the lower
ends if necessary. Bring a
generous amount of salted,
sugared water to the boil.
Boil the spears for 5-10 minutes, depending on thick-
ness, until still firm. Drain
well.
2. Heat the butter in a frying-
pan. Gently fry the shallot
and wholewheat grains.
Season with salt and pepper.
3. Heat the grill to high.
4. Transfer the asparagus
spears into an ovenproof
dish. Sprinkle first with
wholewheat grains, then
with Parmesan.
5. Beat the cream with the
egg yolks and pour over the
cheese. Quickly brown the
asparagus under the grill.
Recommended drink:
dry Grey Burgundy from
Franconia or Baden.

LEEKS TOPPED WITH GORGONZOLA

SERVES 4 ■■
*Preparation and cooking
time: 45 minutes
Kcal per portion: 375
P = 15g, F = 31g, C = 10g*

*4 young leeks
salt and white pepper
1 medium carrot
30g/1oz butter
100ml/4 fl oz single cream
freshly grated nutmeg
150g/5½oz Gorgonzola cheese
2 egg yolks
butter for the dish*

1. Trim off the roots, remove
and reserve the green parts
from the leeks. Cut in half,
wash thoroughly and blanch
in boiling salted water for
about 3 minutes. Remove
and drain well.
2. Trim, wash and finely dice
the carrot, together with the
green parts of the leeks.
Heat the butter in a flameproof casserole and sweat
the diced vegetables.
Season with salt and pepper.
3. Heat the oven to
200°C/400°F/Gas Mark 6.
4. Bring the cream, salt, pepper and nutmeg to the boil in
a saucepan. Press the
Gorgonzola through a sieve
into the cream. Bring back to
the boil, then remove from
the heat and beat in the egg
yolks.
5. Butter an ovenproof dish
and put in the leeks. Cover
with the diced vegetables.
Pour over the cream. and
bake in the centre of the
oven for about 15 minutes or
until cooked.
An accompaniment to roast
beef or veal.

QUARK AND VEGETABLE STRUDEL

SERVES 4 ■ ■ ■

Preparation and cooking time: 50 minutes
Relaxing time: 2 hours
Kcal per portion: 1085
P = 41g, F = 77g, C = 56g

FOR THE PASTRY:
300g/10oz wholemeal flour
pinch of salt
1 egg
1 egg yolk
125g/5oz crème fraîche
75g/3oz butter
1 egg yolk
4 tbsps single cream

FOR THE FILLING:
100g/4oz kohlrabi
100g/4oz carrots
100g/4oz courgettes
500g/1lb2oz quark or curd cheese
4 eggs
2 tbsps chopped kohlrabi leaves
2 tbsps chopped carrot leaves
100g/4oz roast pistachio nuts
white pepper
freshly grated nutmeg

1. For the pastry, sift the flour and salt on to the work top. Make a hollow in the centre. Place the egg, egg yolk and cream in the hollow. Dot the butter, in small knobs, around the edge. Using a round-bladed knife, first cut the fat into the flour. Quickly knead to a smooth dough, working from the outside inwards. Wrap in foil and chill for 2 hours.
2. For the filling, peel the kohlrabi and carrot. Cut the ends from the courgettes. Chop everything into thin sticks. Blanch in plenty of boiling salted water and drain thoroughly in a sieve.
3. Put the quark or curd cheese into a bowl. Stir until smooth and gradually add the eggs, chopped kohlrabi and carrot leaves, pistachio nuts and drained vegetables.

Season with salt, pepper and nutmeg.
4. Heat the oven to 200°C/400°F/Gas Mark 6.
5. Roll out the dough on a floured board into as thin a square as possible. Cover with the quark and vegetable mixture and roll up.

TIP

The strudel can be served either as a side dish or as a main course, possibly with a herb sauce. Toasted sunflower seeds can be added to the quark mixture instead of roasted pistachio nuts.

6. Butter a baking sheet and put the strudel on it with the join underneath. Heat together the egg yolks and cream. Brush the strudel with the mixture. Bake in the centre of the oven for 15-20 minutes until golden.
Recommended drink: dry Sylvaner.

Put the quark, eggs, pistachio nuts and chopped leaves into a bowl and stir.

Stir the vegetables into the quark mixture.

Spread the quark and vegetable mixture over the rolled-out pastry.

Before baking, brush the strudel with a mixture of egg yolk and cream.

BAKED POTATOES WITH MUSHROOM FILLING

SERVES 4 ■

Preparation and cooking time: 1 hour 10 minutes
Kcal per portion: 345
P = 7g, f = 24g, C = 25g

4 large floury potatoes
200g/7oz mushrooms
1 shallot
45g/1½oz butter
150g/5½oz crème fraîche
salt and white pepper
150g/5½oz fresh bean sprouts

1. Heat the oven to 200°C/400°F/Gas Mark 6. Thoroughly wash the potatoes and wrap, unpeeled, in aluminium foil. Bake for about 1 hour, until cooked.
2. Meanwhile wipe and finely chop the mushrooms;

TIP

The potatoes look attractive served in the open aluminium foil. In summer, the potato parcels can also be barbecued.

finely dice the shallot. Heat the butter in a frying-pan, add the mushrooms and shallot and brown lightly over a medium heat. Stir in the crème fraîche. Season with salt and pepper and bring to the boil. Add the bean sprouts and heat quickly in the mushroom sauce.
3. Take the potatoes out of the oven. Unwrap and cut off a lid. Hollow out the potatoes a little and fill with the mushroom mixture.

Quick-and-easy Recipes

*T*he quick recipes in this chapter are proof that there's no magic about fast food. Barely half an hour is all that's needed to produce an attractively served vegetable side-dish or main course. Aubergines with Garlic, Curried Chinese Leaves with Almonds, Cheese-topped Fennel with a nut crust: all can become complete meals for those who are happy not to eat meat, particularly when complemented by a bowl of salad or a nourishing dessert. If time is short frozen vegetables can be used instead of fresh ones, making the preparation and cooking times even quicker.

Aubergines with Garlic
(see recipe on page 84)

AUBERGINES WITH GARLIC

(see photo on page 83)

SERVES 4 ■
*Preparation and cooking
time: 30 minutes
Kcal per portion: 225
P = 3g, f = 19g, C = 10g*

600g/1¼lbs aubergines
5 tbsps olive oil
4 garlic cloves
500g/1lb2oz canned chopped
    tomato
salt and pepper
2 tsps thyme, fresh or dried

1. Wash the aubergines and remove the stalk ends. First quarter lengthways, then cut into slices about 1cm/½ inch thick. Heat the olive oil in a large frying-pan. and fry until golden. Remove from the pan.
2. Crush the garlic and stir into the oil remaining in the pan. Sweat until golden.

TIP

This vegetable dish also tastes delicious cold. It could then be seasoned with a little red wine vinegar or lemon juice.

3. Add the tomatoes and cook over a high heat until reduced by a third.
4. Return the aubergines to the frying-pan. Season with salt, pepper and thyme and cook for a further 10 minutes.
For a complete meal add 500g/1lb2oz minced steak and serve with potatoes.
An accompaniment to leg of lamb or chicken.

CAULIFLOWER WITH HAZELNUT BUTTER

SERVES 4 ■
*Preparation and cooking
time: 30 minutes
Kcal per portion: 385
P = 6g, F = 38g, C = 6g*

1 medium cauliflower (about
    750g/1½lbs)
salt and pepper
juice of ½ lemon
125g/5oz butter
5 tbsps ground hazelnuts
freshly grated nutmeg

1. Remove any leaves from the cauliflower, divide it into the smallest possible florets and wash.
2. Bring a generous amount of water, seasoned with salt and lemon juice, to the boil. Add the cauliflower florets, bring to the boil, then simmer for 8 minutes, until still firm.
3. Melt the butter in a flame-proof casserole. Sprinkle in the ground hazelnuts and cook until the butter foams. Season with salt, pepper and nutmeg.
4. Using a slotted spoon, remove the cauliflower from the cooking liquid and drain thoroughly. Arrange on a plate and pour over the hot hazelnut butter. Serve immediately.
Almonds, walnuts or pistachio nuts can be used instead of hazelnuts.
Gorgonzola cream sauce also goes very well with cauliflower, instead of the nut butter, with scrambled eggs and ham as an accompaniment.
Serve with game.

CURRIED CHINESE LEAVES WITH ALMONDS

SERVES 4 ■
*Preparation and cooking
time: 25 minutes
Kcal per portion: 195
P = 6g, F = 14g, C = 11g*

1 large onion
2 tbsps oil
1 head Chinese leaves (about
    1kg/2¼lbs)
3 garlic cloves
salt and pepper
2 tbsps curry powder
750g/1½lb can tomatoes
2 tbsps flaked almonds
15g/½oz butter
1 bunch coriander or flat-
    leaved parsley

1. Chop the onion. Heat the oil in a large frying-pan and sweat the onion until transparent.
2. Meanwhile quarter the Chinese leaves lengthways, remove the stalk and slice across into 5mm/¼ inch strips. Wash and drain well.
3. Crush the garlic, add to the chopped onion and sweat briefly. Add the Chinese leaves. Cook, covered, for 3 minutes.
4. Season the vegetables with salt and pepper. Sprinkle with the curry powder. Add the tomatoes, together with the juice. Cover and cook for 10 minutes over a low heat.
5. Meanwhile heat the butter in a non-stick frying-pan and stir-fry the almonds until golden.
6. Rinse the coriander or parsley, pull off the leaves, pat dry, and just before serving, sprinkle over the curried Chinese leaves together with the almonds.
Accompaniment:
rice, preferably a mixture of long-grain and wild rice.
Recommended drink:
buttermilk.

BROCCOLI WITH SMOKED PORK

SERVES 4 ■
*Preparation and cooking
time: 25 minutes
Kcal per portion: 175
P = 14g, F = 12g, C = 2g*

600g/1¼lbs broccoli, fresh or
    frozen
salt and pepper
1 tbsp oil
1 medium onion
200g/7oz thickly sliced
    smoked pork
freshly grated nutmeg

1. Trim fresh broccoli, divide into florets and wash. Slice the stalks. Thaw frozen broccoli and cut into small florets.
2. Bring a large saucepan of salted water to the boil and cook the broccoli for 7 minutes so that it is still firm.

TIP

Without the pork the broccoli also makes a good side dish with fish and poultry. The pork can be replaced by prawns and the vegetables served with fish dishes.

Cool in ice-cold water and drain well.
3. Meanwhile heat the oil in a large high-sided frying-pan. Chop the onion and sweat until transparent.
4. Finely dice the pork. Add to the frying-pan with the broccoli. Season with salt, pepper and nutmeg. Cover and cook for a further 7 minutes.
An accompaniment to meat balls or potato pancakes.

CHARD WITH BALSAMIC VINEGAR

SERVES 4
Preparation and cooking time: 25 minutes
Kcal per portion: 155
P = 4g, F = 13g, C = 6g

750g/1½lbs chard
30g/1oz butter
3 garlic cloves
salt and pepper
generous pinch of cayenne
4 tbsps crème fraîche
2 tbsps balsamic vinegar or
  1 tbsp red wine vinegar

1. Wash the chard and cut off the end of the stalks. Cut or pull the leaves from the stalks. Slice the stalks into 1cm/½ inch strips.

> **TIP**
>
> *Chard makes a good starter, either hot or cold.*

2. Heat the butter in a large frying-pan. Add the stalk strips and sweat, covered, over a low heat for 8 minutes.
3. Crush the garlic, and add to the stalks. Stir in the chard leaves. Season with salt, pepper and cayenne.
4. Add the crème fraîche and vinegar. Stir and bring to the boil.
The vegetables can be sprinkled with toasted pine nuts or grated Parmesan.
Accompaniment:
to poached eggs served with mashed potato and lots of chives. Also tasty with Parma ham or cold roast beef.

Cut off the end of the chard stalks.

Cut out the hard leaf end.

Slice the chard stalks into 1cm/½ inch strips.

First sweat the tender stalk strips in butter over a low heat. Then stir in the green leaves.

CREAMY LEEKS TOPPED WITH CHEESE

SERVES 4
Preparation and cooking time: 30 minutes
Kcal per portion: 460
P = 19g, f = 39g, C = 9g

750g/1½lbs leeks
salt and white pepper
butter for the dish
freshly grated nutmeg
250g/8oz quark or curd
  cheese
200ml/7 fl oz single cream
6 tbsps grated Gouda cheese
3 tbsps sunflower seeds

1. Trim the leeks and cut off the ends. Slit lengthways and rinse well under cold running water.
2. Heat the oven to 240°C/475°F/Gas Mark 9.
3. Cut the leeks diagonally into 1cm/½ inch pieces. Blanch for 3 minutes in boiling salted water. Cool in ice-cold water and drain well in a sieve.
4. Butter a large shallow baking dish and arrange the leeks in it. Season with salt, pepper and nutmeg.
5. In a bowl, mix together the quark or curd cheese, cream, grated cheese and sunflower seeds. Season with salt, pepper and nutmeg; spread over the leeks. Bake in the centre of the oven for 15 minutes until golden.
Accompaniment:
mashed potato with lots of chives. Serves 8 as a starter, browned in individual dishes.
Recommended drink:
white wine spritzer.

CHEESE-TOPPED FENNEL WITH A NUT CRUST

SERVES 2
Preparation and cooking time: 30 minutes
Kcal per portion: 1145
P = 37g, F = 98g, C = 29g

750g/1½lbs fennel bulbs
salt and pepper
butter for the dish
200g/7oz crème fraîche
150g/5½oz grated Gouda
  cheese
100g/4oz ground hazelnuts
freshly ground black pepper

1. Wash the fennel bulbs. Cut off and reserve any leaves. Cut the bulbs lengthways into slices about 1cm/½ inch thick.
2. Cook the fennel in boiling salted water for 3 minutes. Remove using a slotted spoon and drain well.
3. Heat the oven to 220°C/425°F/Gas Mark 7.
4. Butter a large ovenproof dish and arrange the fennel slices so that they overlap.
5. Put the crème fraîche into a bowl. Add the cheese and hazelnuts and mix together. Season well with salt and pepper. Spread evenly over the fennel.
6. Bake in the centre of the oven for 15 minutes, until golden. Sprinkle with reserved fennel leaves.
This dish can be made more substantial by sandwiching well-mashed canned tuna between the fennel slices. Pistachio nuts can be used instead of hazelnuts.
Accompaniment:
French bread or mashed potato.
Recommended drink:
light white wine from Friuli or Verdicchio.

BRAISED ASPARAGUS IN CHERVIL SAUCE

SERVES 2 ■

Preparation and cooking time: 30 minutes
Kcal per portion: 380
P = 15g, F = 30g, C = 18g

1kg/2¼lbs asparagus
45g/1½oz butter
salt and white pepper
juice of 1 lemon
2 tbsps maple syrup
100g/4oz chervil
2 egg yolks
300g/10oz yoghurt

1. Scrape the lower part of the asparagus stalks and cut off the ends. Cut the stalks diagonally into pieces about 4cm/1½ inches long. Set the tips to one side.
2. Heat the butter in a large frying-pan. Sweat the asparagus, covered, without the tips, for 15 minutes over a medium heat. After 5 minutes, add salt and pepper. Drizzle with lemon juice and maple syrup.
3. Meanwhile rinse the chervil, pat dry and snip off the stalks. Reserve a few sprigs for garnishing. Blend the remaining chervil in a liquidiser with the egg yolks and yoghurt, to make a smooth sauce. Season with salt and pepper.
4. About 5 minutes before the end of the cooking time, add the asparagus tips to the frying-pan.
5. Arrange the asparagus on four warmed plates, with a dollop of sauce in the centre. Garnish with chervil leaves.
Accompaniment: new potatoes. This quantity serves four as a side dish and is tasty with poached salmon.
Recommended drink: claret.

STIR-FRIED ASPARAGUS

SERVES 4 ■

Preparation and cooking time: 30 minutes
Kcal per portion: 315
P = 7g, f = 28g, C = 8g

500g/1lb2oz asparagus
250g/8oz mange-tout
salt
3 tbsps oil
3 tbsps sesame seeds
3 tbsps soy sauce
1 tbsp very dry sherry
1 punnet mustard and cress

1. Peel only the lower third of the asparagus and cut off the ends of the stalks. Wash briefly and chop into 3cm/1½ inch pieces. Wash the mange-tout and snip off the ends.
2. Blanch the asparagus in boiling salted water for 3 minutes. Cool in ice-cold water and drain. Do the same with the mange-tout, but blanch for only 1 minute.
3. Heat the oil in a wok or large frying-pan. Fry the sesame seeds until golden, stirring constantly.
4. Add the asparagus and the mange-tout peas. Cook for 5 minutes over a low heat, stirring constantly. Drizzle with the soy sauce and sherry.
5. Rinse the mustard and cress under running water. Using kitchen scissors, snip the leaves over the vegetables and stir in.
An accompaniment to fillet of veal or grilled salmon. Can also be served as a vegetarian main course for two, with brown rice or new potatoes.

KOHLRABI IN GORGONZOLA SAUCE

SERVES 4 ■

Preparation and cooking time: 25 minutes
Kcal per portion: 520
P = 23g, F = 44g, C = 8g

6 kohlrabi (about 750g/1½lbs)
salt and pepper
butter for the dish
250ml/8 fl oz single cream
300g/10oz Gorgonzola cheese
freshly grated nutmeg
lemon juice
1 bunch chervil

1. Peel the kohlrabi and halve it. Slice it thinly, preferably in a food processor or using a mandolin. Put the slices in a saucepan with boiling salted water and cook for 3 minutes. Remove with a slotted spoon and drain well.
2. Heat the oven to 220°C/425°F/Gas Mark 7.
3. Butter a large ovenproof dish and arrange the kohlrabi slices so that they overlap.
4. Bring the cream to the boil in a small saucepan. Add the Gorgonzola and melt, stirring constantly. Season with salt, pepper, nutmeg and lemon juice.
5. Rinse the chervil and pat dry. Pull the leaves from the stalks and sprinkle most of them over the kohlrabi slices. Pour over the sauce and brown in the centre of the oven for 10 minutes.
6. Before serving sprinkle with the reserved chervil leaves.
An accompaniment to medallions of veal or poached egg. Can also be served as a vegetarian main course for two with potatoes or sesame rice.

SWEET AND SOUR CARROTS

SERVES 4 ■

Preparation and cooking time: 30 minutes
Kcal per portion: 150
P = 2g, F = 10g, C = 14g

750g/1½lbs carrots
salt and pepper
45g/1½oz butter
3 tbsps maple syrup
juice of 1 lemon
pinch of cumin
1 carton mustard and cress

1. Peel the carrots and cut diagonally into 1cm/½ inch thick slices. Put into a saucepan, just cover with

> **TIP**
>
> *Half of the carrots can be replaced by courgettes. Use fresh mint instead of mustard and cress for an unusual flavour.*

water, add salt and bring to the boil. Cook for 8 minutes over a low heat.
2. Tip the carrots into a sieve and drain well.
3. Heat the butter in a large frying-pan. Add the maple syrup and bring to the boil. Add the carrots and sweat for 5 minutes. Sprinkle with the lemon juice. Season with salt, pepper and cumin.
4. Rinse the mustard and cress under running water. Snip the leaves directly into the frying-pan.
An accompaniment to cold roast beef or roast chicken. Can also be served as a starter on a bed of fresh spinach, sprinkled with toasted sesame seeds.

MIXED PEPPERS WITH SAUSAGE

SERVES 4 ■
Preparation and cooking time: 25 minutes
Kcal per portion: 805
P = 32g, F = 55g, C = 44g

1 large onion
2 tbsps olive oil
750g/1½lbs mixed red, green and yellow peppers
125ml/4 fl oz tomato juice
salt and pepper
1 tsp paprika
generous pinch of cayenne
250g/8oz kabanos or peperone sausage
l bunch flat-leaved parsley

1. Slice the onion into thin rings. Heat the olive oil in a large frying-pan and sweat the onion rings until transparent.
2. Halve, core, de-seed and wash the peppers. Slice across into narrow strips and add to the frying-pan. Pour in the tomato juice. Season with salt, pepper, paprika and cayenne. Cook gently for 15 minutes.
3. Skin the sausage and slice, not too thickly. Combine with the vegetables and cook for 5 minutes.
4. Rinse, pat dry and roughly chop the parsley. Just before serving, mix with the other ingredients.
Instead of spicy sausage, you could use cooked ham, sliced into strips.
Accompaniment:
mashed potato.
Recommended drink:
light red wine, e.g. Chianti or Beaujolais-Villages.

Halve the peppers lengthways. Remove the core and seeds, then wash.

Thinly slice the pepper halves.

Pour the tomato juice over the strips of pepper, season and cook for 15 minutes.

Peel and slice the sausage. Add to the vegetables and heat for a further 5 minutes.

COURGETTES WITH TURKEY STRIPS

SERVES 2 ■
Preparation and cooking time: 30 minutes
Kcal per portion: 420
P = 55g, F = 18g, C = 9g

400g/14oz turkey fillet
30g/1oz butter
salt and white pepper
freshly grated nutmeg
450g/1lb courgettes
3 garlic cloves
250ml/8 fl oz vegetable stock
1 bunch flat-leaved parsley

1. Slice the turkey into thin strips.
2. Heat the butter in a large frying-pan. Fry the turkey strips over a high heat until golden brown. Season with salt and pepper, sprinkle with nutmeg and set aside.
3. Cut the stalk ends from the courgettes. Wash and slice directly into the butter remaining in the pan. Cook gently until golden.
4. Crush the garlic and add to the courgette slices.
5. Pour in the stock and bring to the boil. Add salt and pepper. Cover and cook gently for 5 minutes.
6. Meanwhile rinse, pat dry and roughly chop the parsley. Add the turkey strips to the courgette slices, with their meat juices and reheat briefly.
7. Just before serving stir in the parsley.
Chicken or pork can be used instead of the turkey fillets.
Accompaniment:
mashed potato.
Recommended drink:
dry cider.

MUSHROOM FRITTATA

SERVES 4 ■ ■
Preparation and cooking time: 30 minutes
Kcal per portion: 250
P = 13g, F = 20g, C = 4g

1 medium onion
3 tbsps olive oil
750g/1½lbs oyster or button mushrooms
2 garlic cloves
salt and pepper
1 bunch chives
5 eggs

1. Heat the oil in a medium-sized high-sided frying-pan. Finely dice the onion and sweat over a low heat until transparent.
2. Meanwhile, wipe the mushrooms and slice finely. Add to the frying-pan and sweat for 10 minutes over a medium heat. Crush the garlic and add to the pan; season with salt and pepper.
3. Finely chop the chives. Beat the eggs and stir in the chives. Pour over the mushrooms. Allow to set over a low heat, shaking the pan from time to time so that the mixture does not stick.
4. After about 7 minutes, slide the frittata on to a lid or plate. Turn and slide back into the frying-pan and fry for a further 10 minutes, until cooked.
The frittata looks attractive cut into portions like a cake. It can also be served cold as a starter.
Accompaniment: tomato salad with spring onions.

SAVOY CABBAGE WITH SESAME SEEDS AND BEAN SPROUTS

(see photo on page 21)

SERVES 4 ■
*Preparation and cooking time: 30 minutes
Kcal per portion: 180
P = 6g, F = 16g, C = 4g*

300g/10oz Savoy cabbage
250g/8oz mushrooms
3 tbsps soya oil
2 garlic cloves
2 tbsps sesame seeds
150g/5½oz fresh bean sprouts
salt and pepper
generous pinch of cayenne
3 tbsps dry sherry
3 tbsps soy sauce

1. Remove the thick outer leaves from the cabbage. Quarter the cabbage and cut out the thick central stalk. Cut the quarters crossways into 5mm/¼ inch strips. Wash and drain.
2. Wipe and trim the mushrooms. Using an egg slicer, slice finely.
3. Heat the soya oil in a wok or large high-sided frying-pan. Fry the mushrooms briefly. Crush the garlic and add to the pan. Add the strips of cabbage and sprinkle with the sesame seeds.
4. Briefly rinse the bean sprouts and add to the cabbage.
5. Season the vegetables with salt, pepper and cayenne. Pour in the sherry and soy sauce. Cover and cook for 10 minutes over a medium heat.
This dish can be enhanced by browning some minced meat with the mushrooms – about 100g/4oz per person.
Accompaniment: rice.
Recommended drink: dry sherry.

SPINACH WITH FETA AND PINE NUTS

SERVES 4 ■
*Preparation and cooking time: 30 minutes
Kcal per portion: 445
P = 14g, F = 41g, C = 6g*

600g/1¼lbs spinach, fresh or frozen
1 small onion
2 tbsps olive oil
3 garlic cloves
4 tbsps pine nuts
salt and pepper
1 tsp oregano
300g/10oz Feta cheese

1. Wash fresh spinach and snip off the stalks. Remove frozen spinach from its packaging.
2. Chop the onion finely. Heat the oil in a large saucepan, add the onion and sweat until transparent.
3. Crush the garlic cloves and add to the onion. Add the spinach and sweat for 10 minutes.
4. Sprinkle with the pine nuts. Season with salt, pepper and oregano.
5. Finely dice the Feta or crumble it between your fingers. Sprinkle over the spinach and cook for 5 minutes over a very low heat.
Instead of pine nuts, flaked almonds can be used.
An accompaniment to grilled lamb chops.

MANGE-TOUT WITH LEMON SAUCE

SERVES 4 ■
*Preparation and cooking time: 20 minutes
Kcal per portion: 325
P = 9g, F = 24g, C = 17g*

600g/1¼lbs mange-tout
salt and white pepper
1 small onion
15g/½oz butter
1 tbsp very dry sherry
200g/7oz crème fraîche
juice of ½ lemon
2 spring onions (optional)

1. Wash the mange-tout and snip off the ends. Blanch in boiling salted water for 1 minute. Cool in ice-cold water and drain well.
2. Finely chop the onion. Heat the butter in a large saucepan and sweat the

> **TIP**
> *If serving this dish as a starter the mange-tout can be combined with 200g/7oz prawns. Then it makes enough to serve 8.*

onion until transparent. Pour in the sherry and heat until reduced almost completely.
3. Add the crème fraîche and lemon juice. Cook gently for 3 minutes, then season with salt and pepper.
4. Add the mange-tout to the sauce and heat for 5 minutes.
5. Optional: chop two spring onions into rings and stir into the dish.
Accompaniment: buttered rice.
Recommended drink: Schillerwein from Baden-Württemberg or rosé.

SPRING CABBAGE IN SHERRY CREAM SAUCE

SERVES 4 ■
*Preparation and cooking time: 25 minutes
Kcal per portion: 410
P = 5g, F = 35g, C = 8g*

1 small spring cabbage (450g/1lb)
4 spring onions
30g/1oz butter
5 tbsps very dry sherry
250ml/8 fl oz double cream
1 tbsp Worcestershire sauce
salt and white pepper
2 tbsps sunflower seeds

1. Trim and quarter the cabbage, removing the thick central stalk. Cut the quarters crossways into very fine strips. Wash and drain thoroughly.
2. Trim and wash the spring onions. Chop into fine rings.
3. Heat the butter in a large saucepan and sweat the onions. Add the spring cabbage and fry, stirring, for 5 minutes.
4. Pour in the sherry, then stir in the cream. Season with Worcestershire sauce, salt and pepper. Cover and simmer over a medium heat for 10 minutes.
5. Meanwhile dry-fry the sunflower seeds in a non-stick frying-pan until golden. Taste the vegetables and season again if necessary. Sprinkle over the sunflower seeds.
The sherry can be replaced by white wine or sparkling wine. Pumpkin seeds can be used instead of sunflower seeds.
An accompaniment to fillet of veal or steamed shellfish, such as scampi.

*Q*uick preparation and short but gentle cooking – that's the beauty of a microwave oven, whether you are cooking Celery in White Wine, Asparagus with Mange-tout or hearty Hungarian Potato Goulash. There is simply no better way of cooking tender vegetables. The delicious flavours of the dishes contained in this chapter are an integral part of the microwave cooking programme. For best results remember that vegetable dishes prepared in the microwave oven have to be stirred once during cooking, that it is better to use several small containers than one large one and that round rather than rectangular cooking dishes are best.

Okra with Tomatoes
(see recipe on page 100)

HUNGARIAN POTATO GOULASH

SERVES 4 ■
Microwave alone
Preparation and cooking
time: 40 minutes
Kcal per portion: 295
P = 5g, F = 20g, C = 23g

600g/1¼lbs waxy potatoes
2 red peppers
2 large onions
50g/2oz rindless smoked
*   streaky bacon*
2 tbsps oil
salt and pepper
1 tbsps paprika
1 tsp caraway seeds
2 sprigs marjoram
250ml/8 fl oz strong beef
*   stock*
3 tbsps soured cream
½ bunch parsley

1. Peel, wash and finely dice the potatoes. Wash and halve the peppers; remove cores and seeds. Dice into 1cm/½ inch squares. Finely chop the onions.
2. Finely dice the bacon. Place in a microwave dish with the oil. Brown for 3-4 minutes at 600 watts.
3. Add the diced vegetables. Season with salt, pepper, paprika, caraway and the marjoram leaves. Pour in the stock. Cover and cook for 17-20 minutes at 600 watts, stirring from time to time.
4. Stir the cream into the vegetables and cook, uncovered, for 4-5 minutes at 600 watts, until thickened.
5. Chop the parsley and sprinkle over the dish. Leave to stand for a few minutes before serving. For a spicier flavour, add finely chopped chillies.
An accompaniment to sausages or fried chops.

CREAMY POTATOES

SERVES 4 ■
Microwave alone
Preparation and cooking
time: 30 minutes
Kcal per portion: 485
P = 6g, F= 38g, C = 29g

750g/1½lbs floury potatoes
1 onion
1 garlic clove
30g/1oz butter
salt and white pepper
freshly grated nutmeg
400ml/14 fl oz single cream
a few chervil leaves

1. Peel and wash the potatoes. Chop into 1cm/½ inch cubes. Finely dice the garlic. Put both into a microwave dish with the butter. Fry for 2-3 minutes at 600 watts, until transparent.
2. Add the diced potato and season with salt, pepper and

> **TIP**
>
> *The potato pieces should be about the same size so that they cook evenly. Do not forget to reset the microwave after stirring.*

nutmeg. Pour in the cream. Cover and cook for 15-18 minutes at 600 watts. After 5 minutes, uncover, stir once and finish cooking uncovered.
3. Sprinkle the chervil leaves over the dish. Leave to stand for a few minutes longer.
Serve with rissoles or sausages.

BAVARIAN CABBAGE

SERVES 4 ■
Microwave alone
Preparation and cooking
time: 40 minutes
Kcal per portion: 180
P = 3g, F = 16g, C = 6g

½ head white cabbage
*   (400g/14oz trimmed)*
50g/2oz rindless smoked
*   streaky bacon*
2 tbsps oil
1 tsp sugar
1 tsp caraway seeds
250ml/8 fl oz ham stock
1 tbsp white wine vinegar
salt and pepper

1. Cut the stalk from the white cabbage. Remove limp outer leaves. Wash the cabbage and slice into thin strips.
2. Finely dice the bacon. Put in a large microwave dish with oil and sugar. Glaze for 4-5 minutes at 600 watts, stirring once.
3. Add the white cabbage, stir well and sprinkle with caraway seeds. The cabbage should not be piled too high. Pour in the stock and vinegar. Cover and cook for 15-18 minutes at 600 watts. Uncover, stir and finish cooking uncovered. Leave to stand for a few more minutes before serving. Season with salt and pepper if needed.
After about 10 minutes of the cooking time, thicken, if desired, with a little flour and water.
Serve with grilled sausages or roast pheasant.

KOHLRABI WITH GARDEN PEAS

SERVES 4 ■
Microwave alone
Preparation and cooking
time: 30 minutes
Kcal per portion: 140
P = 4g, F = 9g, C = 8g

3 young kohlrabi with leaves
1 small onion
45g/1½oz butter
5 tbsps dry white wine
salt and white pepper
150g/5½oz fresh shelled peas
1 tbsp chopped parsley

1. Remove the leaves from the kohlrabi. Reserve the tender inner leaves. Peel the bulbs, cut into thin slices and then into strips.
2. Chop the onion and put into a microwave dish with 20g/¾oz butter. Fry,

> **TIP**
>
> *Frozen peas can be used instead of fresh ones, and crème fraîche in place of butter.*

uncovered, for 2 minutes at 600 watts. Add the strips of kohlrabi and pour in the wine. Season with salt and pepper. Cover and cook for 6-8 minutes at 600 watts, stirring once.
3. Add the peas, cover, and cook for a further 3-4 minutes at 600 watts.
4. Carefully cut the kohlrabi leaves into thin strips. Stir into the vegetables with the remaining butter and the parsley.
An accompaniment to roast veal.

EXOTIC LENTILS

SERVES 4 ■
Microwave alone
Preparation and cooking
time: 30 minutes
Soaking time: a few hours
Kcal per portion: 300
P = 8g, F = 19g, C = 20g

125g/5oz green lentils
1 large carrot
2 celery stalks
1 onion
1-2 garlic cloves
4 tbsps oil
125ml/4 fl oz dry white wine
salt and pepper
2 sprigs thyme
1 bay leaf
2 tbsps crème fraîche
1 tbsp chopped parsley

1. Cover the lentils with plenty of cold water and soak for 4 hours.
2. Trim and wash the carrot and celery; dice very finely. Chop the onion and the garlic finely. Put them all into a large microwave dish with the oil. Brown for 5 minutes at 600 watts, stirring once.
3. Drain the lentils and add to the dish. Pour in the white wine and season with salt and pepper. Add the thyme and bay leaf. Cover and cook for 6-8 minutes at 600 watts, stirring from time to time.
4. Uncover and stir the crème fraîche into the vegetables. Reduce, uncovered, for a further 4-5 minutes at 600 watts.
5. Remove the herbs and leave the vegetables to stand for a few minutes longer. Serve sprinkled with parsley. To make the dish creamier, blend some of the lentils in a liquidiser.
An accompaniment to pork or Polish sausage.

Place the finely chopped vegetables and the oil in a microwave dish.

Mix the soaked, drained lentils with the browned vegetables and pour in the white wine.

After half of the cooking time, stir in the crème fraîche.

OKRA WITH TOMATOES

(see photo on page 95)

SERVES 4 ■■
Microwave alone
Preparation and cooking
time: 45 minutes
Kcal per portion: 280
P = 9g, F = 24g, C = 32g

400g/14oz okra
2 tbsps white wine vinegar
salt and pepper
1 onion
1 garlic clove
6 tbsps olive oil
500g/1lb2oz beefsteak
* tomatoes*
2 sprigs thyme
125ml/4 fl oz white wine
2 tbsps chopped parsley

1. Wash the okra. Carefully remove the ends, using a sharp knife. Take care not to damage the flesh. Arrange side by side on a rectangular plate. Drizzle with vinegar and sprinkle with salt. Leave for at least 30 minutes.
2. Meanwhile finely chop the onion and garlic. Put them with the oil in a microwave dish. Fry for 2 minutes at 600 watts, until transparent.
3. Wash the tomatoes. Cut a cross in the top and put, dripping wet, in a microwave dish. Put them in the microwave for 2-3 minutes at 600 watts. Rinse in cold water. Then peel, seed, chop and add to the onion. Add the thyme, salt and pepper. Pour in the white wine. Cook gently, uncovered, for 6-8 minutes at 600 watts.
4. Mix the okra with the tomato sauce, cover and cook for 6-8 minutes at 600 watts, stirring once gently. Leave to stand for a few minutes longer. Serve sprinkled with parsley.
An accompaniment to roast chicken or grilled fish.

Carefully remove the tops of the okra with a sharp knife.

Put the okra on a shallow dish, drizzle with vinegar and sprinkle with salt. Leave to marinate for 30 minutes.

Stir the okra into the tomato sauce.

ONIONS STUFFED WITH VEAL

SERVES 2 ■■
Microwave alone
Preparation and cooking
time: 50 minutes
Kcal per portion: 595
P = 28g, F = 37g, C = 32g

2 Spanish onions
200g/4oz minced veal
2 tbsps uncooked rice
1 tbsp chopped parsley
2 tbsps tomato purée
salt and pepper
1 tsp paprika
100g/4oz crème fraîche
2 tbsps oil
5 tbsps dry white wine

1. Peel the onions. Place in a microwave dish with 250ml/8 fl oz water. Cover and cook for 4-5 minutes at 600 watts, turning once.
2. Mix together the veal, rice, parsley and 1 tablespoon of tomato purée. Season with salt, pepper and ¼ tsp paprika.
3. Cut a lid from the onions. Hollow out the inner flesh with a teaspoon. Leave at least two layers around the outside. Finely chop the onion flesh and mix half of it with the meat mixture. Stuff the onions with the mixture and put in a microwave dish.
4. Stir together the crème fraîche, oil, wine, remaining tomato purée and paprika. Pour a little of the mixture over each onion. Distribute the rest, with the remaining onion, around the onions.
5. Cover and cook for 20-25 minutes at 600 watts.
Recommended drink: lager.

BEETROOT WITH HORSERADISH

SERVES 4 ■
Microwave alone
Preparation and cooking
time: 35 minutes
Kcal per portion: 130
P = 2g, F = 8g, C = 12g

500g/1lb2oz raw beetroot
1 onion
45g/1½oz butter
salt and pepper
2 tbsps freshly grated horseradish
1 tbsp balsamic vinegar
1 tbsp maple syrup

1. Wash, peel and coarsely grate the beetroot. Dice the onion finely and put with the butter in a microwave dish. Fry, uncovered, for 2 min-

Peel the beetroot and grate coarsely in a food processor.

utes at 600 watts, until transparent.
2. Add the beetroot, salt and pepper. Cover and cook for 8 minutes at 600 watts.
3. Stir the horseradish, vinegar and syrup into the vegetables. Cook, uncovered, for a further 4-6 minutes at 600 watts.
An accompaniment to boiled beef.

LEEK AND BACON

SERVES 4 ■
Microwave alone
Preparation and cooking
time: 25 minutes
Kcal per portion: 275
P = 4g, F = 27g, C = 4g

2 large leeks (about 500g/1lb2oz)
75g/3oz rindless smoked streaky bacon
1 tbsp oil
salt and white pepper
generous pinch of stock granules
freshly grated nutmeg
125ml/5 fl oz single cream
1 tbsp lemon juice

1. Remove the roots from the leeks. Cut off almost all the green parts. Halve the leeks lengthways, wash thoroughly and cut into 5mm/¼ inch slices.
2. Finely dice the bacon. Put the bacon and the oil into a large microwave dish. Fry, uncovered, for 3-4 minutes at 600 watts, until the fat is transparent.
3. Add the leeks. They should not be piled too high. Season with salt, pepper, stock granules and nutmeg; pour in the cream. Cover and cook for 8-10 minutes at 600 watts. After 5 minutes, uncover, stir and continue cooking uncovered. Season with the lemon juice.
An accompaniment to sausages or boiled beef.

MIXED PEPPERS

SERVES 4 ■
Microwave alone
Preparation and cooking
time: 40 minutes
Kcal per portion: 225
P = 3g, F = 19g, C = 10g

2 small red peppers
2 small yellow peppers
2 small green peppers
1 Spanish onion
1 garlic clove
2 large beefsteak tomatoes
5 tbsps olive oil
2 sprigs thyme
1 bay leaf
salt and pepper
1 tbsp chopped parsley

1. Halve, core and de-seed the peppers. Slice the flesh into thin strips. finely dice the garlic.

> **TIP**
>
> *This dish can be enhanced by adding green or black olives.*

2. Cut a cross in the top of the tomatoes. Wash and put in a microwave dish dripping wet. Put in the microwave for 3-4 minutes at 600 watts. Cool in cold water, peel and halve. Remove the stalk ends and seeds.
3. Place all the vegetables in a large microwave dish. Do not pile too high. Pour over the oil. Add the herbs and season with salt and pepper. Cover and cook for 18-20 minutes at 600 watts, stirring from time to time.
4. Remove the herbs and sprinkle with parsley.
An accompaniment to boiled beef or steak.

ASPARAGUS WITH MANGE-TOUT

SERVES 4 ■
Microwave alone
Preparation and cooking
time: 40 minutes
Kcal per portion: 95
P = 5g, F = 7g, C = 7g

500g/1lb2oz white asparagus
125ml/4 fl oz water
pinch of sugar
salt
30g/1oz butter
200g/7oz mange-tout
a few sprigs of chervil
a little grated orange zest

1. Peel the asparagus stalks. Cut off the ends and chop into 5cm/2 inch pieces. Reserve the tips. Place the

Carefully peel the asparagus spears, using an asparagus peeler or swivel vegetable peeler.

Mix the mange-tout with the pre-cooked asparagus.

Before serving, mix orange zest, chervil leaves and butter into the vegetables.

> **TIP**
>
> *The thickness of the asparagus spears and its quality determine how long it will take to cook.*

rest in a microwave dish. Pour in the water. Add salt, sprinkle with sugar and add 10g/¼oz butter. Cover and cook for 5-6 minutes at 600 watts.
2. Meanwhile, snip the ends off the mange-tout and wash. Mix the mange-tout and asparagus tips with the rest of the asparagus. Cover and cook for a further 4-5 minutes at 600 watts.
3. Pull off the chervil leaves. Mix into the vegetables, together with the orange zest and remaining butter. Leave to stand, covered, for a few minutes longer.
An accompaniment to veal or turkey steak, baked plaice or sole.

SCORZONERA IN CARAWAY SAUCE

SERVES 2 ■
Microwave alone
Preparation and cooking
time: 1 hour
Kcal per portion: 340
P = 5g, F = 32g, C = 7g

1l/1¾ pints water
2 tbsps vinegar
500g/1lb2oz scorzonera
salt and white pepper
1 tbsp caraway seeds
200ml/7 fl oz single cream
1 tsp balsamic vinegar
juice and zest of ½ lemon
1 tbsp chopped parsley

1. Put the water and vinegar into a large bowl. Wash and peel the scorzonera. Place in the bowl of water and vinegar so that it does not discolour.
2. Chop the scorzonera into even-sized pieces. Place in a microwave dish and pour in 250ml/8 fl oz water. Add salt and half the caraway seeds.
3. Cover and cook for 20-25 minutes at 600 watts. At the end of the cooking time, remove the vegetables from the microwave. Leave to stand, covered, for a few more minutes.
4. During this time put the cream, the remaining caraway seeds, vinegar, lemon juice and zest, salt and pepper in a microwave dish. Reduce by half for 8-10 minutes at 600 watts, until smooth.
5. Drain the scorzonera in a sieve and mix into the cream sauce. Heat, uncovered, for 3-4 minutes. Serve sprinkled with parsley.
An accompaniment to roast beef, steak or escalopes.

CELERY IN WHITE WINE

SERVES 2 ■
Microwave alone
Preparation and cooking
time: 30 minutes
Kcal per portion: 280
P = 3g, F = 21g, C = 8g

1 head celery (about
    500g/1lb2oz)
2 shallots
50g/2oz butter
salt and white pepper
125ml/4 fl oz dry white wine
½ tsp flour
1 tbsp chopped herbs (parsley,
    basil, tarragon, chives)

1. Trim the celery. Cut off any leaves and reserve. Separate the stalks and wash. Chop into 2cm/¾ inch pieces.
2. Dice the shallots and put in a microwave dish with 20g/¾oz butter. Fry for 2 minutes at 600 watts until transparent. Then add the celery. Season with salt and pepper. Pour in the white wine. Cover and cook for 10 minutes at 600 watts.
3. Knead the remaining butter with the flour. Stir into the vegetables. Reduce, uncovered, for 4-5 minutes at 600 watts.
Serve sprinkled with herbs and finely chopped celery leaves.
An accompaniment to braised dishes or sweetcorn rissoles.

> **TIP**
>
> *In a conventional oven, this would take twice as long to cook.*

GREEK-STYLE MUSHROOMS

SERVES 2 ■

Microwave alone
Preparation and cooking
time: 25 minutes
Kcal per portion: 305
P = 7g, F = 23g, C = 6g

500g/1lb2oz mushrooms
2 small onions
1 bay leaf
1 sprig thyme
generous pinch of coriander
juice of ½ lemon
3 tbsps olive oil
125ml/4 fl oz dry white wine
salt and white pepper
1 tbsp chopped parsley

1. Wipe the mushrooms and slice. Finely dice the onions. Put both in a microwave dish and add the bay leaf, thyme and coriander. Pour in the lemon juice, oil and wine. Season with salt and pepper.

Wipe the mushrooms and cut off the stalk ends.

Place all the ingredients in a microwave dish; they will only need to cook for 15 minutes.

Take care when removing the mushrooms from the oven – the bowl will be very hot.

> ### TIP
> *Mushrooms cooked in this way also taste delicious as a cold starter. Brown mushrooms have a stronger, more aromatic flavour than white ones.*

2. Cover and put into the microwave for 15 minutes at 600 watts, stirring once during this time.
3. Remove the herbs. Stir the parsley into the mushrooms and serve.
An accompaniment to quick-fried meat or grills.

SWISS-STYLE CARROT PURÉE

SERVES 4 ■

Microwave alone
Preparation and cooking
time: 35 minutes
Kcal per portion: 225
P = 3g, F = 16g, C = 16g

300g/10oz floury potatoes
500g/1lb2oz carrots
125ml/5 fl oz single cream
salt
pinch of sugar
30g/1oz butter
2 tbsps finely chopped chervil

1. Peel, wash and finely chop the potatoes and carrots. Put in a microwave dish with the cream. Add the salt and sugar. Cover and cook for 15-18 minutes at 600 watts, stirring from time to time.

> ### TIP
> *If you can get young, bunched carrots in the spring, make sure they have fresh, juicy leaves. Remove the leaves immediately since they draw the juice out of the carrots.*

2. Blend the potato and carrot mixture in a liquidiser. Stir in the butter in small knobs. Put the carrot purée into a bowl and sprinkle with chervil.
An accompaniment to braised beef or sausages.

COURGETTES WITH TOMATO

SERVES 2 ■

Microwave alone
Preparation and cooking
time: 30 minutes
Kcal per portion: 265
P = 6g, F = 23g, C = 8g

2 courgettes (about 250g/8oz)
200g/4oz button mushrooms
2 beefsteak tomatoes
2 shallots
1 tbsp oil
20g/¾oz butter
1 sprig thyme
salt and pepper
½ tsp paprika
2 tbsps crème fraîche
2 tbsps chopped parsley

1. Wash the courgettes and cut off the ends. Wipe the mushrooms. Slice both vegetables finely.
2. Cut a cross in the top of the tomatoes. Place dripping wet in a microwave dish, cover and put in the microwave for 2-3 minutes at 600 watts. Then rinse in cold water, peel and dice finely, without the stalk ends and seeds.
3. Finely chop shallots and put with the oil and butter in a microwave dish. Fry for 2 minutes at 600 watts, until transparent.
4. Add the sliced courgettes and mushrooms. Sprinkle with individual thyme leaves. Season with salt, pepper and paprika. Stir in the crème fraîche, cover and cook for 4 minutes at 600 watts.
5. Add the diced tomato. Stir and cook, uncovered, for a further 4-5 minutes at 600 watts.
6. Sprinkle with parsley and leave to stand for a little while longer before serving. An accompaniment to rissoles or quick-fried meat.

Lean Cuisine

*A*s far as vegetables are concerned lean cuisine has an added advantage. Eating light healthy food does not mean having to do without your favourite dishes. In many cases a dish designed as an accompaniment can even be transformed into a main course. Simply increase the amount of vegetables, herbs and other ingredients if you prefer plant products to meat products, to produce a balanced vegetarian meal. This applies just as much to Asparagus Ragoût with Broccoli or Tommato and Potato Stew as it does to appetising Mixed Vegetables in Coconut Milk.

Fennel and Pears
(see recipe on page 122)

LEEK AND CARROT MEDLEY

SERVES 4 ■

Preparation and cooking time: 40 minutes
Kcal per portion: 135
P = 2g, F = 12g, C = 6g

3 medium leeks (about
    500g/1lb2oz)
3 medium carrots (200g/7oz)
3 tbsps olive oil
salt and white pepper
125ml/4 fl oz strong chicken
    stock
juice of ½ lemon
1 tbsp chopped parsley

1. Remove the roots from the leeks. Halve lengthways, wash thoroughly under run-

> **TIP**
>
> *This also tastes delicious cold. Yoghurt flavoured with garlic can be served with it, if desired.*

ning water and cut into 1cm/½ inch pieces. Scrub or scrape the carrots. Slice first lengthways, then cut into narrow strips about 5cm/2 inches long.
2. Heat the oil in a large flameproof casserole. Fry the leeks over a medium heat until golden. Season with salt and pepper and pour in the stock. Cover and simmer for about 10 minutes over a low heat.
3. Stir in the carrot and cook for about 15-20 minutes.
4. Season the vegetables with lemon juice and, if necessary, more salt and pepper. Sprinkle with parsley.
An accompaniment to any meat dish.

CARROTS WITH SHERRY

SERVES 2 ■

Preparation and cooking time: 30 minutes
Kcal per portion: 220
P = 3g, F = 15g, C = 9g

1 bunch young carrots with
    leaves
1 shallot
20g/¾oz butter
salt and white pepper
3 tbsps dry sherry
20g/¾oz pine nuts

1. Remove the leaves from the carrots reserving a few small ones. Scrub and finely slice the carrots. Finely dice the shallot.
2. Heat the butter in a small flameproof casserole. Sweat the shallot over a medium heat until transparent. Add the sliced carrot and brown lightly, stirring constantly. Add salt, then pour in the sherry. Cover and cook over a medium heat. The vegetables should still be firm.
3. Meanwhile dry-fry the pine nuts in a small frying-pan. Finely chop the carrot leaves.
4. Season the carrots with pepper. Sprinkle with carrot leaves and pine nuts.
An accompaniment to roast chicken or braised veal.

SHALLOTS AND PEAS

SERVES 2 ■

Preparation and cooking time: 45 minutes
Kcal per portion: 195
P = 8g, F = 9g, C = 21g

250g/8oz shallots
20g/¾oz butter
½ tsp sugar
6 tbsps strong chicken stock
200g/7oz fresh shelled peas
salt and white pepper
1 tbsp chopped parsley

1. Heat the butter in a flame-proof casserole. Quarter the shallots, put in the pan and sprinkle with sugar. Glaze, stirring constantly, over a low heat until golden brown. Pour in the stock, cover, and simmer for about 10 minutes.
2. When the shallots have become syrupy and are almost cooked, add the peas. Season with salt and pepper. Cook for about 5 minutes over a low heat. Serve sprinkled with parsley. frozen peas can be used instead of fresh peas.
An accompaniment to veal ragoût or braised chicken.

FRENCH BEANS WITH BLACK OLIVES

SERVES 4 ■

Preparation and cooking time: 40 minutes
Kcal per portion: 215
P = 5g, F = 12g, C = 16g

750g/1½lbs young French
    beans
4 small shallots
2 tbsps olive oil
2 thyme sprigs
salt and pepper
125ml/4 fl oz dry white wine
50g/2oz stoned black olives
2 tbsps chopped parsley

1. Snip the ends off the beans and wash. Leave small

> **TIP**
>
> *The cooking time depends on the size and tenderness of the beans. Always test their crispness during cooking.*

beans whole, snap larger ones in half. Chop or quarter the shallots.
2. Heat the olive oil in a flameproof casserole and brown the shallots. Add the beans and thyme sprigs. Season with salt and pepper and pour in the white wine. Cover and simmer over a medium heat. After about 5 minutes stir in the olive halves, then cook until the beans are done but still firm.
3. Discard the thyme and sprinkle with parsley.
An accompaniment to lamb chops or roast lamb.

ASPARAGUS RAGOÛT
WITH BROCCOLI

ASPARAGUS RAGOÛT WITH BROCCOLI

SERVES 4 ■

Preparation and cooking time: 50 minutes
Kcal per portion: 195
P = 5g, F = 18g, C = 5g

500g/1lb2oz white asparagus
250g/8oz broccoli
salt and white pepper
pinch of sugar
30g/1oz butter
125ml/5 fl oz single cream
1 tsp flour
pinch of cayenne pepper
a little grated lemon zest
lemon juice to taste
1 egg yolk
1 tbsp finely chopped chives

Peel the asparagus and divide the broccoli into florets.

1. Carefully peel the asparagus spears. If necessary, cut off the ends, then chop.

> **TIP**
>
> *A light meal can be produced by mixing cooked peeled prawns with the vegetables.*

Thicken the asparagus sauce with beaten egg yolk.

Mix the cooked vegetables into the sauce.

Wash the broccoli and divide into small florets. Finely chop the stalks.
2. Bring a generous amount of water to the boil, containing salt, sugar and 10g/¼oz butter. Boil the asparagus for about 10-15 minutes, depending on the thickness of the spears, so that they are still firm. Boil the broccoli florets and stalk pieces in boiling salted water. They should still be firm.
3. Drain the asparagus spears and reserve the water. Measure out 500ml/16 fl oz of the asparagus cooking water. Mix with the cream and cook over medium heat until reduced by half.

4. Knead the remaining butter with the flour. Using a whisk, beat this into the boiling asparagus stock to thicken it. Cook for a few minutes over a high heat. Season with salt, pepper, cayenne, lemon zest and lemon juice.
5. Add the asparagus and the well-drained broccoli to the sauce. Whisk the egg yolk with a little sauce and use to thicken the ragoût. If necessary, season again, then sprinkle with chives.
An accompaniment to pork escalopes.

CHICORY IN ORANGE BUTTER

SERVES 4 ■

Preparation and cooking time: 30 minutes
Kcal per portion: 85
P = 2g, F = 6g, C = 5g

4 heads chicory (each 125g/5oz)
30g/1oz butter
1 tsp sugar
juice and grated zest of 1 orange
salt
cayenne pepper
a few mint leaves
orange segments to garnish (optional)

1. Remove limp outer leaves from the chicory and cut the heads in half. Remove the bitter cores.

> **TIP**
>
> *With only 30 calories per 100g chicory is an extremely low-calorie vegetable, although rich in minerals. Its slightly bitter taste is pleasantly reduced by the addition of orange juice.*

Remove the limp leaves from the chicory.

Carefully cut the bitter core from the chicory halves.

Toss the chicory halves in the orange butter.

2. Heat the butter in a flame-proof casserole. Add the sugar, orange zest and orange juice. Season with a pinch of salt and cayenne. Heat through quickly.
3. Toss the chicory halves in the orange butter. Cover and cook, cut surfaces down, for about 10 minutes. Baste with the braising juices from time to time.
4. Serve garnished with orange segments if desired. An accompaniment to veal or turkey steaks.

CUCUMBER WITH FISH STUFFING

SERVES 2 ■■
Preparation and cooking time: 45 minutes
Kcal per portion: 200
P = 23g, F = 4g, C = 4g

1 medium cucumber (about 600g/1¼lbs)
salt and white pepper
250g/8oz cod fillet
1 egg white
1 tbsp crème fraîche
2 tbsps finely chopped dill
pinch of cayenne pepper
juice of ½ lemon
125ml/4 fl oz strong fish stock

1. Partially peel the cucumber, leaving green stripes behind. Cut into four pieces, about 6cm/2½ inches long. Hollow them out and sprin-

> **TIP**
>
> *If you wish to serve a sauce with the cucumber, thicken the fish stock with crème fraîche.*

kle inside and outside with salt. Finely dice the remaining cucumber.
2. For the fish stuffing, cut the fish into pieces and blend well in a liquidiser. Thoroughly mix in the egg white, crème fraîche and 1 tablespoon dill. Season with salt, pepper, cayenne and lemon juice.
3. Stuff the cucumber pieces with the mixture. Place in a steamer and arrange the diced cucumber around them.
4. Pour the fish stock into the base of the saucepan. Place the steamer over the stock. Cover and steam for about 10 minutes. Serve sprinkled with dill.

TOMATO AND POTATO STEW

SERVES 4 ■
Preparation and cooking time: 50 minutes
Kcal per portion: 255
P = 8g, F = 12g, C = 30g

1 onion
1-2 garlic cloves
500g/1lb2oz beefsteak tomatoes
2 tbsps olive oil
1 sprig thyme
1 sprig rosemary
salt and pepper
500g/1lb2oz floury potatoes
8 tbsps chicken stock
1 tbsp chopped parsley
1 tbsp chopped basil

1. Finely dice the onion and garlic. Blanch, peel, core and chop the tomatoes.
2. Heat the oil in a flameproof casserole and lightly brown the onion and garlic. Add the tomatoes, thyme and rosemary. Season with salt and pepper. Cover and cook over a low heat for about 5 minutes.
3. Meanwhile wash and finely dice the potatoes. Stir into the tomato mixture and pour over the stock. Cover and cook over a low heat for about 30 minutes, stirring from time to time. Season again and serve sprinkled with parsley and basil.
An accompaniment to rissoles or fried chops.

SPICY MIXED PEPPERS

SERVES 4 ■
Preparation and cooking time: 40 minutes
Kcal per portion: 185
P = 5g, F = 9g, C = 16g

2 green peppers
2 red peppers
1 Spanish onion
2 garlic cloves
4 anchovy fillets
2 tbsps olive oil
salt and pepper
½ tsp herbes de provence
125ml/4 fl oz dry white wine
100g/4oz canned sweetcorn
2 tbsps chopped parsley

1. Wash and halve the peppers; remove the cores and seeds. Chop the halves into small squares. Dice the onion and garlic; finely chop the anchovies.
2. Heat the oil in a large non-stick frying-pan. Lightly brown the anchovies and garlic. Gradually add the vegetables, stirring constantly, and cook over a medium heat for a few minutes. Season with salt and pepper and sprinkle with the herbs. Pour in the wine. Cover and cook over a low heat for about 15-20 minutes, stirring from time to time.
3. Stir in the sweetcorn and bring to the boil over a high heat. Stir in the parsley just before serving.
An accompaniment to quick-fried meat.

SWEET AND SOUR BEETROOT

SERVES 2 ■
Preparation and cooking time: 50 minutes
Kcal per portion: 230
P = 2g, F = 15g, C = 14g

400g/14oz raw beetroot
4 small shallots
2 tbsps oil
1 tsp coriander seeds
salt and white pepper
1 tbsp maple syrup
1 tsp balsamic vinegar
5 tbsps red wine
a few coriander sprigs

1. Wash and peel the beetroot. Cut into 5-mm/¼ inch slices, then into strips. Quarter the shallots.
2. Heat the oil in a flameproof casserole and brown the shallot quarters.

> **TIP**
>
> *Beetroot is also delicious served with cold creamy yoghurt or soured cream. When buying be sure to get the raw vegetable, as beetroot is often sold pre-cooked for use in salads.*

3. Add the beetroot and crushed coriander seeds. Season with salt and pepper. Pour in the maple syrup, balsamic vinegar and red wine. Stir well, cover and cook for about 20-30 minutes.
4. Serve sprinkled with individual coriander leaves.
An accompaniment to boiled beef or sweetcorn rissoles.

OYSTER MUSHROOMS WITH TOMATOES

SERVES 2 ◼
*Preparation and cooking
time: 25 minutes
Kcal per portion: 220
P = 4g, F = 16g, C = 12g*

300g/10oz oyster mushrooms
1 small onion
1 garlic clove
2 tbsps oil
salt and pepper
1 sprig oregano
4 tbsps dry white wine
2 beefsteak tomatoes
1 tbsp chopped parsley or
    basil

1. Cut the ends off the oyster mushrooms. Wipe, pat dry and divide into pieces. Finely dice the onion and garlic.
2. Heat the oil in a non-stick frying-pan. Lightly brown the onion and garlic. Add the mushrooms and sweat for a few minutes, turning them in the oil. Sprinkle with salt,

> **TIP**
>
> *Lay slices of
> Mozzarella over
> the cooked
> vegetables and
> cover for a few
> minutes to melt
> the cheese.*

pepper and individual oregano leaves. Pour in the wine, cover and cook over a low heat for about 10 minutes.
3. Meanwhile blanch and peel the tomatoes. Dice finely, without the stalk ends or core. Scatter over the mushrooms and heat briefly. Serve sprinkled with herbs.

SAVOY CABBAGE ROLLS WITH CHANTERELLE MUSHROOMS

SERVES 2 ◼◼
*Preparation and cooking
time: 45 minutes
Kcal per portion: 260
P = 16g, F = 17g, C = 8g*

4 large clean Savoy cabbage
    leaves
salt and pepper
250g/8oz chanterelle
    mushrooms
1 shallot
20g/¾oz butter
150g/5½oz quark or curd
    cheese
2 tbsps chopped herbs (basil,
    parsley, chervil)
30g/1oz Cheddar cheese,
    grated
125ml/4 fl oz chicken stock
1 tbsp soured cream

1. Blanch the cabbage leaves in plenty of boiling salted water for a few minutes. Remove from the water using a slotted spoon. Plunge briefly into ice-cold water, then drain.
2. Wipe the mushrooms and halve larger ones if necessary. Dice the shallot finely. Heat the butter in a non-stick frying-pan and fry the shallot until transparent. Add the mushrooms and brown lightly, stirring constantly.
3. Let the mushrooms cool slightly. Heat the oven to 200°C/400°F/Gas Mark 6.
4. Mix together the quark or curd cheese, herbs and cheese. Add the mushrooms. Season generously with salt and pepper.
5. Spread out the Savoy cabbage leaves. Spread over the mushroom mixture. Fold both sides of each leaf over the stuffing. Roll up from end to end and put side by side in a baking dish. Pour over the stock, cover and cook for about 25 minutes. Ten minutes before the end of the

*After cooling, stir the browned
mushrooms and shallots into the
herb and quark mixture.*

*Spread the mushroom and quark
mixture over the Savoy cabbage
leaves. Fold the long edges
inwards, then roll up.*

cooking time remove the lid, spoon the juices over the rolls and brush with the soured cream.
If fresh chanterelles are unavailable, ceps or button mushrooms can be used.
An accompaniment to game. Can also be served on its own as a starter or a vegetarian main course. In the latter case double the quantities.

SPRING ONIONS WITH MUSHROOMS

SERVES 2 ◼
*Preparation and cooking
time: 35 minutes
Kcal per portion: 185
P = 4g, F = 18g, C = 2g*

1 bunch spring onions
250g/8oz button mushrooms
1 tbsp sesame oil
salt and white pepper
generous pinch of ground
    lemon grass
generous pinch of ground
    coriander
generous pinch of ground
    turmeric
1-2 tbsps soy sauce
a few coriander sprigs

1. Trim and wash the spring onions. Chop into thin, diagonal slices, including some of the green parts. Wipe and finely slice the mushrooms.
2. Heat the oil in a wok or

> **TIP**
>
> *If you like ethnic
> cooking, you
> should have
> coriander in your
> herb garden. It
> thrives well and
> adds an
> interesting
> flavour to many
> dishes.*

high-sided frying-pan. Stir-fry the onions briefly.
3. Add the mushrooms, salt and pepper. Sprinkle with the spices. Stir-fry until the vegetables are cooked but still firm. Season with the soy sauce and serve garnished with coriander sprigs.
An accompaniment to fried fish or turkey steaks.

GOLDEN CAULIFLOWER

SERVES 2 ■
Preparation and cooking time: 35 minutes
Kcal per portion: 245
P = 5g, F = 20g, C = 8g

1 small cauliflower (about 500g/1lb2oz)
1 onion
1 garlic clove
1 dried chilli
2 tbsps oil
1 tsp curry powder
generous pinch of ground saffron
salt and white pepper
3 tbsps rice wine or dry sherry
100g/4oz Greek yoghurt
a few chervil sprigs

1. Trim the cauliflower and divide into small florets. Finely dice the onion and garlic. De-seed and finely dice the chilli.
2. Heat the oil in a wok or high-sided frying-pan and sweat the onion and garlic

---

TIP

To make a light, exotic meal, mix prawns into this dish.

---

until transparent. Add the chilli, curry powder and saffron and fry briefly.
3. Add the cauliflower florets and season with salt and pepper. Cook over a medium heat, stirring constantly, until golden. Pour in the rice wine or sherry. Cover and cook over a low heat for about 10 minutes, stirring from time to time.
4. Stir the yoghurt until smooth and mix into the vegetables. Sprinkle with chervil. An accompaniment to white fish or fried scampi.

MIXED VEGETABLES IN COCONUT MILK

SERVES 4 ■
Preparation and cooking time: 45 minutes
Kcal per portion: 160
P = 5g, F = 12g, C = 8g

4 small shallots
1 garlic clove
3 celery stalks
2 small carrots
100g/4oz mushrooms
150g/5½oz Chinese leaves
100g/4oz mange-tout
3 tbsps oil
salt and pepper
1 tsp finely grated ginger root
½ tsp ground lemon grass
generous pinch of cayenne pepper
generous pinch of sambal ulek
125ml/4 fl oz coconut milk (ready-made)
1 tbsp chopped parsley

1. Cut the shallots into wedges and finely chop the garlic. Trim and wash the other vegetables.
2. Chop the celery into thin slices. Chop the carrots, mushrooms and Chinese leaves into thin strips. Leave the mange-tout whole.
3. Heat the oil in a wok or high-sided frying-pan. Brown the vegetables, one after another, stirring constantly. Season with salt, add the spices and pour in the coconut milk. Bring to the boil and cook over a low heat for a few minutes. The vegetables should be cooked but still firm.
4. Serve sprinkled with parsley.
An accompaniment to oriental-style meat dishes.

STIR-FRIED KOHLRABI

SERVES 2 ■
Preparation and cooking time: 30 minutes
Kcal per portion: 405
P = 8g, F = 36g, C = 12g

2 medium kohlrabi (about 500g/1lb2oz)
1 small onion
2 tbsps oil
½ tsp mild curry powder
2 tbsps soy sauce
2 tbsps sunflower seeds

1. Remove any leaves from the kohlrabi and set aside. Peel the kohlrabi, slice thinly, then cut into strips. Finely dice the onion.
2. Heat the oil in a wok or high-sided frying-pan and sweat the onion until transparent. Add the strips of kohlrabi and fry gently over a medium heat, stirring constantly. Sprinkle with curry powder, pour over the soy sauce and continue to stir-fry until the kohlrabi is cooked.
3. Dry-fry the sunflower seeds in a second frying-pan.
4. Finely slice the reserved kohlrabi leaves. Sprinkle over the vegetables, with the sunflower seeds.
An accompaniment to curried chicken breast.

FRIED CELERIAC WITH SESAME SEED CRUST

SERVES 2 ■
Preparation and cooking time: 1 hour
Kcal per portion: 325
P = 25g, F = 21g, C = 12g

about 400g/14oz celeriac
1 small egg
20g/¾oz cracked wheat
30g/1oz sesame seeds
salt and white pepper
2 tbsps oil

1. Wash the celeriac; leave it whole and un-peeled. Boil for about 40 minutes in plenty of boiling salted water, until cooked but not too soft.
2. Cool the celeriac briefly in cold water, then pull off the skin or peel.
3. Chop the celeriac into 1cm/½ inch slices. Beat the egg with a fork. Combine the cracked wheat and sesame seeds. Lightly dust

---

TIP

Cooking the celeriac in the pressure-cooker saves a great deal of time. Peel while still hot, when the skin is easier to remove.

---

the celeriac slices with salt and pepper. Turn the slices first in the egg, then in the sesame seed mixture.
4. Heat the oil in a large non-stick frying-pan. Fry the celeriac slices over a medium heat for about 3 minutes on each side, until golden.
An accompaniment to roast venison or medallions of venison. Can also be served as a light meal with cranberries.

COURGETTE
PATTIES

COURGETTE PATTIES

SERVES 4 ■

*Preparation and cooking
time: 30 minutes
Kcal per portion: 190
P = 6g, F = 16g, C = 2g*

*2 medium courgettes (about
    400g/14oz)
1 small onion
1 garlic clove
½ bunch parsley
100g/4oz Feta cheese
1 egg
salt and pepper
3 tbsps oil*

1. Wash the courgettes. Cut off the ends and grate the flesh coarsely.
2. Finely dice the onion and garlic. Chop the parsley and mash the cheese.
3. Mix all these ingredients together. Beat the egg. Add to the other ingredients and

---

TIP

*Mix some
coarsely chopped
sunflower seeds
into the mixture.*

---

mix thoroughly. Season the mixture generously with salt and pepper.
4. Heat the oil in a large non-stick frying-pan. Using a tablespoon, place small balls of the mixture in the hot fat. Press flat with the back of a spoon and fry over a medium heat for about 3-4 minutes on each side. Drain on absorbent paper and serve immediately.
An accompaniment to roast lamb or veal. Can also be served as a meal for two with rémoulade sauce.

COURGETTES STUFFED WITH CHICKEN AND PRAWNS

SERVES 4 ■

*Preparation and cooking
time: 1 hour
Kcal per portion: 230
P = 25g, F = 9g, C = 11g*

*4 medium courgettes (each
    about 200g/7oz)
1 tbsp oil
2 tbsps chopped onion
300g/10oz chicken breast
1 tbsp finely chopped dill
1 egg
1 tbsp breadcrumbs
100g/4oz cooked peeled
    prawns
salt and white pepper
1 tbsp curry powder
freshly grated ginger root
cayenne pepper
15g/½oz butter
125ml/4 fl oz strong chicken
    stock*

1. Wash the courgettes. Halve lengthways and hollow out with a spoon, leaving a thin shell. Finely chop the flesh.
2. Heat the oil in a non-stick frying-pan. Sweat the onion with the courgette.
3. Heat the oven to 200°C/400°F/Gas Mark 6.
4. Finely grind the chicken in a liquidiser or food processor. Mash into a smooth meat stuffing with the courgette mixture, dill, egg and breadcrumbs. Stir in the prawns. Season well with salt, pepper, curry powder, ginger and cayenne. Stuff the mixture into the hollowed-out courgette halves.
5. Butter a large baking dish and put in the courgettes. Dot the stuffing with butter and bake for about 30 minutes. After 15 minutes, pour over the chicken stock.

Halve the courgettes lengthways. Hollow out and finely chop the flesh.

Mash together the processed chicken, fried vegetables, dill, egg and breadcrumbs.

Mix the prawns into the meat stuffing; add seasoning and spices.

Fill the hollowed out courgette halves with the chicken and prawn mixture.

TOMATOES STUFFED WITH FETA CHEESE

SERVES 4 ■ ■

*Preparation and cooking
time: 1 hour
Kcal per portion: 145
P = 4g, F = 12g, C = 4g*

*8 medium ripe tomatoes
salt and pepper
1 onion
2 garlic cloves
1 thyme sprig
1 oregano sprig
2 parsley stalks
100g/4oz Feta cheese
1 egg
1 tbsp breadcrumbs
1-2 tbsps olive oil*

1. Cut a lid from the tomatoes and reserve. Hollow out the tomatoes using a small spoon. Season the insides with salt and pepper.
2. Heat the oven to 200°C/400°F/Gas Mark 6.
3. For the stuffing, finely dice the onion and garlic. Pull the leaves from the thyme and oregano. Finely chop, together with the parsley. Mash the Feta with a fork or blend in a liquidiser. Add the egg and the breadcrumbs. Mix to a smooth paste with the other ingredients. If necessary, season with salt and pepper.
4. Stuff the tomatoes with the mixture and cover with the lids. Brush a small baking dish with some of the oil. Put in the tomatoes and brush with the remaining oil. Cook in the centre of the oven for about 25-30 minutes.
Accompaniment:
green salad and unpeeled boiled potatoes. Can also be served cold as a starter.

FENNEL AND PEARS

(see photo on page 108)

SERVES 2 ■
*Preparation and cooking
time: 35 minutes
Kcal per portion: 260
P = 6g, f = 9g, C = 28g*

---

*2 small fennel bulbs (about
    300g/10oz)
2 pears
juice of ½ lemon
20g/¾oz butter or margarine
salt and white pepper
cayenne pepper
125ml/4 fl oz dry white wine
50g/2oz shelled peas*

---

1. Wash and trim the fennel bulbs. Cut off and reserve any green leaves. Halve and thinly slice the bulbs. Peel, halve and core the pears.

The fennel leaves can be used for garnishing.

> **TIP**
>
> *The pears used
> for this dish
> should not be
> too soft.*

Thinly slice the fennel bulbs and the pears.

Slice the halves lengthways and sprinkle with lemon juice.
2. Heat the butter or margarine in a flameproof casserole. Fry the fennel strips lightly. Season with salt, pepper and a pinch of cayenne; pour in the wine. Cover and simmer for about 15 minutes.
3. Add the pear slices and peas. Cover and cook for just a few minutes.
4. Finely chop the reserved fennel leaves and sprinkle over the vegetables.
An accompaniment to Italian-style braised veal.

Add the pear slices and peas to the braised strips of fennel.

CELERY WITH MOZZARELLA

SERVES 4 ■
*Preparation and cooking
time: 1 hour
Kcal per portion: 245
P = 5g, F = 9g, C = 16g*

---

*2 heads celery (each about
    400g/14oz)
30g/1oz butter
salt and white pepper
125ml/4 fl oz dry white wine
4 beefsteak tomatoes
10 stoned black olives
6-8 basil leaves
100g/4oz Mozzarella cheese*

---

1. Cut the bottom and any green leaves from the celery. Cut in half lengthways.
2. Heat the butter in a large flameproof casserole. Turn the celery halves in the butter, season with salt and pepper and pour in the wine. Cover and simmer gently for about 20 minutes.
3. Meanwhile blanch, peel, core and finely dice the tomatoes. Slice the olives and cut the basil leaves into thin strips. Combine with the diced tomato. Season with salt and pepper. Cut the Mozzarella into thin slices.
4. Heat the grill to medium.
5. Turn the celery over so that the cut surfaces face upward. Cover with the tomato mixture, then with cheese. Brown under the grill for 10 minutes.
An accompaniment to fillet steak or rissoles. Can be served with mashed potato as a vegetarian main course for two.

SPINACH WITH YOGHURT

SERVES 4 ■
*Preparation and cooking
time: 35 minutes
Kcal per portion: 90
P = 3g, F = 8g, C = 2g*

---

*500g/1lb2oz young spinach
1 onion
2-3 garlic cloves
2 tbsps oil
1 small dried chilli
a little freshly grated ginger
    root
1 tsp curry powder
salt and white pepper
175g/6oz Greek yoghurt
tomato strips to garnish*

---

1. Trim the spinach and remove the thicker stalks. Thoroughly wash the leaves several times and drain.
2. Finely dice the onion and one garlic clove. Heat the oil in a wok or high-sided frying-pan. Sweat the onion and garlic until transparent.
3. De-seed and finely chop the chilli. Add to the pan with the grated ginger and curry powder. Lightly brown over a medium heat. Stir in the spinach leaves, cover and leave for a few minutes until they collapse.
4. Meanwhile crush the remaining garlic cloves and mix with the yoghurt. Season generously with salt and pepper.
5. Arrange the spinach in rings on warmed plates. Pour the garlic yoghurt into the centre. If desired, sprinkle with a little curry powder, toasted almonds or pistachio nuts. Garnish with thin strips of tomato.
An accompaniment to grilled kebabs.

Index

The Complete
VEGETARIAN
COOKBOOK

Chris Hardisty

Colour
Library
Direct

CONTENTS

The publishers would like to thank the following people who supplied recipes and without whom this book would not have been possible: Chris Hardisty, Rosie Brook, Pam Knutson, Freda Hooker, Pauline Robertshaw, D.M. Arnot, Val Shaw, Brian Holmes, Vivien Margison, Isabel Wilson, Marianne Vaney, Ian Jones, Wendy Godden, Joan Davis, Jo Wright, Isabel Booth, Alison Ray, Susan Mills, Kate Allen, Pat McGlashan, Deirdre Kuntz, Suzanne Ross, Joan Davies, Merle Millan, Ann Bohren, Winifred Allen, Sumitra Gopal and Sally Halon.

Photography by Peter Barry
Food prepared and styled by Helen Burdett
Designed by Claire Leighton and Judith Chant
Typesetting and graphics by Julie Smith
Edited by Jillian Stewart

4945
This edition published in 1998 by Colour Library Direct,
a division of Quadrillion Publishing Ltd.,
Godalming Business Centre, Woolsack Way,
Godalming, Surrey, England, GU7 1XW
Printed and bound in Singapore
ISBN 1-85833-583-3

INTRODUCTION

There's a revolution taking place – a food revolution. A decade or so ago vegetarians were seen as weirdos, now everybody knows one and almost four million of us are one. The numbers are growing so fast – doubled in the past year – that before long, carnivores will only be able to do it with other consenting adults in private.

The scale of change is extraordinary. The results of a major Vegetarian Society food survey, carried out by Bradford University, shows that apart from 28,000 becoming vegetarian every week, over 4½ million people eat no red meat and over 9 million have drastically reduced their meat intake. And if that isn't dramatic enough, 40 per cent of the population have considered becoming vegetarian.

People come to vegetarianism for different reasons: some out of compassion for animals, mostly reared in appalling conditions and slaughtered barbarically; some out of environmental concern; some because of Third-World impoverishment; and others for reasons of health.

Vegetarians have lower rates of obesity, and suffer less from coronary heart disease, high blood pressure, cancer of the bowel and a host of other disorders than their meat-eating counterparts. The professional debate isn't any longer about whether vegetarians are healthier than meat eaters, but why they are! Even the government's own health advisers recommend that we cut down on fats generally and in particular saturated fats by substituting them with polyunsaturated fats; that we reduce salt and sugar intake and increase fibre and complex carbohydrates.

In simple language this means that we should cut down on meat and animal products and eat more fresh vegetables and fruit; include plenty of bread, pasta, rice, pulses, grains and potatoes in our meals and keep processed foods to a minimum. In fact, what they're describing is a vegetarian diet! The World Health Organisation goes even further than this and recommends – albeit in polite and very guarded language – that meat should now be considered an optional extra.

There are thousands of ingredients from around the world that most meat-eaters simply ignore, but which can open up a whole new taste experience. Across India and the East millions of people eat nothing but vegetarian food, while the Japanese diet contains very little meat, and traditional African and Middle Eastern foods are largely meat-free.

So what's the outcome of this move towards vegetarianism? Millions of people reluctantly munching away at muesli and lentil burgers, hating every minute of it? Not a bit! As this book is about to reveal to you, vegetarian eating is about imagination and experimentation, diversity and change. Start to look beyond the 'something and two veg', use your imagination and you will discover dishes more delicious than you ever dreamed.

The Vegetarian Society only endorses the use of free-range eggs and vegetarian cheeses (those made with non-animal rennet) and although it was once difficult to find anything other than vegetarian Cheddar you will now find a large selection of vegetarian cheeses in health food stores, so try to use these wherever possible.

Our choice of food has enormous influence not only on our health, but on the lives of others and on the earth itself. And it all starts here!

JULIET GELLATLEY
THE VEGETARIAN SOCIETY

SNACKS & STARTERS

Vegetarian snacks and starters offer endless opportunities for the cook to use his or her imaginative flair – whether it's a salad, stuffed vegetables, or a risotto, the scope is limitless. It is always best to look on any snack or starter as a mini main course where garnishing and presentation are concerned. This applies to the starter in particular, as it introduces the meal and should give a taste of things to come.

Starters can consist of almost anything you wish to serve as long it does not clash with the main course. Try to balance a substantial main dish with a light starter and vice versa. Many main dishes can be served in small portions as starters, or as snacks. Pay attention to the ingredients and try not to duplicate them in the first course and the main dish. For example, if your main course does not include raw food, serve a mixed salad, or if your main dish is salad based, serve a hot starter such as soup.

Home-made soups are delicious, and as well as being the perfect starter, the heartier ones can be served with bread as a one-course meal. Making soup was once thought to be fiddly and time-consuming. Not so now with the aid of a liquidiser, although if you do not have one it is possible to press the soup through a sieve to produce a creamy soup. Most vegetables are suitable for use in soups, so this is a perfect way of using up almost any ingredients you may have to hand. Soup also keeps well and often tastes better the day after it has been cooked!

FENNEL AND WALNUT SOUP

*A delicious and unusual combination makes this
soup perfect for special occasions.*

SERVES 4

1 bulb chopped fennel
1 head chopped celery
1 large onion, chopped
1 tbsp olive or sunflower oil
75g/3oz walnuts, crushed
1150ml/2 pints vegetable stock, bean
  stock or water
45ml/3 tbsps Pernod
140ml/¼ pint single cream
Salt and pepper
Parsley to garnish

1. Sauté the fennel, celery and onion in the oil over a low heat.

2. Add the walnuts and stock and simmer for half an hour.

3. Liquidise the simmered ingredients together and return to the pan.

4. Add the Pernod, single cream and salt and pepper.

5. Reheat gently and serve garnished with parsley.

TIME: Preparation takes about 15 minutes, cooking takes about 1 hour 10 minutes.

SERVING IDEA: Celery leaves may be used as a garnish if no parsley is available.

VARIATION: Other nuts such as cashews or almonds may be used in place of walnuts.

WATCHPOINT: Do not allow the soup to boil after adding the cream and Pernod.

CREAM OF CARROT SOUP

A classic soup which is suitable for any occasion.

SERVES 4

1 large onion, chopped
2 cloves garlic, crushed
1 tbsp olive oil
450g/1lb carrots, chopped
1 tsp mixed herbs
850ml/1½ pints stock
140ml/¼ pint soured cream
Salt and pepper

1. Sauté the chopped onion and garlic in the oil until transparent.

2. Add the carrots, mixed herbs and stock.

3. Bring to the boil and simmer for about 30 minutes until the carrots are soft.

4. Cool a little and then liquidise until smooth.

5. Add the soured cream, season to taste and mix thoroughly.

6. Heat through gently and serve.

TIME: Preparation takes about 10 minutes, cooking takes 35 minutes.

WATCHPOINT: Do not allow the soup to boil after adding the soured cream.

VARIATION: For a richer soup, omit the soured cream and add a swirl of double cream just before serving.

WILD RICE SOUP

A meal in itself when served with granary bread and a green salad.

SERVES 4

50g/2oz wild rice
420ml/¾ pint water
2 onions, chopped
1 tbsp butter or ghee
2 sticks celery, chopped
½ tsp dried thyme
½ tsp dried sage
850ml/1½ pints water or vegetable stock
2 tsps Vecon (vegetable stock)
1 tbsp shoyu (Japanese soy sauce)
6 small potatoes, peeled and roughly
  chopped
1 carrot, finely diced
Milk or single cream

---

1. Add the wild rice to the water, bring to the boil, reduce the heat and simmer for 40-50 minutes until the rice has puffed and most of the liquid has been absorbed.

2. Sauté the onions in the butter until transparent.

3. Add the celery, thyme and sage and cook for 5-10 minutes.

4. Add the water, vecon, shoyu and potatoes.

5. Simmer for 20 minutes or until the potatoes are cooked.

6. Blend the mixture in a liquidiser until smooth.

7. Return to the pan, add the carrot and wild rice.

8. Add the milk or cream to thin the soup to the desired consistency.

9. Reheat gently and serve.

TIME: Preparation takes about 15 minutes. Cooking takes 30 minutes plus 40 minutes to cook the wild rice.

COOK'S TIP: You can prepare and cook the soup whilst the wild rice is cooking. Add the rice to the soup at the end of the cooking time.

FREEZING: Cook a large quantity of wild rice and freeze in small portions. Add to the soup or other dishes as needed.

VARIATION: Toast some flaked almonds and sprinkle on top of the soup before serving.

SPINACH AND APPLE SOUP

The two main flavours complement each other
perfectly in this hearty soup.

SERVES 4

25g/1oz butter or margarine
1 small onion, chopped
25g/1oz wholemeal flour
570ml/1 pint vegetable stock
450g/1lb spinach, shredded
225g/8oz apple purée
280ml/½ pint milk
Salt and freshly ground black pepper
Pinch of nutmeg
Lemon juice
Natural yogurt
A little parsley, finely chopped

1. Melt the butter in a large saucepan and fry the onion until soft.

2. Add the flour and cook to a roux.

3. Add the stock slowly, stir well and simmer for 10 minutes.

4. Add the spinach and cook until tender.

5. Cool slightly and mix in the apple purée.

6. Place all the ingredients in a liquidiser and blend until smooth.

7. Return to the pan and reheat slowly together with the milk.

8. Add the salt, pepper, nutmeg and lemon juice to taste.

9. Serve in individual bowls with the yogurt swirled on the top and garnished with chopped parsley.

TIME: Preparation takes 15 minutes, cooking takes 15 minutes.

COOK'S TIP: The apple purée can be omitted if not available but it adds an unusual flavour to the soup.

VARIATION: If there is no vegetable water available for the stock, a teaspoonful of Vecon (vegetable stock) or a stock cube can be mixed with 1 pint of boiling water instead.

EASY LENTIL SOUP

*A good old-fashioned soup which is sure
to please all the family.*

SERVES 4-6

225g/8oz split red lentils
25g/1oz butter or margarine
1 medium onion, peeled and finely
    chopped
2 stalks celery, finely diced
2 carrots, scrubbed and finely diced
Grated rind of 1 lemon
1150ml/2 pints light vegetable stock
Salt and freshly ground black pepper

1. Pick over the lentils and remove any stones. Rinse well.

2. Heat the butter or margarine in a pan and sauté the onion for 2-3 minutes.

3. Add the diced celery and carrots and let the vegetables sweat for 5-10 minutes.

4. Stir in the lentils, add the lemon rind, stock and salt and pepper to taste.

5. Bring to the boil, reduce the heat and simmer for 15-20 minutes until the vegetables are tender.

6. Roughly blend the soup in a liquidiser, it should not be too smooth.

7. Check the seasoning and reheat gently.

TIME: Preparation takes about 10 minutes, cooking takes 15-20 minutes.

SERVING IDEA: Sprinkle with cheese and serve with hot toast.

FREEZING: Freeze for up to 3 months.

19

GARDEN VEGETABLE SOUP

A hearty soup perfect for those cold winter nights.

SERVES 4-6

1 tbsp margarine
½ head fennel, finely chopped
3 medium carrots, diced
1 medium onion, chopped
2-3 cloves garlic, crushed
1 parsnip, diced
Salt and pepper
2 heaped tsps dried parsley
1 tbsp tomato purée
1 large potato, diced
1150ml/2 pints vegetable stock
50g/2oz frozen peas

1. Melt the margarine in a large pan and add the fennel, carrots, onion, garlic, parsnip and seasoning.

2. Cover and allow to 'sweat' over a very low heat for 10-15 minutes, stirring occasionally.

3. Add the parsley, tomato purée, potato and stock.

4. Stir well, bring to the boil and simmer for 20-30 minutes until the vegetables are tender.

5. Just before serving, add the frozen peas.

6. Bring back to the boil and serve immediately.

TIME: Preparation takes 15 minutes, cooking takes about 35 minutes.

SERVING IDEA: Serve with crusty rolls or French bread.

VARIATION: If fennel is not available, use 2 or 3 sticks of finely chopped celery.

SPLIT PEA SOUP

A classic soup which looks extra special with
a swirl of yogurt on top.

SERVES 6

225g/8oz split peas
3 pints vegetable stock or water plus a
   stock cube
50g/2oz margarine
1 large onion, chopped
3 sticks celery, chopped
2 leeks, finely sliced
2 medium potatoes, peeled and diced
1 medium carrot, finely chopped,
Salt and pepper

1. Cook the peas in the stock for 10-15 minutes.

2. Meanwhile, melt the margarine and sauté the onion, celery and leeks for a few minutes.

3. Add to the peas and stock together with the potatoes and carrot and bring back to the boil.

4. Simmer for 30 minutes.

5. Season well and liquidise until smooth.

TIME: Preparation takes about 10 minutes, cooking takes 40 minutes.

SERVING IDEA: If the vegetables are chopped small enough you can serve this as a chunky soup.

COOK'S TIP: If you do not have a liquidiser you can pass the soup through a sieve although it will not be quite as thick.

FRENCH ONION SOUP

This soup tastes best if cooked the day
before it is needed and then reheated as required.

SERVES 4

---

3 medium onions
50g/2oz butter or margarine
25g/1oz plain flour or soya flour
1ltr/1¾ pints boiling vegetable stock or
    water plus 2 stock cubes
Salt and pepper

Topping
4 slices French bread, cut crosswise
50g/2oz Cheddar cheese, grated
25g/1oz Parmesan cheese, grated

---

1. Slice the onions very finely into rings.

2. Melt the butter in a pan, add the onion rings and fry over a medium heat until well browned.

3. Mix in the flour and stir well until browned.

4. Add the stock and seasoning and simmer for 30 minutes.

5. Toast the bread on both sides.

6. Combine the cheese, and divide between the bread slice; grill until golden brown.

7. Place the slices of bread and cheese in the bottom of individual soup dishes and spoon the soup over the top.

8. Serve at once.

TIME: Preparation takes 10 minutes, cooking takes 30 minutes.

VARIATION: For a special occasion, add a tablespoonful of brandy to the stock.

WATCHPOINT: The onions must be very well browned, as this gives the rich colour to the soup.

SWEET POTATO SOUP

Warm up your winter nights with this heartening soup.

SERVES 4-6

50g/2oz butter or margarine
1 large onion, finely chopped
450g/1lb sweet potato, peeled and diced
225g/8oz carrots, peeled and diced
1 tbsp chopped coriander
1 lemon, zest and juice
850ml/1½ pints stock
Pepper

1. Melt the butter or margarine and cook the onion until transparent.

2. Add the sweet potato and carrots and allow to 'sweat' over a very low heat for 10-15 minutes, stirring occasionally.

3. Add the coriander, lemon zest, juice of half the lemon, stock and pepper.

4. Cover and simmer for 30-40 minutes.

5. Liquidise until almost smooth, but leaving some texture to the soup.

6. Return to the pan and reheat until piping hot.

7. Garnish with coriander leaves and serve immediately.

TIME: Preparation takes 15 minutes, cooking takes 40-55 minutes.

SERVING IDEA: Serve with granary rolls.

COOK'S TIP: Fresh coriander may be kept in a jug of water in a cool place. It can also be frozen for use when fresh is not available.

CRUDITÉS

A great favourite served with delicious dips to accompany.

SERVES 6-8

Choose from the following vegetable selection:

Cauliflower, broccoli - divided into small florets

Carrots, celery, courgettes, cucumber – cut into matchstick pieces

Chicory – separate the blades

Mushrooms – sliced or quartered

Peppers, kohlrabi, fennel – sliced

Radishes, spring onions, cherry tomatoes – leave whole

Tomato and Cheese Dip

1 tbsp butter or margarine
1 tbsp grated onion
225g/8oz tomatoes, peeled and diced
50g/2oz Cheddar cheese, grated
50g/2oz breadcrumbs
1 egg, beaten
½ tsp dried mustard
Salt and pepper
2-4 tbsps Greek yogurt

Creamed Curry Dip

1 tbsp mango chutney
6 tbsps home-made or good quality mayonnaise
1 tsp curry paste
2 tbsp double cream
Pinch ground cumin

Avocado Dip

2 ripe avocados
1 onion, diced
½ clove garlic, crushed
2 tbsps lemon juice
Salt and pepper

Tomato and Cheese Dip

1. Melt the butter and gently fry the onion for 2 or 3 minutes until soft.

2. Add the tomatoes, cover and simmer for 10 minutes.

3. Add the cheese, breadcrumbs and egg and cook for a further minute, stirring all the time, until thickened. Do not allow to boil.

4. Add the mustard and seasoning and blend or liquidise until smooth.

5. Mix in enough Greek yogurt to ensure a smooth 'dipping' consistency and store in the refrigerator until required.

Creamed Curry Dip

1. Chop the pieces of mango with a sharp knife and place in a bowl.

2. Add the other ingredients and mix well.

3. Refrigerate until required.

Avocado Dip

1. Peel the avocados, remove the stones and chop the flesh roughly.

2. Process or liquidise together with the onion, garlic and lemon juice until smooth.

3. Season to taste and refrigerate until required.

TIME: Preparation takes 30 minutes, cooking takes 15 minutes.

PARSNIP FRITTERS

These tasty fritters make a nice change for lunch or a light snack.

SERVES 4

100g/4oz plain unbleached flour
2 tsps baking powder
1 tsp salt
½ tsp pepper
1 egg
140ml/¼ pint milk
1 tbsp melted butter
680g/1½lbs cooked parsnips, finely
   diced
Oil or clarified butter for frying

1. Sift together the flour, baking powder, salt and pepper.

2. Beat the egg and mix with the milk and melted butter.

3. Stir this mixture into the dry ingredients.

4. Stir in the cooked parsnips.

5. Divide the mixture into 16 and shape into small fritters.

6. Fry in oil or clarified butter until browned on both sides.

TIME: Preparation takes 10 minutes, cooking takes about 5-8 minutes per batch.

VARIATION: Courgettes, sweetcorn, onions or aubergine may be substituted for the parsnips.

SERVING IDEA: Serve with yogurt sauce or make them slightly larger and serve as a main course with salad.

RED LENTIL SOUFFLÉ

Serve this tasty soufflé as a starter or with watercress or salad for a light lunch.

SERVES 4

100g/4oz red lentils
1 bay leaf
280ml/½ pint water
25g/1oz margarine or butter
75ml/2½ fl.oz double cream
2 egg yolks (size 3)
3 egg whites (size 3)
50g/2oz grated Cheddar cheese (optional)
Salt and pepper
Pinch of paprika

1. Pick over the lentils and remove any stones. Rinse well.

2. Place the lentils, bay leaf and water in a pan and bring to the boil.

3. Simmer for 20 minutes or until the lentils are soft.

4. Remove the bay leaf and beat the lentils until they are very smooth.

5. Beat in the margarine, cream and egg yolks.

6. Beat the egg whites until very stiff and fold into the mixture.

7. Season and fold in the grated cheese.

8. Pour into a well greased souffle dish and sprinkle with a little paprika.

9. Bake in a preheated oven 190°C/375°F/ Gas Mark 5 for approximately 20 minutes or until the souffle is well risen, firm and brown.

10. Serve immediately.

TIME: Preparation takes about 15 minutes, cooking takes 40 minutes.

VARIATION: Add a good pinch of mixed herbs to the lentils whilst cooking.

MIXED NUT BALLS

*This versatile dish can be made in advance and
refrigerated until required for cooking.*
SERVES 8

60g/2½ oz ground almonds
60g/2½ oz ground hazelnuts
60g/2½ oz ground pecan nuts
75g/3oz wholemeal breadcrumbs
100g/4oz Cheddar cheese, grated
1 egg, beaten
4-5 tbsps dry sherry or 2 tbsps milk and 3
   tbsps dry sherry
1 small onion, finely chopped
1 tbsp grated fresh ginger
1 tbsp fresh parsley, chopped
1 small red or green chilli, finely chopped
1 medium red pepper, diced
1 tsp sea salt
1 tsp freshly ground black pepper

1. Mix the almonds, hazelnuts and pecan
nuts together with the breadcrumbs and
the cheese.

2. In another bowl, mix the beaten egg
with the sherry, onion, ginger, parsley,
chilli and red pepper.

3. Combine with the nut mixture and add
the salt and pepper.

4. If the mixture is too dry, add a little
more sherry or milk.

5. Form into small 2cm/1-inch balls.

6. Do not preheat the oven.

7. Arrange the balls on a well greased
baking tray and bake at 180°C/350°F/Gas
Mark 4 for about 20-25 minutes, until
golden brown.

TIME: Preparation takes about 20 minutes, cooking takes 20-25 minutes.

SERVING IDEA: Serve on individual plates on a bed of chopped lettuce. Garnish with slices
of lemon and hand round your favourite sauce in a separate bowl.

HUMMUS

A classic starter which also makes the perfect snack.

SERVES 4

225g/8oz cooked chick peas (reserve stock)
4 tbsps light tahini
Juice of 2 lemons
6 tbsps olive oil
3-4 cloves garlic, crushed
Salt to taste

1. Put the cooked chick peas into a blender together with 140ml/¼ pints of the reserved stock.

2. Add the tahini, lemon juice, half of the olive oil, the garlic, and salt.

3. Blend until smooth, adding a little more stock if it is too thick.

4. Leave to stand for an hour or so to let the flavours develop.

5. Serve on individual dishes with the remaining olive oil drizzled over the top.

TIME: Preparation takes 10 minutes, standing time takes 1 hour.

SERVING IDEA: Serve sprinkled with paprika and garnished with wedges of lemon. Accompany the hummus with warm pitta bread.

BULGAR BOATS

This pretty starter can easily be taken on picnics.

SERVES 6

50g/2oz green lentils
100g/4oz bulgar
1 red pepper
1 green pepper
1 medium onion
50g/2oz pine nuts (dry roasted in a pan)
2 tsps dried salad herbs (tarragon, chives
   or parsley)
Juice and rind of 1 lemon
Salt
Freshly ground black pepper
Cos lettuce to serve

1. Remove any grit or stones from the lentils and rinse well.

2. Cover with plenty of water and boil for about 20 minutes - do not overcook.

3. Place the bulgar wheat in a mixing bowl and cover with boiling water. Leave for about 10 minutes - the grain will then have swollen, softened and absorbed the water.

4. Dice the peppers and chop the onion finely.

5. Drain the lentils and add to the wheat, together with the peppers, nuts, onion, herbs, lemon juice and rind, salt and pepper.

6. Using one large lettuce leaf per person, spoon the salad into the centre of the leaves and arrange on a large serving dish garnished with wedges of lemon.

TIME: Preparation takes 15 minutes, cooking takes 20 minutes.

VARIATION: Cashews or peanuts could be used instead of pine nuts. The bulgar mixture could be served in 'parcels' of lightly blanched cabbage leaves.

COOK'S TIP: If the salad is not required immediately, cover and refrigerate until required.

FENNEL AND ORANGE CROUSTADE

A delicious mixture which is simple to prepare.

SERVES 4

4 x 1-inch thick slices wholmeal bread
Oil for deep frying
2 fennel bulbs (reserve any fronds)
4 oranges
1 tbsp olive oil
Pinch salt
Chopped fresh mint for garnishing

1. Trim the crust off the bread and cut into 7.6cm/3-inch squares.

2. Hollow out the middles, leaving evenly shaped cases.

3. Heat the oil and deep fry the bread until golden brown.

4. Drain the bread well on absorbent kitchen paper. Leave to cool.

5. Trim the fennel bulbs and slice thinly. Place in a mixing bowl.

6. Remove all the peel and pith from the oranges and cut into segments - do this over the mixing bowl to catch the juice.

7. Mix the orange segments with the fennel.

8. Add the olive oil and salt and mix together thoroughly.

9. Just before serving, divide the fennel and orange mixture evenly between the bread cases and garnish with fresh mint and fennel fronds.

TIME: Preparation takes 15 minutes, cooking takes 5 minutes.

VARIATION: Serve the salad on individual plates sprinkled with croutons.

COOK'S TIP: The salad can be made in advance and refrigerated until required but do not fill the cases until just before serving.

CARROT AND SWEETCORN MEDLEY

*A delicious combination which is perfect as a
light starter or summer snack.*

SERVES 6

450g/1lb carrots
1 clove garlic, crushed
2-3 tbsps lemon juice
Salt
Freshly ground black pepper
350g/12oz tinned sweetcorn
Lettuce
1 knuckle size piece of fresh root ginger,
    grated
Few black olives, stones removed

1. Scrub and grate the carrots and place in
a mixing bowl.

2. Combine the garlic, lemon juice, salt
and pepper in a screw topped jar and
shake well.

3. Mix the dressing with the grated carrot
and add the sweetcorn.

4. Put a little finely shredded lettuce in the
bottom of individual stem glasses and
arrange the carrot and sweetcorn mixture
over the top.

5. Garnish with grated ginger and olives.

6. Chill for 30 minutes before serving.

TIME: Preparation takes 15 minutes, chilling takes 30 minutes.

SERVING IDEA: Serve with wholemeal bread and butter triangles.

VARIATION: To use as an accompaniment to a main course - arrange the carrot
on a wide serving plate, leaving an indentation in the centre. Fill this with
the sweetcorn and garnish with ginger and olives.

Date, Apple and Celery Starter

A healthy dish with a tasty mix of flavours.

SERVES 4

2 dstsp desiccated coconut
2 crisp eating apples
3-4 sticks celery
75g/3oz dates
2 tbsps natural yogurt
Salt and pepper
Pinch of nutmeg

1. Toast the coconut in a dry frying pan over a low heat until it is golden brown, then put to one side.

2. Core and dice the apples and chop the celery finely.

3. Plunge the dates into boiling water, drain and chop finely.

4. Combine the apples, celery and dates in a mixing bowl.

5. Add the yogurt, seasoning and nutmeg and mix thoroughly so that the salad is coated completely.

6. Transfer to a serving bowl and garnish with the toasted coconut.

7. Serve at once.

TIME: Preparation takes 10 minutes, cooking takes 2-3 minutes.

SERVING IDEA: Serve individual portions on a bed of watercress.

COOK'S TIP: Red skinned apples add colour to this salad.

MUSHROOMS AND TOFU IN GARLIC BUTTER

A quick and delicious starter.

SERVES 4

225g/8oz button mushrooms
2.5cm/1" root ginger
225g/8oz smoked tofu
100g/4oz butter
4 small cloves garlic, crushed
2 tbsps chopped parsley

1. Wipe the mushrooms with a damp cloth.

2. Peel and grate the root ringer.

3. Cut the smoked tofu into small 1.2cm./ ½ " squares.

4. Melt the butter in a frying pan.

5. Add the crushed garlic and ginger and fry gently for two minutes.

6. Add the mushrooms and cook gently for 4-5 minutes until the mushrooms are softened.

7. Finally, add the smoked tofu and heat through.

8. Divide between 4 individually heated dishes, sprinkle with chopped parsley and serve at once.

TIME: Preparation takes 10 minutes, cooking takes 12 minutes.

SERVING IDEA: Serve with french bread or crusty wholemeal rolls.

VARIATION: Substitute asparagus tips for the button mushrooms.

SAVOURY TOMATOES

An ideal starter for slimmers.

SERVES 4

4 large Spanish tomatoes
4 tbsps cottage cheese
1 tsp ground cumin
1 green pepper, de-seeded and diced
Seasoning
50g/2oz pumpkin seeds
1 bunch watercress

1. Slice off the tops of the tomatoes.

2. Remove the seeds and leave upside down to drain.

3. Rub the cottage cheese through a sieve to achieve a smooth consistency, add a little milk if necessary.

4. Stir in the cumin, pepper and seasoning.

5. Divide the mixture into four and stuff the tomatoes.

6. Dry roast the pumpkin seeds in a frying pan until they are lightly browned. Sprinkle over the tomatoes.

7. Chill until required.

8. Serve on a bed of watercress.

TIME: Preparation takes 10 minutes.

SERVING IDEA: Serve with very thin slices of brown bread and butter.

VARIATION: Use cream cheese in place of the cottage cheese.

DHINGRI KARI (MUSHROOM CURRY)

An ideal snack or supper dish.

SERVES 4

225g/8oz leeks, finely sliced
2 cloves garlic, crushed
½ tsp grated ginger
2 tsps curry powder
1 tsp garam masala
2 tbsps oil
450g/1lb mushrooms, cut into quarters
100g/4oz creamed coconut, grated
1 tbsp lemon juice

1. Fry the leeks, garlic, ginger and spices in the oil until soft.

2. Add the mushrooms and cook over a low heat until soft.

3. Add the grated coconut and cook gently until the coconut has completely dissolved, adding a little water if the mixture appears too dry.

4. Stir in the lemon juice and sufficient salt to taste.

5. Serve on a bed of rice.

TIME: Preparation takes 15 minutes, cooking takes about 20 minutes.

SERVING IDEA: Serve with a tomato and onion salad.

POTATO NESTS

*An ideal supper dish and an excellent
way of using up leftover cooked potatoes.*

SERVES 2

1 onion, finely chopped
450g/1lb potatoes, cooked in their skins
A little milk
Knob of butter
Seasoning
2 eggs
25g/1oz cheese, grated

1. Cook the onion in a little water until softened. Drain.

2. Peel the cooked potatoes and mash them with the milk, butter and seasoning.

3. Add the drained onion and mix well.

4. Divide the mixture into two and make 'nests' on a greased baking sheet.

5. Crack an egg into each nest and sprinkle with grated cheese.

6. Bake at 200°C/400°F/Gas Mark 6 for 20-25 minutes or until the eggs are set.

TIME: Preparation takes 10 minutes, cooking takes 25-30 minutes.

SERVING IDEA: Garnish with parsley and serve with beans and grilled tomatoes or a salad.

VARIATION: The nests may be filled with chopped leftover nut roast mixed with a mushroom or tomato sauce and a few freshly chopped herbs.

FILO CRACKERS

*Serve these delicious snacks anywhere –
buffets, picnics, or drinks parties.*

SERVES 4

50g/2oz dried mixed fruit
25g/1oz figs, chopped
50g/2oz ground almonds
50g/2oz dates, chopped
50g/2oz walnuts, chopped
1 tbsp brown sugar
½ tsp ground cinnamon
Zest and juice of 1 orange
25g/1oz melted butter plus 13g/½ oz
    melted butter
16 sheets filo pastry, approximately
    20.3cm x 8" square

1. Put the mixed fruit, figs, ground almonds, dates and walnuts into a mixing bowl.

2. Add the sugar, cinnamon, zest and juice of the orange and the 25g/1oz melted butter. Mix together well and set to one side.

3. Use two sheet together for each cracker. Divide the mixture into 8 and place one portion of the filling in the centre of each sheet.

4. Fold the base of the filo over the filling and roll up.

5. Twist the ends of the filo roll where there is no filling, to form a cracker shape.

6. Place on a greased baking tray and brush generously with the remaining melted butter.

7. Cook at 200°C/400°F/Gas Mark 6 for 20 minutes or until the crackers are golden brown and crisp.

TIME: Preparation takes 20 minutes, cooking takes 20 minutes.

SERVING IDEA: Serve with orange wedges.

COOK'S TIP: Frozen filo pastry may be purchased at most large supermarkets.
Allow 2 hours to defrost at room temperature or 3 minutes in a microwave.

WATCHPOINT: A little extra care must be taken when handling filo pastry and it must
always be kept well wrapped before use to avoid drying out.

IMAM BAYILDI

Imam Bayildi means "the priest has fainted".
Apparently the dish was so delicious that the
priest fainted with delight!

SERVES 4

2 large aubergines
Salt
150ml/5fl.oz olive oil
2 onions, peeled and finely chopped
2 cloves garlic, crushed
250g/9oz tomatoes, skinned and chopped
½ tsp mixed spice
Juice of ½ lemon
1 tsp brown sugar
1 tbsp chopped parsley
1 tbsp pine kernels
Salt and pepper

1. Halve the aubergines lengthways, and scoop out the flesh with a sharp knife leaving a substantial shell so they do not disintegrate when cooked.

2. Sprinkle the shells with a little salt and leave upside down on a plate for 30 minutes to drain away any bitter juices.

3. Meanwhile, heat half the oil in a saucepan and fry the onion and garlic until just softened.

4. Add the scooped out aubergine flesh, tomatoes, mixed spice, lemon juice, sugar, parsley, pine kernels and a little seasoning.

5. Simmer for about 20 minutes until the mixture has thickened.

6. Wash and dry the aubergine shells and spoon the filling into the halves.

7. Place side by side in a buttered ovenproof dish.

8. Mix the remaining oil with 140ml/¼ pint water and a little seasoning.

9. Pour around the aubergines and bake at 180°C/350°F/Gas Mark 4 for 30-40 minutes or until completely tender.

TIME: Preparation takes 25 minutes, cooking takes 1 hour.

SERVING IDEA: Serve hot or cold garnished with fresh herbs and accompanied by chunks of wholemeal bread. If serving cold, chill for at least 2 hours before serving.

CAULIFLOWER AND BROCCOLI SOUFLETTES

Serve as a winter-time starter or as a main meal with rice salad and ratatouille.

SERVES 6

350g/12oz cauliflower
350g/12oz broccoli
50g/2oz margarine
50g/2oz brown rice flour
420ml/¾ pint milk
50g/2oz Cheddar cheese, grated
1 large egg, separated
Good pinch of nutmeg

1. Break the cauliflower and broccoli into small florets and steam until just tender - about 7-10 minutes.

2. Melt the margarine, remove from the heat and gradually add the flour. Stir to a roux and add the milk gradually, blending well to ensure a smooth consistency.

3. Return the pan to the heat and stir until the sauce thickens and comes to the boil.

4. Cool a little and add the egg yolk and cheese, stir well and add nutmeg to taste.

5. Whip the egg white until stiff and fold carefully into the sauce.

6. Place the vegetables into 6 small buttered ramekin dishes and season.

7. Divide the sauce evenly between the dishes and bake immediately at 190°C/375°F/Gas Mark 5 for about 35 minutes until puffed and golden.

8. Serve at once.

TIME: Preparation takes 15 minutes, cooking takes 50 minutes.

SALADS FOR ALL SEASONS

'To remember a successful salad is generally to remember a successful dinner; at all events, the perfect dinner necessarily includes the perfect salad.'

George Ellwanger
Pleasures of the Table 1903

Raw vegetables have always been an important part of our diet and for optimum health it is important that raw food in some form be eaten every day. We are lucky nowadays to find a wide variety of salad ingredients available all year round, although they do tend to be expensive out of season. Today the choice of produce is endless and with organically grown produce you can be sure that the vegetables and the soil have not been treated with chemical sprays or pesticides. Nearly all vegetables are suitable for use in salads, and eaten this way they provide more nutrients than cooked vegetables. Even with careful cooking, valuable vitamins and minerals can be lost.

Vegetables are a valuable source of fibre, vitamins and minerals and, although in most cases they are 80 per cent water, the other 20 per cent contains carbohydrates, fat and protein. To many people, a salad is just a random mix of lettuce, cucumber and tomato. A good salad, however, should be pleasing to the eye as well as the palate. It can be as vibrant as you wish, using red, green, and orange peppers, tomatoes, spring onions, carrots and lettuce, or it can be a tranquil mix of greens using lettuce, cabbage, cucumber, avocado, spring onions and green peppers. The list of ingredients that can be used in salads is as long as your own imagination, so experiment and you will find a salad for every season and every occasion.

GREEK SALAD

*A great favourite which has the added
advantage of being easy to prepare.*

SERVES 4

2 tomatoes
½ green pepper
¼ cucumber
2 sticks celery, finely sliced
1 tsp fresh basil, finely chopped
Few crisp leaves of lettuce
100g/4oz Feta cheese, diced
16 black olives

Dressing
4 tbsps olive oil
2 tbsps lemon juice
1 clove garlic, crushed
Large pinch oregano
Salt and pepper

1. Cut each tomato into eight pieces and
put into a large mixing bowl.

2. Chop the pepper and cucumber
roughly. Add to the tomato together with
the celery and chopped basil.

3. Mix together the oil, lemon juice, garlic,
oregano and seasoning, and pour over the
salad.

4. Mix well to coat all the vegetables.

5. Arrange a few leaves of lettuce in the
bottom of a serving bowl, and pile the
salad on the top, followed by the cheese
cubes.

6. Garnish with olives.

TIME: Preparation takes 15 minutes.

SERVING IDEA: Serve with pitta bread.

VARIATION: Add a few croutons just before serving.

TABOULEH

*This is a traditional salad from the Middle East. The main
ingredient is bulgar which is partially cooked cracked wheat and
only needs soaking for a short while before it is ready to eat.*

SERVES 6

175-200g/6-7oz bulgar wheat
1 tsp salt
350ml/12fl.oz boiling water
450g/1lb tomatoes, chopped
½ cucumber, diced
3-4 spring onions

Dressing
50ml/2fl.oz olive oil
50ml/2fl.oz lemon juice
2 tbsps fresh mint
4 tbsps fresh parsley
2 cloves garlic, crushed

1. Mix the bulgar wheat with the salt, pour over the boiling water and leave for 15-20 minutes. All the water will then be absorbed.

2. Mix together the ingredients for the dressing and pour over the soaked bulgar.

3. Fold in lightly with a spoon.

4. Leave for two hours or overnight in a fridge or cool place.

5. Add the salad ingredients and serve.

TIME: Preparation takes about 20 minutes, standing time is about 2 hours.

COOK'S TIP: A few cooked beans can be added to make this dish more substantial.

SERVING IDEA: Serve with flans, cold pies and roasts.

PASTA AND AVOCADO SALAD

The perfect lunch or supper salad for guests.

SERVES 4

225g/8oz pasta shapes
3 tbsps mayonnaise
2 tsps tahini
1 orange
½ medium red pepper, chopped
1 medium avocado
Pumpkin seeds to garnish

1. Cook the pasta until soft and leave to cool.

2. Mix together the mayonnaise and tahini.

3. Segment the orange and chop into small pieces, retain any juice.

4. Chop the pepper.

5. Stir the mayonnaise mixture, pepper and orange (plus juice) into the pasta.

6. Just before serving, cube the avocado and stir in carefully.

7. Serve on an oval dish, decorated with pumpkin seeds.

TIME: Preparation takes 10 minutes, cooking takes about 35 minutes.

WATCHPOINT: Do not peel the avocado until required as it may discolour.

VARIATION: Green pepper may be used in place of the red pepper.

LOLLO ROSSO SALAD

A colourful variation of a Greek Salad.

SERVES 4

½ Lollo Rosso lettuce
3 medium tomatoes, diced
1 red pepper, chopped
1 green pepper, chopped
3 sticks celery, diced
⅓ cucumber, diced
175g/16oz Cheshire cheese
16 black olives

Dressing
1 tbsp tarragon vinegar
3 tbsps olive oil

1. Wash the lettuce and dry it well. Break into pieces with your fingers and put it into a large bowl.

2. Add the tomatoes, pepper, celery, cucumber and cheese.

3. Mix together the vinegar and olive oil, and pour over the salad.

4. Mix gently.

5. Divide the salad between 4 individual dishes and place 4 olives on the top of each one.

TIME: Preparation takes about 10 minutes.

SERVING IDEA: Serve for lunch with crusty rolls or French bread.

VARIATION: If you do not like olives, substitute havled, de-seeded black grapes.

COOK'S TIP: To keep celery crisp, wash well and place the sticks in a jug of cold water in the refrigerator.

MARINATED CARROT SALAD

The perfect light lunch dish or accompaniment to burgers or roasts.

SERVES 4-5

450g/1lb carrots
1 medium onion
1 medium green pepper

Dressing
100ml/4fl.oz tomato juice
100ml/4fl.oz olive oil
100ml/4fl.oz cider vinegar
2 tsps brown sugar
1 level tsp dry mustard power
Seasoning

1. Peel the carrots and cut into matchsticks.

2. Cover with water, bring to the boil and simmer for 4-5 minutes. Drain and allow to cool a little.

3. Slice the onion finely into rings.

4. Cut the pepper into strips.

5. Mix together the dressing ingredients until well blended.

6. Combine the carrots with the onion and pepper and pour the dressing over the top.

7. Marinate overnight, stirring occasionally.

8. Serve garnished with chopped parsley and lemon slices.

TIME: Preparation takes 10 minutes, cooking takes 5 minutes. Marinate overnight.

SERVING IDEA: Serve with cubed cheese and bread to mop up the juices.

VARIATION: If you do not have any tomato juice, use the juice from a tin of tomatoes.

BAVARIAN POTATO SALAD

*It is best to prepare this salad a few hours in advance to
allow the potatoes to absorb the flavours.*

SERVES 4-6

900g/2lbs tiny new potatoes
4 tbsps olive oil
4 spring onions, finely chopped
1 clove garlic, crushed
2 tbsps fresh dill, chopped or 1 tbsp dried
2 tbsps wine vinegar
½ tsp sugar
Seasoning
2 tbsps chopped fresh parsley

1. Wash the potatoes but do not peel, put
them into a pan, cover with water and
boil until just tender.

2. Whilst the potatoes are cooking, heat
the olive oil in a frying pan and cook the
spring onions and garlic for 2-3 minutes
until they have softened a little.

3. Add the dill and cook gently for a
further minute.

4. Add the wine vinegar and sugar, and
stir until the sugar melts. Remove from the
heat and add a little seasoning.

5. Drain the potatoes and pour the
dressing over them whilst they are still
hot.

6. Allow to cool and sprinkle with the
chopped parsley before serving.

TIME: Preparation takes 15 minutes, cooking takes 15 minutes.

SERVING IDEA: Serve with cold roasts.

CUCUMBER AND PINEAPPLE SALAD

*If you do not have fresh pineapple, use tinned
pineapple without added sugar.*

SERVES 4

2 dstsps raisins
2 tbsps pineapple juice
275g/10oz cucumber
1 red pepper
150g/6oz pineapple
3 tbsps French dressing
1 tsp fresh mint, finely chopped
1 dstsp sesame seeds

1. Soak the raisins in the pineapple juice for at least half an hour.

2. Slice the cucumber finely.

3. Cut the pepper in half, de-seed, remove the core and chop finely.

4. Chop the pineapple into cubes.

5. Arrange the cucumber on a serving dish.

6. Mix the pepper, pineapple and raisins together and pile in the centre of the cucumber.

7. Mix the mint into the French dressing and pour over the salad just before serving.

8. Sprinkle the sesame seeds over the top.

TIME: Preparation takes 10 minutes, soaking takes 30 minutes.

SERVING IDEA: Serve with flans and roasts.

SPINACH SALAD

Serve with a simple main course.

SERVES 4-6

450g/1lb spinach
1 medium red cabbage
1 medium onion
100g/4oz apricots
6 tbsps French dressing
50g/2oz toasted sunflower seeds

1. Wash the spinach and drain well.

2. First remove the outer leaves and core, then slice the cabbage finely.

3. Slice the onion finely and cut the apricots into slivers.

4. Tear the spinach leaves with the finger into bite-sized pieces and put into a serving dish.

5. Add the sliced cabbage, onion and apricots.

6. Pour over the dressing and mix together thoroughly.

7. Sprinkle with sunflower seeds and serve.

TIME: Preparation takes 15 minutes.

WATCHPOINT: Spinach leaves bruise easily so take care when washing and tearing the leaves.

COOK'S TIP: If using dried apricots, soak beforehand in a little fruit juice.

CARROT AND CELERY SALAD

*The addition of quartered hard boiled eggs will make this
salad into a very substantial first course.*

SERVES 4

225g/8oz carrots
100g/4oz celery
1 red pepper
75g/3oz walnuts
4 tbsps sweetcorn
1 level tsp paprika
¼ tsp chilli powder
4 tbsps French dressing

1. Scrub the carrots and then dice.

2. Slice the celery finely.

3. Remove the core and seeds from the pepper and then dice.

4. Put the carrots, celery and pepper into a serving bowl and add the walnuts and sweetcorn.

5. Mix the paprika and chilli powder into the French dressing and pour over the salad.

6. Mix well and refrigerate for 30 minutes before serving.

TIME: Preparation takes 10 minutes, chilling takes 30 minutes.

SERVING IDEA: Serve as an accompaniment to pasta and grain dishes.

SUNSET SALAD

Serve this colourful salad with cold nut roasts, raised pies or quiche.

SERVES 4-6

3 dessert apples
350g/¾ lb celery
4 medium mushrooms
75g/3oz walnuts
Lettuce leaves
75g/3oz alfalfa sprouts
75g/3oz black grapes

Dressing
125ml/4fl.oz mayonnaise
50ml/2fl.oz plain yogurt
Seasoning

1. Cut the unpeeled apples into quarters and remove the core. Dice roughly.

2. Dice the celery and slice the mushrooms.

3. Chop the walnuts into quarters.

4. Mix the mayonnaise and yogurt together and season.

5. Put the apples, celery, mushrooms and walnuts into a bowl and fold in the dressing.

6. Line a serving dish with well washed lettuce and spread the sprouts around the outer edge.

7 Pile the salad in the centre and garnish with the grapes.

TIME: Preparation takes 15 minutes.

COOK'S TIP: Use red skinned apples and lettuce tinged with red e.g. Lollo Rosso to give colour to your salad.

SEELI SALAD

Serve this very attractive salad for a party or as part of a buffet.

SERVES 4-6

1 large red cabbage
1 green pepper, de-seeded and chopped
½ small pineapple, peeled and finely
  chopped
Segments from 2 medium oranges
6 spring onions, finely chopped
3 sticks celery, chopped
75g/3oz hazelnuts, roughly chopped
75g/3oz sprouted aduki beans

Dressing
100ml/4fl.oz mayonnaise
50ml/2fl.oz Greek yogurt
Seasoning

1. Remove any tough or discoloured outer leaves from the cabbage.

2. Remove the base so that the cabbage will stand upright, and cut about a quarter off the top.

3. Using a sharp knife, scoop out the inside of the cabbage leaving 0.6cm/¼ " for the shell. Set the shell aside.

4. Discard any tough pieces and shred the remaining cabbage very finely.

5. Put the shredded cabbage into a large bowl together with the pepper, pineapple, orange segments, spring onions, celery, hazelnuts and beans.

6. Mix the mayonnaise, yogurt and seasoning together and carefully fold into the vegetables and fruit.

7. Put the mixture into the cabbage shell and place on a serving dish garnished with parsley.

TIME: Preparation takes 20 minutes.

WATCHPOINT: If preparaing in advance, refrigerate the salad and dressing separately and mix them together just before serving.

VARIATION: Walnuts may be used in place of hazelnuts but add them when mixing the salad and dressing together.

83

GREEN PEPPER SALAD

*Serve in individual dishes as a starter accompanied by
crusty brown bread or as a light lunch with bread and chunks of cheese.*

SERVES 4-6

3 medium green peppers
3 medium tomatoes
2 medium onions
75g/3oz sprouted lentils
Black grapes for garnish
Dressing
4 tbsps olive oil
2 tbsps red wine vinegar
2 tsps cumin
½ tsp fresh coriander, chopped

1. Core and slice the peppers finely.

2. Slice the tomatoes and onions.

3. Arrange the peppers, tomatoes and onions alternately on a round serving dish and sprinkle the lentil sprouts over the top.

4. Mix all the ingredients for the dressing together well and pour over the vegetables.

5. Cover and leave to marinade for at least 1 hour at room temperature before serving.

6. Just before serving, garnish with halved black grapes.

TIME: Preparation takes 10 minutes. Standing time is 1 hour.

COOK'S TIP: You can prepare this salad in advance and refrigerate until required but remove from the refrigerator 30 minutes before serving.

WATCHPOINT: Make sure you only sprout whole lentils, red split lentils will not sprout.

SPROUTED LENTIL SALAD

A quick and easy salad.

SERVES 4-6

225g/8oz broccoli florets
1 red pepper
225g/8oz sprouted lentils
50g/2oz sultanas
4-6 tbsps French dressing
1 tsp freshly grated ginger

1. Cover the broccoli florets with boiling water and leave to stand for 5 minutes. Drain and cool.

2. Core and de-seed the pepper and dice roughly.

3. Arrange the sprouted lentils on a serving dish.

4. Mix together the broccoli florets, pepper and sultanas and pile in the centre.

5. Mix the grated ginger with the French dressing and pour over the salad.

6. Serve at once.

TIME: Preparation takes 15 minutes.

SERVING IDEA: Serve with pastry based dishes.

VARIATION: Cauliflower florets may be used in place of broccoli.

BROCCOLI AND CAULIFLOWER SALAD

Serve this simple salad with crackers.

SERVES 4

1 red pepper
275g/10oz broccoli
275g/10oz cauliflower
1 tbsp roasted almond flakes

Dressing
4 tbsps Greek yogurt
2 tbsps lemon juice
2 tbsps olive oil
Salt and pepper
Pinch of nutmeg

1. De-seed the pepper and cut into matchstick pieces.

2. Wash and trim the broccoli and cauliflower and break into small florets.

3. Place the pepper, broccoli and cauliflower in a mixing bowl.

4. Combine the yogurt, lemon juice, olive oil, seasoning and nutmeg in a screw top jar and shake well.

5. Spoon the dressing over the salad and mix together well.

6. Divide the mixture between 4 individual serving plates and garnish with the almond flakes.

TIME: Preparation takes 10 minutes.

VARIATION: Omit the nutmeg from the dressing and add a few freshly chopped herbs.

Mount Carmel Salad

Serve as an accompaniment to a hot main dish.

SERVES 4-6

100g/4oz carrots, peeled
1 green pepper
50g/2oz apricots
1 tbsp sesame seeds
225g/8oz beansprouts
4 tbsps French dressing
2 tbsps pineapple juice

1. Cut the carrots into matchsticks.

2. De-seed and slice the pepper thinly.

3. Cut the apricots into slivers.

4. Toast the seasame seeds in a dry pan over a low heat until they are golden brown and give off a delicious aroma.

5. Place the carrots, pepper, apricots and beansprouts in a serving dish.

6. Mix the French dressing with the pinapple juice and fold into the salad.

7. Sprinkle the sesame seeds over the top.

8. Serve at once.

TIME: Preparation takes 10 minutes.

COOK'S TIP: Use beansprouts which are at least 2.5cm/1" long for this recipe.

SMOKED TOFU SALAD

A tasty main course salad. Serve with granary bread.

SEVES 4-6

225g/8oz broccoli florets
100g/4oz mushrooms
100g/4oz pineapple
4 tbsps sweetcorn
4-6 tbsps French dressing
1 packet smoked tofu, cut into cubes

1. Cover the broccoli florets with boiling water and leave to stand for 5 minutes. Drain and allow to cool.

2. Wipe the mushrooms with a clean cloth and slice thinly.

3. Cut the pineapple into small pieces.

4. Put the broccoli, mushrooms, pineapple and sweetcorn into a large bowl together with the French dressing.

5. Mix carefully.

6. Divide the salad between 4 individual dishes and place the smoked tofu on top.

7. Serve at once.

TIME: Preparation takes 15 minutes.

VARIATION: Omit the tofu and serve as a side salad with savoury flans.

COOK'S TIP: If using plain tofu, marinate for a few hours in equal parts of shoyu sauce and olive oil, together with 1 crushed clove of garlic and 1 tsp of fresh grated ginger.

MAIN MEALS

The main course has traditionally been regarded as the focal point of a meal and the principal source of protein. This is not always the case with a vegetarian meal. For example, pasta alone does not supply enough protein, and nuts or seeds, pulses or some dairy produce needs to be added with the pasta or at some other stage during the meal. If a soup containing lentils or beans, or garnished with grated cheese were followed by a simple pasta dish with a tomato sauce, this would give an adequate supply of protein.

Equally, the same pasta dish followed by a dessert containing milk or eggs would give an equal amount of protein. It's also not always necessary to have one main dish plus two vegetables. Try making smaller portions of one or two main dishes and a couple of starters to give variety and provide an interesting and satisfying meal.

Many of the recipes in this section are easy to make and can be prepared in advance if required. Suggested accompaniments are given, but these are only guidelines, and seasonal vegetables should be used when they are at their cheapest and best. A vegetarian main course is generally much cheaper to produce than a meat meal so you can afford to serve a wide range of dishes or spoil your guests with an exotic dessert.

INDIAN VEGETABLE CURRY

*A wonderfully tasty curry which has the added
advantage of freezing well.*

SERVES 4

Spices
2 tsps turmeric
1 tsp cummin
1 tsp mustard seed
1 tsp fenugreek
4 tsps coriander
½ tsp chilli powder
1 tsp ginger
1 tsp black peppercorns

1lb onions, finely chopped
Ghee or vegetable oil (vary amount to suit
   – about 4 tbsps)
½ pint sterilised milk
2 tbsps white wine vinegar
400g/1 x 14oz tin tomatoes, liquidised
   with their juice
1 tbsp tomato purée
2 tsps brown sugar
1 tsp vegetable bouillon powder or 1
   stock cube dissolved in little boiling
   water
900g/2lbs chopped mushrooms or mixed
vegetables (e.g. mushrooms, cauliflower,
carrots, potatoes, okra)

1. Grind all the spices together, this amount will make 3 tbsps of curry powder.

2. Fry the onions in the ghee or vegetable oil until golden.

3. Add the ground spices, lower the heat and cook for 3 minutes, stirring all the time.

4. Add the milk and vinegar and stir well.

5. Add the liquidised tomatoes, tomato purée, sugar and stock.

6. Bring to the boil, cover and simmer very gently for 1 hour.

7. Add the vegetables and cook until tender – about 30 minutes.

TIME: Preparation takes 30 minutes, cooking takes 1 hour 30 minutes.

SERVING IDEA: Serve with boiled brown rice, chappatis and Cucumber Raita. Cucumber Raita – combine diced cucumber with yogurt, a little chopped mint, a pinch of chilli powder, cumin and seasoning to taste.

FREEZING: The curry sauce will freeze well for up to 3 months so it is well worth while making double the quantity.

LECSO

A popular recipe from Hungary.

SERVES 4-6

---

2 medium green peppers
2 medium yellow peppers
1 large onion, finely sliced
2-3 tbsps sunflower oil
2 tbsps paprika
3 medium tomatoes, skinned and
    quartered
2 eggs, well beaten

---

1. Wash the peppers, core them and cut into strips.

2. Fry the onion in the oil for 1-2 minutes until just coloured.

3. Add the paprika, and stir well.

4. Add the peppers and fry for about 2 minutes.

5. Add the tomatoes and fry for a further minute.

6. Add the beaten eggs and seasoning.

7. Stir well until just cooked.

8. Serve immediately on a bed of rice.

TIME: Preparation takes 10 minutes, cooking takes about 10 minutes.

SERVING IDEA: Lecso can be served with boiled potatoes instead of rice.

VARIATION: Red peppers may be used in place of the yellow peppers.

NUTTY POTATO CAKES

This is the perfect way to use up left over potatoes.

MAKES 8 CAKES

450g/1lb potatoes
15g/½ oz margarine or butter
A little milk
75g/3oz mixed nuts, finely ground
25g/1oz sunflower seeds, finely ground
2 tbsps spring onions, finely chopped
Freshly ground black pepper
Wholemeal flour for coating
Oil for frying

1. Peel the potatoes, cut into pieces and boil until just soft.

2. Drain and mash with the butter and milk to a creamy consistency.

3. Add the nuts, seeds, onions and pepper to taste.

4. If necessary, add a little more milk at this stage to give a soft texture which holds together.

5. Form into 8 cakes.

6. Coat with flour and fry quickly in as little oil as possible.

7. Drain on kitchen roll.

8. Serve hot.

TIME: Preparation takes 10 minutes, cooking takes 25 minutes.

SERVING IDEA: Serve with a green salad and sliced tomatoes in an oil and fresh basil dressing.

VARIATION: Dry roast the sunflower seeds until golden brown, before grinding.

101

CARROT AND CASHEW NUT ROAST

*A delicious roast to serve hot, but the full flavour of
the caraway seeds and lemon are more prominent
when the roast is served cold.*

SERVES 6

1 medium-sized onion, chopped
1-2 cloves garlic, crushed
1 tbsp olive or sunflower oil
450g/1lb carrots, cooked and mashed
225g/8oz cashew nuts, ground
100g/4oz wholewheat breadcrumbs
1 tbsp light tahini
1½ tsps caraway seeds
1 tsp yeast extract
Juice of ½ a lemon
2½ fl.oz/65ml stock from the carrots or
    water
Salt and pepper

1. Fry the onion and garlic in the oil until soft.

2. Mix together with all the other ingredients and season to taste.

3. Place the mixture in a greased 900g/2lb loaf tin.

4. Cover with foil and bake at 180°C/350°F/Gas Mark 4 for 1 hour.

5. Remove the foil and bake for a further 10 minutes.

6. Leave to stand in the baking tin for at least 10 minutes before turning out.

TIME: Preparation takes 20 minutes, cooking takes 1 hour 10 minutes.

FREEZING: This loaf can be frozen at the end of Step 3. When required, remove
from the freezer and thaw overnight in the refrigerator then continue from
Step 4 or freeze at the end of Step 6.

SERVING IDEA: Serve hot with roast potatoes and a green vegetable, or
cold with a mixed green salad.

STUFFED MARROW

This makes a nice change from the more common stuffed vegetables.

SERVES 4

1 medium marrow
6 tbsps fresh brown breadcrumbs
2-4 tbsps milk
4 eggs, hard boiled
100g/4oz grated cheese
Salt and pepper
Pinch of freshly grated nutmeg
1 egg, beaten
A little margarine or butter
Parsley and 1 red pepper for garnish

1. Wash the marrow well, cut in half lengthwise and scoop out the seeds.

2. Place in a well greased baking tin or dish.

3. Soak the breadcrumbs in the milk.

4. Chop the hard-boiled eggs and add to the breadcrumbs together with the cheese, seasoning and nutmeg.

5. Bind the mixture with the beaten egg.

6. Pile into the marrow halves and dot with knobs of margarine or butter.

7. Pour a little water around the marrow and bake in a moderate oven, 190°C/375°F/Gas Mark 5 for 35-40 minutes until the marrow is tender and the top is nicely browned. (If the top is browning too quickly, cover with greaseproof paper.)

8. Serve on a large dish garnished with parsley and red pepper rings.

TIME: Preparation takes 25 minutes, cooking takes 35-40 minutes.

SERVING IDEA: For a special occasion garnish with cranberries and surround with sliced red or yellow peppers, chopped lettuce and watercress.

COOK'S TIP: If the marrow is old it may be better to partly bake the shell before adding the filling.

STUFFED COURGETTES

*Serve as a starter or accompany with a parsley
sauce and potatoes for a light lunch.*

SERVES 4

4 medium courgettes
2 tbsps olive oil
1 onion, very finely chopped
100g/4oz carrots, grated
½ tsp paprika
1 tsp cumin seeds
¼ tsp turmeric
¼ tsp asafetida powder (optional)
100g/4oz creamed coconut, grated

1. Wash the courgettes and cut in half lengthwise.

2. Using a teaspoon, remove the flesh leaving about 0.6cm/¼ " shell.

3. Chop the flesh finely.

4. Heat the oil and sauté the onion for a few minutes.

5. Add the carrots, courgette flesh and spices and cook, stirring frequently, for a further 5 minutes until softened.

6. Remove from the heat and stir in the creamed coconut.

7. Divide the mixture between the courgette shells making sure that it covers the exposed part of the flesh.

8. Place the courgettes in a greased ovenproof casserole and cook at 190°C/ 375°F/Gas Mark 5 for 45 minutes until the courgette shells are soft.

9. Serve immediately.

TIME: Preparation takes 10 minutes, cooking takes 55 minutes.

COOK'S TIP: Creamed coconut can be bought at delicatessens, health food shops and most supermarkets. Asafetida powder is available from Indian shops.

BUTTER BEAN ROAST

*A combination of simple ingredients makes this
a useful recipe for mid-week meals.*

SERVES 4

225g/8oz dried butter beans
2 large onions
A little oil for frying
175g/6oz mushrooms, sliced
100g/4oz cooked rice
1 egg, beaten
1 tbsp freshly chopped parsley
1 tsp dried mixed herbs
Salt and pepper

1. Soak the beans overnight, change the water and cook until soft – about 1-1¼ hours.

2. Drain and mash the beans thoroughly.

3. Slice the onions finely and fry in a little oil until golden brown, adding the mushrooms after 10 minutes.

4. Mix all the ingredients together in a bowl.

5. Place the mixture in a greased 450g/1lb loaf tin and bake at 190°C/375°F/Gas Mark 5 for 30 minutes or until browned on top.

TIME: Preparation takes 10-15 minutes, bean cooking takes 1-1¼ hours, and cooking takes 30 minutes for roast.

SERVING IDEA: Serve with potatoes and salad.

FREEZING: Prepare to the end of Step 4. Place the mixture in the loaf tin, cover with foil and freeze for up to 2 months. To de-frost, remove from freezer 8 hours before required and allow to defrost at room temperature. Cook as above.

VALENCIA LOAF

This loaf is delicious served with an apple sauce and a variety of vegetables.

SERVES 6

---

2 large onions
75ml/3fl.oz oil
75g/3oz spaghetti
50g/2oz brown breadcrumbs
225g/8oz ground almonds
2 eggs, beaten
1 tsp sage
Rind and juice of 1 lemon
Salt and pepper

---

1. Peel and slice the onions and fry in the oil for 10 minutes over a low heat.

2. Cook the spaghetti in boiling, salted water until *al dente*.

3. Drain the spaghetti and add the onion, breadcrumbs, almonds, eggs, sage, lemon juice and rind. Season to taste.

4. Stir carefully and put into a lined and greased 900g/2lb loaf tin.

5. Cover and bake in a moderate oven 190°C/375°F/Gas mark 5 for 1 hour.

6. Turn out onto a serving dish and remove the lining paper carefully.

7. Cut into thick slices and serve immediately.

TIME: Preparation takes 15 minutes, cooking takes 1 hour 20 minutes.

VARIATION: 50g/2oz of soya flour mixed with a little water may be used in place of the eggs.

DEEP MUSHROOM PIE

*A delicious pie and so adaptable. Serve with
salad or potatoes and a green vegetable.*

SERVES 4

Filling
1 tbsp vegetable oil
350g/¾ lb mushrooms, cleaned and
    chopped
225g/8oz mixed nuts, finely milled
2 medium onions, peeled and finely
    chopped
100g/4oz wholewheat breadcrumbs
2 eggs, beaten
1 tsp dried thyme or 2 tsps fresh
1 tsp dried marjoram or 2 tsps fresh
1 tbsps shoyu (Japanese soy sauce)
Salt and pepper to taste
Small quantity of stock to achieve right
    consistency if necessary

Pastry
350g/12oz wholewheat flour
Pinch of salt
1 tsp baking powder (optional)
100g/4oz solid vegetable fat
100ml/4fl.oz water plus extra boiling
    water as necessary
Beaten egg to glaze

1. Heat the oil in a large saucepan and gently fry the onion until soft.

2. Add the finely chopped mushrooms and cook until the juices begin to run.

3. Remove from the heat and add all the other filling ingredients to form a thick, but not dry, consistency adding a little stock or water if necessary. Allow to cool.

4. To prepare the pastry, first sift the flour, salt and baking powder into a large mixing bowl.

5. Cut the fat into small pieces and melt in a saucepan. Add the cold water and bring to a fierce, bubbling boil.

6. Immediately pour into the centre of the flour and mix vigorously with a wooden spoon until glossy.

7. When the mixture is cool enough to handle, use hands and knead it into a ball.

8. Divide the mixture into two-thirds and one-third, placing the one-thirds portion in an oiled plastic bag to prevent drying out.

9. Use the two-thirds portion to line the base and sides of a 19cm/7" spring mould, pressing it down and moulding it into position.

10. Spoon in the mushroom filling, press down firmly making a "dome" shape.

11. Roll out the remaining pastry to just larger than the tin and place on top of the pie, pinching the edges together to seal.

12. Trim off excess pastry and glaze generously with beaten egg.

13. Cut or prick vents in the lid to allow the steam to escape.

14. Bake at 220°C/425°F/Gas Mark 7 for 20 minutes. Reduce to 190°C/375°F/Gas Mark 5 and bake for a further hour.

15. Unmould and serve on an attractive platter surrounded by watercress and twists of lemon and cucumber.

TIME: Preparation takes about 35 minutes, cooking takes 1 hour 20 minutes.

Spinach, Corn and Nut Raised Pie

An attractive pie which is suitable for family meals and entertaining.

SERVES 6

450g/1lb spinach
1 onion, chopped
2 tbsps oil
100g/4oz hazelnuts, finely chopped
100g/4oz brazil nuts, finely chopped
100g/4oz wholemeal breadcrumbs
100g/4oz sweetcorn
1 tsp oregano
½ tsp sage
1 tbsp freshly chopped parsley
1 tsp shoyu (Japanese soy sauce)
2 tbsps tahini
280ml/½ pint stock
Salt and pepper

Pastry
325g/12oz wholemeal flour
1 tsp baking powder
100g/4oz vegetable fat
175ml/6fl.oz water
Pinch of salt

1. Steam the spinach until soft. Drain well and chop finely.

2. Fry the onion in the oil until soft.

3. Mix together all the dry ingredients, add the shoyu, tahini and sufficient stock to give a moist texture.

4. Season to taste.

5. For the pastry, mix together the dry ingredients.

6. Melt the fat in the water and heat until about to boil.

7. Add the liquid to the flour and mix well. Add extra boiling water if the mixture is too dry.

8. Put two thirds of the dough into a 17.8cm/7" pie tin and push into shape.

9. Put the filling into the pie case and press down well.

10. Roll out the remaining dough and make a pie lid.

11. Glaze the top and make two small steam holes.

12. Bake at 210°C/425°F/Gas mark 7 for 20 minutes, reduce the heat to 190°C/375°F/Gas Mark 5 for a further 50 minutes or until golden brown.

TIME: Preparation takes about 40 minutes, cooking takes about 1 hour 15 minutes.

SERVING IDEA: Serve hot with vegetables or cold with salad.

COOK'S TIP: There is no need to grease the pie tin when using hot water pastry.

SWEETCORN AND PARSNIP FLAN

Serve this unusual flan with jacket potatoes
filled with cottage cheese and chives.

SERVES 6

Base
75g/3oz soft margarine
175g/6oz wholemeal flour
1 tsp baking powder
Pinch of salt
4-6 tbsps ice-cold water
1 tbsp oil

Filling
1 large onion, peeled and finely chopped
1 clove garlic, crushed
25g/1oz butter or margarine
2 large parsnips, steamed and roughly
   mashed
175g/6oz sweetcorn, frozen or tinned
1 tsp dried basil
Salt and pepper
3 eggs
140ml/¼ pint milk
75g/3oz grated Cheddar cheese
1 medium tomato, sliced

1. Rub the margarine into the flour, baking powder and salt until the mixture resembles fine breadcrumbs.

2. Add the water and oil and work together lightly. The mixture should be fairly moist.

3. Leave for half an hour.

4. Roll out and line a 25.4cm/10" flan dish.

5. Prick the bottom and bake blind at 210°C/425°F/Gas Mark 7 for about 8 minutes.

6. Meanwhile, sauté the onion and garlic in the butter or margarine until soft and golden.

7. Add the parsnips, sweetcorn and basil and season to taste.

8. Beat the eggs and add the milk.

9. Add to the vegetable mixture and stir over a low heat until the mixture just begins to set.

10. Pour into the flan base and top with the grated cheese and sliced tomato.

11. Bake 190°C/375°F/Gas Mark 5 for 15-20 minutes or until the cheese is golden brown.

TIME: Preparation takes about 40 minutes, cooking takes 30 minutes.

COOK'S TIP: The partial cooking of the whole mixture before placing in the flan base helps to keep the base from becoming soggy and considerably reduces the cooking time.

RATATOUILLE PIE WITH CHEESE AND PEANUT PASTRY

*A colourful dish to make in the autumn when aubergines
and courgettes are cheap and plentiful.*

SERVES 4-6

Ratatouille
2 tbsps olive oil
2 onions, chopped
4 tomatoes, sliced
1 aubergine, sliced
3 courgettes, finely sliced
2 sticks celery, chopped

White sauce
50g/2oz flour
50g/2oz margarine
430ml/¾ pint milk

Pastry
50g/2oz butter
100g/4oz self raising flour
50g/2oz finely grated cheese
50g/2oz finely chopped salted peanuts
A little milk
Beaten egg

1. Put the oil and all the vegetables into a large pan and cook gently for about 20 minutes or until soft.

2. To make the sauce, melt the margarine in a separate pan, stir in the flour and cook for 2 minutes, stirring all the time.

3. Gradually add the milk and bring to boiling point.

4. Stir the sauce into the vegetable mixture and put into an ovenproof dish.

5. Rub the butter into the flour and add the cheese and peanuts.

6. Add a little milk and roll out the pastry.

7. Place on top of the ratatouille mixture, trim and brush with beaten egg.

8. Bake 190°C/375°F/Gas Mark 5 for about 30 minutes or until golden brown.

TIME: Preparation takes 30 minutes, cooking takes 1 hour.

SERVING IDEA: Serve with bundles of julienne vegetables – carrots, swede, turnips etc.

VARIATION: Sliced green pepper can be used in place of the celery.

SWEET POTATO AND FRENCH BEAN PASTIES

These pasties are a tasty addition to any lunch box or picnic basket.

SERVES 4

225g/8oz wholemeal shortcrust pastry
½ medium onion, finely chopped
1 clove garlic, crushed
1 tbsp oil
½ tsp freshly grated ginger
¼ – ½ tsp chilli powder
¼ tsp turmeric
½ tsp ground cumin
1 tsp ground coriander
¼ tsp mustard powder
1 medium-sized sweet potato, cooked and
    finely diced
100g/4oz French beans, chopped into
    1.2cm/½" lengths
2 tbsps water or stock
Salt and pepper

1. Fry the onion and garlic in the oil until soft.

2. Add the ginger and all the spices and stir.

3. Add the diced potato, beans and water or stock and cook gently for 4-5 minutes or until the beans begin to cook.

4. Allow the mixture to cool and season well.

5. Roll out the pastry into 4 circles.

6. Place a quarter of the filling in the centre of each circle and dampen the edges of the pastry with a little water.

7. Join the pastry together over the filling.

8. Make a small hole in each pasty and glaze with milk or egg.

9. Bake for 15-20 minutes at 200°C/400°F/Gas Mark 6.

TIME: Preparation, including making the pastry, takes 25 minutes.
Cooking takes 15-20 minutes.

FREEZING: The pasties will freeze well for up to 2 months. Thaw at room temperature.

COURGETTE AND CARROT LAYER

*Serve with a sprouted salad for a light lunch or glaze
with agar and fresh herbs for a special occasion.*

SERVES 4

450g/1lb carrots, cooked, mashed and
    seasoned
1 medium onion
450g/1lb courgettes, finely chopped
1 tbsp oil
100g/4oz almonds, finely chopped or
    ground
75g/3oz wholemeal breadcrumbs
1 tsp Vecon (vegetable stock) dissolved in
    a little boiling water
1 egg beaten
1 level tsp mixed herbs
1 tbsp tomato purée
1 tbsps shoyu sauce (Japanese soy sauce)
Ground black pepper

1. Grease and line a 450g/1lb loaf tin.

2. Fry the onion and courgettes in the oil, add all the remaining ingredients except the carrot, and mix together well.

3. Place half of the courgette mixture into the loaf tin and press down well.

4. Arrange the carrots on top of this followed by the remaining courgette mixture.

5. Cover with foil and cook for 1 hour at 175°C/350°F/Gas Mark 4.

6. Allow to cool for 10 minutes before removing from tin.

TIME: Preparation, including cooking the carrots, takes 25 minutes.

COOK'S TIP: This mixture makes a delicious filling for a raised pie.

COURGETTE AND SWEETCORN SAVOURY

This is an excellent way to use up leftover pasta.

SERVES 4

1 tbsp oil
1 medium onion, chopped
225g/8oz courgettes, sliced
200g/7oz tin sweetcorn, drained
175g/6oz cooked pasta shapes
Large pinch oregano
1 tbsp tomato purée
Salt and pepper

Sauce
25g/1oz margarine
25g/1oz wholewheat flour
275ml/½ pint skimmed milk
3 tbsps white wine
50g/2oz strong cheese, grated

Topping
25g/1oz wholemeal breadcrumbs
1 dstsp sunflower seeds

1. Heat the oil in a frying pan and sauté the chopped onion until soft.

2. Add the sliced courgettes and brown lightly.

3. Mix in the sweetcorn, cooked pasta, oregano and tomato purée, and stir.

4. Season lightly and transfer the mixture to an oiled ovenproof dish.

5. Make the cheese sauce by melting the margarine and stirring in the flour to make a roux. Cook gently for a few minutes and then pour on the milk and wine, stirring all the time, to make a smooth sauce.

6. Add the grated cheese and stir until it melts into the sauce. Remove from the heat and pour over the vegetable mixture.

7. Top with the breadcrumbs and sunflower seeds.

8. Bake 180°C/350°F/Gas Mark 4 for about 20 minutes until the dish is brown and bubbling.

TIME: Preparation takes about 30 minutes, cooking takes 20 minutes.

SERVING IDEA: Serve with grilled tomatoes and creamed potatoes.

Winter Crumble

*A variety of hearty vegetables topped with oats and
cheese makes the perfect winter meal.*

SERVES 4-6

Topping
75g/3oz butter or margarine
100g/4oz wholewheat flour
50g/2oz rolled oats
100g/4oz Cheddar cheese, grated
¼ tsp salt

175ml/6fl.oz stock or water
280ml/½ pint sweet cider
1 tsp brown sugar
2 carrots, chopped
2 large parsnips, cut into rings
2 sticks celery, chopped
2 heads broccoli, cut into florets
¼ cauliflower, cut into florets
1 dstsp wholewheat flour
2 tbsps chopped parsley
1 medium onion, chopped and fried until
  golden
4 large tomatoes, peeled and sliced
225g/8oz cooked black-eyed beans
Salt and pepper

1. Make the topping by rubbing the butter
into the flour and oats until the mixture
resembles fine breadcrumbs.

2. Stir in the cheese and salt.

3. Mix the stock with the cider and sugar
and put into a large pan with the carrots
and parsnips.

4. Cook until just tender, remove the
vegetables and put aside.

5. Add the celery, broccoli and cauliflower
to the pan, cook until tender, remove and
reserve with other vegetables.

6. Mix the flour with a little water, add to
the cider and cook until thickened, stirring
all the time.

7. Cook for 2-3 minutes, remove from the
heat and add the parsley.

8. Place the onions, vegetables, tomatoes
and beans in a greased casserole and
season well. Pour the sauce over the
mixture.

9. Sprinkle the topping over the top and
press down a little.

10. Cook at 200°C/400°F/Gas mark 6 for
30-35 minutes or until the topping is
golden brown.

TIME: Preparation takes 20 minutes, cooking takes 1 hour 5 minutes.

SERVING IDEA: Serve with roast potatoes.

COOK'S TIP: The casserole can be prepared in advance to the end of Step 9.
Refrigerate until ready to cook.

RATATOUILLE LASAGNE

Serve with crusty rolls and a green salad
for the perfect lunch or supper.

SERVES 4-6

6 strips lasagne verdi or wholemeal
  lasagne
2-3 tbsps olive oil
2 onions, finely chopped
2 cloves garlic, crushed
1 large aubergine, chopped
1 courgette, sliced thinly
1 green pepper, chopped
1 red pepper, chopped
400g/1 x 14oz tin tomatoes, chopped
2-3 tbsps tomato purée
A little vegetable stock
Salt and freshly ground black pepper

White sauce
25g/1oz butter or margarine
25g/1oz wholemeal flour
280ml/½ pint milk

40g/1½ oz Parmesan cheese, grated
Parsley, to garnish

1. Preheat the oven to 180°C/350°F/Gas
Mark 4.

2. Cook the lasagne in boiling, salted
water for 12-15 minutes.

3. Plunge into a bowl of cold water to
prevent overcooking or sticking.

4. Heat the oil and fry the onion and
garlic until soft.

5. Add the aubergine, courgette and
peppers and sauté until soft.

6. Add the tomatoes with their juice and
the tomato purée and simmer until tender.
It may be necessary to add a little stock at
this stage.

7. Season well and set aside.

8. Make the white sauce by melting the
butter in a small saucepan.

9. Add the flour and cook to a roux.

10. Add the milk slowly, stirring
constantly, bring to the boil and simmer
for about 5 minutes. Remove from the
heat.

11. Grease a deep ovenproof dish.

12. Layer the ratatouille and lasagne strips,
starting with the ratatouille and finishing
with a layer of lasagne.

13. Pour over the white sauce and
sprinkle the Parmesan cheese over the
top.

14. Bake in the oven for 35 minutes until
golden. Garnish with parsley before
serving.

TIME: Preparation takes about 20 minutes, cooking takes 1 hour.

VARIATION: If aubergine is not available, 225g/8oz sliced mushrooms may be used instead.

SAVOURY BEAN POT

Serve this exciting mixture with rice or jacket potatoes and a salad.

SERVES 4

2 tbsps vegetable oil
2 vegetable stock cubes, crumbled
2 medium onions, chopped
2 eating apples, peeled and grated
2 medium carrots, grated
3 tbsps tomato purée
280ml/½ pint water
2 tbsps white wine vinegar
1 tbsp dried mustard
1 level tsp oregano
1 level tsp cumin
1 dstsp brown sugar
Salt and pepper
450g/1lb cooked red kidney beans
A little soured cream

1. Heat the oil in a non-stick pan.

2. Add the crumbled stock cubes, onions, apples and carrots.

3. Sauté for 5 minutes, stirring continuously.

4. Mix the tomato purée with the water and add together with all the other ingredients apart from the beans and cream.

5. Stir well, cover and simmer for 2 minutes.

6. Add the beans and tip the mixture into an ovenproof casserole.

7. Cover and cook at 180°C/350°F/Gas Mark 4 for 35-40 minutes.

8. Add a little more water after 20 minutes if necessary.

9. Top with swirls of soured cream and serve.

TIME: Preparation takes 20 minutes, cooking takes 45 minutes.

VARIATION: Use cider vinegar in place of the white wine vinegar.

VEGETABLE STEW WITH HERB DUMPLINGS

The ideal meal to warm up a cold winter's night.

SERVE 4-6

1 large onion
900g/2lbs mixed vegetables (carrot,
    swede, parsnips, turnips,
    cauliflower etc.)
570ml/1 pint stock or water plus a
    stock cube
Salt and pepper
Flour or proprietory gravy powder to
    thicken

Dumplings
100g/4oz wholewheat self-raising flour
50g/2oz vegetarian suet
1 tsp mixed herbs
¼ tsp salt

1. Chop the onion into large pieces.

2. Peel and prepare the vegetables and chop into bite-sized pieces.

3. Put the onion and vegetables into a pan and cover with the stock.

4. Bring to the boil and simmer for 20 minutes.

5. Season to taste.

6. Mix a little flour or gravy powder with a little water and stir into the stew to thicken.

7. Place the ingredients for the dumplings into a bowl and add just enough water to bind.

8. Shape the mixture into 8 small dumplings.

9. Bring the stew to the boil and drop in the dumplings.

10. Cover and allow to simmer for 10 minutes.

11. Serve at once.

TIME: Preparation takes 10 minutes, cooking takes 30 minutes.

SERVING IDEA: Serve with boiled potatoes.

VARIATION: The mixed herbs may be omitted when making the dumplings or chopped fresh parsley and a squeeze of lemon juice may be used instead.

MUSHROOM STROGANOFF

A great favourite which is much appreciated by all age groups.

SERVES 4-6

2 medium onions, sliced
5 sticks celery, chopped
50g/2oz butter or margarine
450g/1lb tiny button mushrooms
½ tsp mixed herbs
½ tsp basil
1 large heaped tbsp unbleached flour
280ml/½ pint stock
Salt and pepper
65ml/2½ fl.oz soured cream or yogurt
Chopped parsley

1. Put the onions and celery into a large pan together with the butter or margarine and sauté over a low heat until the onions are transparent.

2. Add the mushrooms and cook for 2-3 minutes until the juices run.

3. Add the mixed herbs and basil.

4. Stir in the flour and cook for 1 minute.

5. Add the stock and seasoning and allow to cook gently for 8-10 minutes.

6. Remove from the heat, stir in the soured cream and adjust the seasoning if necessary.

7. Heat very gently to serving temperature but do not allow to boil.

8. Garnish with the chopped parsley and serve at once.

TIME: Preparation takes 10 minutes, cooking takes 20 minutes.

COOK'S TIP: If tiny button mushrooms are not available use the larger variety and slice thickly.

SCONE BASED PIZZA

A bumper sized pizza for four hungry people.

SERVES 4-6

Base
90g/3½ oz margarine
200g/7oz wholemeal flour
2 small eggs plus 2 tbsps milk or 4 tbsps
  soya flour mixed with 3 tbsps water
½ tsp mixed herbs
½ tsp dried mustard
Salt and pepper

Topping
A little olive oil
1 tbsp tomato purée
50g/2oz margarine
1 large onion, finely chopped
100g/4oz mushrooms, sliced
1 green or red pepper, finely sliced
4 tomatoes, sliced
2 sticks celery, finely sliced
100g/4oz Cheddar cheese, grated

1. Make the scone mix by rubbing the margarine into the flour until it resembles fine breadcrumbs.

2. Beat the eggs together with the milk.

3. Add to the flour mixture together with the herbs, mustard and seasoning. Knead together to form a ball of dough.

4. Press the mixture evenly over a 25.4cm/ 10" pizza plate.

5. Brush the top with a little olive oil and spread the tomato purée evenly over the top with a knife.

6. Melt the margarine in a frying pan and cook the onions, mushrooms, pepper and celery for 4-5 minutes until softened a little.

7. Pile the mixture on top of the pizza base.

8. Lay the tomatoes evenly over the top and sprinkle on the grated cheese.

9. Bake for 20-25 minutes at 200°C/400°F/ Gas Mark 6 until the cheese is melted and golden brown.

TIME: Preparation takes 20 minutes, cooking takes about 30 minutes.

SERVING IDEA: Garnish with watercress and serve with sweetcorn or a crisp green salad.

FREEZING: Freeze after cooking for up to 2 months. Allow to thaw before reheating in the oven.

EXPRESS VEGETABLE PIE

*Any cooked, left-over vegetables may be
used for this quick and easy pie.*

SERVES 4

1 large onion, peeled and finely chopped
25g/1oz margarine
2 sticks of celery, diced
75g/3oz cashew nuts, chopped and dry
    roasted
675g/1½ lbs mixed frozen vegetables
    (peas, corn, swede, carrot, turnip, diced
    peppers, parsnip etc.)
1 dstsp tomato purée
140ml/¼ pint water or stock
½ -1 tsp yeast extract
Salt and black pepper
3-4 large potatoes
Knob of butter
Little milk

1. Sauté the onion in the margarine
together with the celery and a little water
until just tender.

2. Add the remaining ingredients apart
from the potatoes, butter and milk.

3. Simmer for 3-5 minutes, adding a little
more water if the mixture seems too dry.
Keep hot.

4. Cook the potatoes until soft, mash with
a knob of butter and a little milk, adding
salt and pepper to taste.

5. Turn the vegetable mixture into a
casserole dish and cover completely with
the mashed potato.

6. Fork over the top roughly, dot with
butter and grill for 3-5 minutes until
golden brown.

7. Serve immediately.

TIME: Preparation takes 20 minutes, cooking takes 15 minutes.

SERVING IDEA: Serve with salad, mushrooms and pumpkin seeds.

SAVOURY RICE CAKE

An excellent way to use up left-over rice.

SERVES 2-4

1 medium onion, finely chopped
1 clove garlic, crushed
2 tbsps olive oil
1 tbsp fresh thyme, chopped
1 red pepper, thinly sliced
1 green pepper, thinly sliced
4 eggs, beaten
Salt and pepper
6 tbsps cooked brown rice
3 tbsps natural yogurt
75g/3oz Cheddar cheese, grated

1. Fry the onion and garlic in the olive oil until soft.

2. Add the thyme and pepper and fry gently for 4-5 minutes.

3. Beat the eggs with the salt and pepper.

4. Add the cooked rice to the thyme and pepper followed by the eggs.

5. Cook over a moderate heat, stirring from time to time until the eggs are cooked underneath.

6. Spoon the yogurt on top of the part-set egg and sprinkle the cheese over the top.

7. Put under a moderate grill and cook until puffed and golden.

8. Serve immediately.

TIME: Preparation takes about 15 minutes, cooking takes 15 minutes.

SERVING IDEA: Garnish with fresh thyme and serve with a green salad.

141

QUICK VEGETABLE CHILLI

Serve this tasty chilli with wholemeal baps and salad.

SERVES 4

2 large onions, sliced
1 tbsp olive oil
¾ cloves garlic, crushed
1 tsp chilli powder
400g/1 x 14oz tin tomatoes, chopped
400g/1 x 14oz tin of red kidney beans
1 small red pepper, roughly chopped
1 medium courgette, sliced into chunks
Cauliflower florets
2 carrots, roughly chopped
½ tbsp tomato purée
1 tsp dried, sweet basil
1 tsp oregano
¼ -½ pint stock

1. Sauté the onions in the oil until soft.

2. Add the garlic and cook for 1 minute.

3. Add the chilli powder and cook for a further minute.

4. Add the rest of the ingredients and simmer for 25-30 minutes.

5. Serve on a bed of brown rice.

TIME: Preparation takes about 15 minutes, cooking takes 30 minutes.

VARIATION: Florets of broccoli could be used in place of the cauliflower.

COURGETTES MEDITERRANEAN STYLE

Any other type of cooked bean may be used for this dish.

SERVES 4

3 tbsps olive oil
1 large onion, finely chopped
3 cloves garlic, crushed
1 red pepper, chopped
225g/8oz cooked haricot beans
1 x 400g/14oz tin tomatoes
450g/1lb courgettes, finely sliced
1 level tsp oregano
Seasoning

1. Heat the oil in a pan.

2. Add the onion, garlic and pepper and cook for 4-5 minutes.

3. Add the cooked beans, tinned tomatoes and courgettes. Stir well.

4. Add the oregano and seasoning, and stir again.

5. Cover and cook slowly for 30 minutes.

TIME: Preparation takes 10-15 minutes, cooking takes 40 minutes.

SERVING IDEA: Serve on a bed of white rice.

COOK'S TIP: This dish will reheat well.

OVEN BAKED SPAGHETTI

A convenient way to cook this favourite mid-week meal.

SERVES 4

225g/8oz wholewheat spaghetti, cooked
2 x 400g/14oz tins tomatoes, roughly
  chopped
1 large onion, grated
1 tsp oregano
Seasoning
100g/4oz Cheddar cheese
2 tbsps Parmesan cheese, grated

1. Grease four individual ovenproof dishes and place a quarter of the spaghetti in each one.

2. Pour the tomatoes over the top.

3. Add the onion, sprinkle with oregano and season well.

4. Slice the cheese finely and arrange over the top of the spaghetti mixture.

5. Sprinkle with Parmesan and bake at 180°C/350°F/Gas Mark 4 for 30 minutes.

TIME: Preparation takes 10 minutes, cooking takes 20-25 minutes.

SERVING IDEA: Serve with garlic bread.

WATCHPOINT: When cooking spaghetti remember to add a few drops of oil to the boiling water to stop it sticking together.

COOK'S TIP: Oven Baked Spaghetti may be cooked in one large casserole if required but add 10 minutes to the cooking time.

147

LENTIL MOUSSAKA

Try a taste of the Greek Islands with this classic dish.

SERVES 4-6

150g/5oz green lentils
1 large aubergine, sliced
4-5 tbsps oil
1 large onion, chopped
1 clove garlic, crushed
1 large carrot, diced
4 sticks celery, finely chopped
1-2 tsps mixed herbs
1 x 400g/14oz tin tomatoes
1 dstsp shoyu sauce (Japanese soy sauce)
Black pepper
2 medium potatoes, cooked and sliced
2 large tomatoes, sliced

Sauce
50g/2oz margarine
50g/2oz brown rice flour
425ml/¾ pint milk
1 large egg, separated
50g/2oz grated Cheddar cheese
1 tsp nutmeg

1. Cook the lentils in plenty of water until soft. Drain and reserve the liquid.

2. Fry the aubergine in the oil, drain well and set aside.

3. Sauté the onion, garlic, carrot, celery and a little of the lentil stock.

4. Simmer with the lid on until just tender.

5. Add the lentils, mixed herbs and tinned tomatoes. Simmer gently for 3-4 minutes.

6. Season with the shoyu and pepper.

7. Place a layer of the lentil mixture in a large casserole dish and cover with half of the aubergine slices.

8. Cover the aubergine slices with half of the potato slices and all the tomato.

9. Repeat with the remaining lentils, aubergines and potatoes.

10. To make the sauce, melt the margarine in a saucepan, remove from the heat and stir in the flour to make a roux.

11. Add the milk gradually, blending well, so that the sauce is smooth and lump free.

12. Return to the heat and stir continually until the sauce thickens.

13. Remove the pan from the heat and cool slightly. Add the egg yolk, stir in the cheese and add the nutmeg.

14. Beat the egg white until it is stiff, then carefully fold into the sauce.

15. Pour the sauce over the moussaka, covering the dish completely.

16. Bake at 180°C/350°F/Gas Mark 4 for about 40 minutes until the top is golden brown and puffy.

TIME: Preparation takes 45 minutes, cooking takes 1 hour 10 minutes.

FREEZING: Assemble the mixture without the sauce and freeze. Defrost, add the sauce and cook from Step 14.

SERVING IDEA: Serve with a crunchy green salad or battered mushrooms.

VEGETARIAN PAELLA

Perfect served with crusty bread and a green salad.

SERVES 4-6

4 tbsps olive oil
1 large onion, chopped
2 cloves garlic, crushed
½ tsp paprika
350g/12oz long grain brown rice
1150ml/1½ pints stock
175ml/6fl.oz dry white wine
1 x 400g/14oz tin tomatoes, plus juice,
   chopped
1 tbsp tomato purée
½ tsp tarragon
1 tsp basil
1 tsp oregano
1 red pepper, roughly chopped
1 green pepper, roughly chopped
3 sticks celery, finely chopped
225g/8oz mushrooms, washed and sliced
50g/2oz mange tout, topped and tailed
   and cut into halves
100g/4oz frozen peas
50g/2oz cashew nut pieces
Salt and pepper

1. Heat the oil and fry the onion and garlic until soft.

2. Add the paprika and rice and continue to cook for 4-5 minutes until the rice is transparent. Stir occasionally.

3. Add the stock, wine, tomatoes, tomato purée and herbs and simmer for 10-15 minutes.

4. Add the pepper, celery, mushrooms and mange tout and continue to cook for another 30 minutes until the rice is cooked.

5. Add the peas, cashew nuts and seasoning to taste.

6. Heat through and place on a large heated serving dish.

7. Sprinkle the parsley over the top and garnish with lemon wedges and olives.

TIME: Preparation takes 20 minutes, cooking takes 45 minutes.

COOK'S TIP: To prepare in advance, undercook slightly, add a little more stock or water and reheat. Do not add the peas until just before serving otherwise they will lose their colour.

MOORS AND CHRISTIANS

*This dish, originally from Cuba, is so called
because of the use of black beans and white rice.*

SERVES 4

225g/8oz black beans, soaked overnight
  and cooked until soft
2 tbsps vegetable oil
1 medium onion, chopped
4 cloves garlic, crushed
1 medium green pepper, finely chopped
2 large tomatoes, skinned and finely
  chopped
275g/10oz long grain rice
Salt and pepper
Little bean cooking water if required

1. Drain the cooked beans and mash 3
tbsps to a paste with a fork, adding a little
bean cooking water if necesssary.

2. Heat the oil and fry the onion, garlic
and pepper until soft.

3. Add the tomatoes and cook for a
further 2 minutes.

4. Add the bean paste and stir.

5. Add the cooked beans and rice, and
enough water to cover.

6. Bring to the boil, cover and simmer for
20-25 minutes until the rice is *al dente*.

7. Serve hot.

TIME: Preparation takes 15 minutes. Cooking time, 1-1½ hours for the beans, 25-30
minutes for the finished dish.

SERVING IDEA: Serve with a crisp green salad and crusty bread.

VARIATION: A small tin of tomatoes may be used in place of fresh ones.

PULSES, GRAINS & PASTA

Pulses used to be considered food for the underprivileged, but in recent years their true nutritional value has been recognised and we are now lucky to find a wide selection available – as many as 25 different types – providing a variety of cheap and nutritious dishes.

Dried beans contain protein, vitamins, minerals and fibre and are particularly high in vitamins B1 and B2. They also contain significant amounts of calcium, phosphorous, and iron. Dried pulses should always be washed thoroughly before use. Leave them to stand in water for the time recommended on the packet. Once the pulses have been soaked, transfer to a saucepan and cover with fresh water. Bring to the boil and boil rapidly for the first 10 minutes, turn down the heat and continue boiling slowly until the beans are cooked. To test, remove a bean from the pot, hold between thumb and forefinger and squeeze gently. If the bean yields to the pressure it should be soft enough to eat.

Grains are another important food group. These botanic grasses are the staple food of most of the world, and are the cheapest, most important source of energy. A wide variety of grains are available, but the majority of people still tend to use only a small proportion of them, such as pearl barley, oats and rice. There are many other delicious grains to choose from. Millet, for instance, can be made into a breakfast dish, bulgar salad makes a nice change from rice salad, and buckwheat is excellent in casseroles and roasts.

Home-made pasta is a delight and far superior to its shop-bought relatives. This chapter includes two recipes for fresh pasta which you can incorporate into your repertoire and once you've made your own pasta you'll never want to buy it again.

BLACK AND WHITE BAKE WITH BOULANGERE TOPPING

Serve this hearty dish with lightly steamed vegetables.

SERVES 4

100g/4oz black kidney beans, soaked
  overnight and cooked until tender
1 medium cauliflower, divided into florets
700ml/1¼ pints water
1 bay leaf
280ml/½ pint milk
2 tbsps sunflower oil
1 medium onion, very finely chopped
40g/1½ oz fine wholemeal flour
1 tbsp wholegrain mustard
1 tbsp parsley, chopped
Salt and pepper
350-450g/¾ -1lb potatoes, cooked and cut
  into 5mm/¼ " slices
25g/1oz butter or margarine

---

1. Wash and drain the cauliflower florets.

2. Bring the water to the boil in a large pan, add the bay leaf and a little salt.

3. Plunge the cauliflower into the water, return to the boil, cover and poach the florets for 8-10 minutes until just cooked.

4. Drain, discard the bay leaf and reserve the cooking water.

5. Top up the milk with the cooking water to give 570ml/1 pint.

6. Heat the oil in a small pan and gently sauté the onion until soft.

7. Stir in the flour and cook over a gentle heat for 1-2 minutes.

8. Gradually add the milk and water, stirring all the time to avoid lumps.

9. Add the mustard and cook gently for a further 3 minutes.

10. Drain the cooked beans and return them to a large pan, add the florets and mix well.

11. Pour the mustard sauce over the beans and cauliflower and stir in the chopped parsley and seasoning.

12. Place the mixture in a greased 1½ ltr/3 pint casserole dish.

13. Top with the sliced potatoes, overlapping them slightly, and dot with the butter or margarine.

14. Bake at 180°C/350°/Gas Mark 4 for 20-25 minutes until the top is nicely browned.

TIME: Preparation takes 25 minutes. Cooking time, including the beans, 1 hour 10 minutes.

FREEZING: Freeze the base for 4-6 weeks and add the topping when required.

COOK'S TIP: Choosing the right sort of topping for bakes is most important, it should enhance what is underneath rather than fighting against it.

VEGETARIAN SHEPHERD'S PIE

*The Shepherds Pie will serve 2 people without
any accompaniments and 4 people if served with vegetables.*

SERVES 2-4

100g/4oz brown lentils
50g/2oz pot barley
450ml/¾ pint stock or water
1 tsp yeast extract
1 large carrot, diced
½ onion, chopped finely
1 clove garlic, crushed
50g/2oz walnuts, roughly chopped
1 tsp vegetarian gravy powder or
    thickener
Salt and pepper
450g/1lb potatoes, cooked and mashed

1. Simmer the lentils and barley in 280ml/
½ pint of the stock and yeast extract for
30 minutes.

2. Meanwhile, cook the carrot, onion,
garlic and walnuts in the remaining stock
for 15 minutes or until tender.

3. Mix the gravy powder or thickener with
a little water and add to the carrot
mixture, stir over a low heat until
thickened.

4. Combine the lentils and barley with the
carrot mixture, season and place in an
ovenproof dish.

5. Cover with the mashed potato and cook
at 180°C/350°F/Gas Mark 4 for about 30
minutes until browned on top.

TIME: Preparation takes 15 minutes, cooking takes 1 hour.

SERVING IDEA: Garnish with grilled tomatoes and serve with vegetables in season,
broccoli, sprouts, spring cabbage etc.

BULGAR RISOTTO

*This makes a quick lunch dish and is
particularly handy if unexpected guests call.*

SERVES 3-4

100g/4oz bulgar wheat
1 medium onion, peeled and finely
   chopped
2 sticks celery, finely chopped
1-2 cloves garlic, crushed
12g/½ oz butter
1 small red pepper, diced
1 small green pepper, diced
½ tsp dried mixed herbs
50g/2oz peanuts, chopped
1 tsp vegetable extract dissolved in ¼ cup
   boiling water
2 tsps shoyu sauce (Japanese soy sauce)
75g/3oz sweetcorn
75g/3oz peas
Salt and pepper
Juice of half a lemon

1. Put the bulgar wheat into a bowl and cover with boiling water.

2. Leave for about 10 minutes after which time the water will have been absorbed and the wheat swollen.

3. Meanwhile, place the onion, celery and garlic into a saucepan and sauté for a few minutes in the butter.

4. Add the peppers, herbs, nuts and vegetable extract.

5. Simmer over a low heat for about 8 minutes.

6. Add the bulgar wheat, shoyu, sweetcorn, peas and seasoning and mix together well.

7. Continue cooking for a further 5 minutes.

8. Mix in the lemon juice and transfer to a heated serving dish.

9. Serve immediately.

TIME: Preparation takes 15 minutes, cooking takes 20 minutes.

SERVING IDEA: Serve with a crisp green salad.

WATCHPOINT: If the risotto is too dry, add a little more water or stock.

MILLET RISSOLES WITH YOGURT SAUCE

*Rissoles are always popular and yogurt
sauce makes these even more tempting!*

MAKES ABOUT 15

1 medium onion, peeled and finely
chopped
1 clove garlic, crushed
1 tsp dried mixed herbs or 2 tbsps freshly
chopped parsley
Oil
150g/5oz millet flakes
300-450ml/½ -¾ pint water
1 tbsp tomato purée
1 tsp vegetable extract
75g/3oz Cheddar cheese, grated
¼ tsp paprika
Salt and pepper
Wholemeal breadcrumbs

Sauce
10fl.oz/½ pint Greek yogurt
2 tbsps freshly chopped parsley
Salt and pepper
Pinch of paprika
A little lemon juice (optional)

1. Sauté the onion, garlic and mixed herbs
in a little oil until soft.

2. Place the millet flakes in a separate pan
with the water, bring to the boil and
simmer gently, stirring constantly until a
thick texture results.

3. Cool a little.

4. Add the remaining rissole ingredients,
except the breadcrumbs, and mix together
well.

5. Shape into rissoles and coat with the
crumbs.

6. Fry in very shallow oil on both sides
until crisp and golden.

7. To make the sauce, mix all the
ingredients together well.

TIME: Preparation takes 15 minutes, cooking takes 15 minutes.

SERVING IDEA: Serve with the sauce handed round separately.

VARIATION: Vary the flavour of the rissoles by using freshly chopped
mint instead of the mixed herbs or parsley.
Fresh basil also makes a delicious alternative.

PEANUT RISOTTO

Use this mixture to stuff cabbage, spinach or vine leaves.

SERVES 4

1 large onion, chopped
1 clove garlic, crushed
1 tbsp vegetable oil
150g/6oz short grain brown rice
100g/4oz peanuts, roughly chopped
100g/4oz mushrooms, sliced
570ml/1 pint boiling water
100g/4oz fine beans
25g/1oz raisins
2 tsps dried oregano
2 tsps lemon juice
Salt and pepper

1. Fry the onion and garlic in the oil for 3-4 minutes.

2. Add the rice and peanuts to toast for 1-2 minutes.

3. Add the mushrooms and cook for a further 3-4 minutes, then add the boiling water, stir once and simmer for 30 minutes.

4. Add the beans, raisins, herbs, lemon juice and seasoning and cook for a further 5-10 minutes.

TIME: Preparation takes 10 minutes, cooking takes 50 minutes.

SERVING IDEA: Serve garnished with lemon wedges and parsley.

VARIATION: Use this mixture to stuff cabbage, spinach or vine leaves.

SAVOURY GRAIN CASSEROLE

Serve as a complete meal for 2 people or serve accompanied with lightly steamed vegetables for 4 people.

SERVES 2-4

75g/3oz brown rice
75g/3oz split peas
2 sticks celery, very finely chopped
1 medium onion, very finely chopped
100g/4oz mushrooms, chopped
1 x 400g/14oz tin tomatoes, drained and chopped or 225g/8oz tomatoes, peeled and chopped
½ tsp dill seeds
½ tsp thyme
2 tbsps shoyu sauce (Japanese soy sauce)
1 egg, beaten
100g/4oz Cheddar cheese, grated

1. Cover the rice with water and cook for 10-15 minutes; drain.

2. Cover the split peas with water and cook for 20 minutes until just tender but not mushy; drain.

3. Meanwhile, combine the celery, onion, mushrooms, tomatoes, dill, thyme, shoyu and the egg in a large bowl.

4. Stir in the rice and peas.

5. Place the mixture in a greased ovenproof casserole dish and cook for 45 minutes at 180°C/350°F/Gas Mark 4.

6. Remove from the oven and sprinkle with the grated cheese.

7. Return to the oven for 10 minutes until the cheese has melted.

8. Serve at once.

TIME: Preparation takes 10 minutes, cooking takes 1 hour 45 minutes.

SERVING IDEA: Garnish with a few whole cooked button mushrooms or grilled tomatoes.

BUTTER BEAN AND SPINACH ROLL WITH LEMON CRUST

*The lemon crust gives just the right edge of flavour to
make the whole dish a little bit special.*

SERVES 4

225g/8oz butter beans, soaked overnight
  and cooked until tender
225g/8oz fresh spinach
½ tsp freshly grated nutmeg
Salt and freshly ground black pepper
50g/2oz Cheddar cheese, grated
1 egg, beaten
1 tsp sunflower oil
50g/2oz fresh breadcrumbs
1 tbsp sesame seeds
Grated rind of 1 lemon
2 tsps lemon juice

1. Preheat the oven to 200°C/400°F/Gas Mark 6.

2. Drain the cooked beans, transfer to a large bowl and mash well.

3. Wash and trim the spinach. Using a pan with a close fitting lid, cook the spinach, with no added water, for 5 minutes.

4. When cooked and cool enough to handle, chop the spinach finely and add the nutmeg and seasoning.

5. Stir the grated cheese and beaten egg into the mashed butterbeans.

6. Place a sheet of cling film on the working surface and spread the bean mixture over it in a rectangle measuring roughly 17.8cm x 27.9cm/7" x 11".

7. Cover the bean layer with the chopped spinach.

8. With the short end towards you, lift the edge of the cling film and gently roll the mixture into a cylinder, using the film to support the roll.

9. In a bowl, rub the oil into the breadcrumbs and stir in the sesame seeds and lemon rind.

10. Spread the breadcrumb mixture over the working surface and roll the butter bean roll over it until it is well covered.

11. Transfer the roll to a greased baking sheet, sprinkle with the lemon juice and bake for 15-20 minutes until the crust is crisp and golden.

TIME: Preparation takes 15 minutes. Cooking time, including the beans, 1 hour 30 minutes.

SERVING IDEA: Serve with a colourful mixed pepper salad.

169

BUTTER BEANS AND MUSHROOMS AU GRATIN

*You can vary the flavour of this dish by
substituting other kinds of beans.*

SERVES 4

175g/6oz butter beans, soaked overnight
   and cooked until soft
75g/3oz butter
1 tbsp lemon juice
Salt and pepper
225g/8oz mushrooms, separate the caps
   from the stalks
25g/1oz wholemeal breadcrumbs
25g/1oz grated cheese
Sauce
50g/2oz margarine
50g/2oz flour
280ml/½ pint milk

1. Mix the beans with 50g/2oz of the
butter, lemon juice and salt and pepper.

2. Place the mixture in the bottom of a pie
dish.

3. Melt the remaining butter in a pan and
fry the mushroom caps for about 5
minutes.

4. Make the sauce by melting the
margarine and stirring in the flour, cook
for about 2 minutes and then gradually
add the milk, stirring all the time until the
sauce thickens.

5. Chop the mushroom stalks and add to
the sauce, pour this over the beans.

6. Place the cooked mushroom caps,
underside upwards, on the top and
sprinkle with the breadcrumbs and
cheese.

7. Bake in a moderate oven, 190°C/375°F/
Gas Mark 5, for about 15 minutes until the
top is brown.

TIME: Preparation takes 15 minutes, cooking takes 35 minutes.

SERVING IDEA: Serve with lightly steamed green vegetables.

CHICKPEA STEW

*You can use tinned chickpeas for this recipe
but the dried ones have a much nicer flavour.*

SERVES 4

1 large onion, finely chopped
1 large carrot, diced
1 tbsp vegetable oil
2 large potatoes, peeled and diced
400g/1 x 14oz tin of tomatoes
1 tsp dried basil
Freshly ground black pepper
225g/8oz cooked chickpeas

1. Place the onion, carrot and oil in a pan and fry gently for about 5 minutes.

2. Add the potatoes, tomatoes and their juice, herbs and pepper.

3. Cover and simmer gently for about 30 minutes or until the potatoes are soft. Stir occasionally to make sure that the potatoes do not stick to the bottom of the pan.

4. Add the cooked chickpeas and warm through gently.

TIME: Preparation takes about 20 minutes, cooking takes 35-40 minutes.

SERVING IDEA: Serve with cooked green vegetables such as broccoli, peas or spring cabbage.

CHICKPEA BURGERS

These burgers are nice cold and are useful for a packed lunch or picnic.

SERVES 4

450g/1lb cooked chickpeas or 2 x 14oz cans chickpeas
1 onion, finely chopped
2 cloves garlic, crushed
2 medium potatoes, cooked and mashed
2 tbsps shoyu sauce (Japanese soy sauce)
1 dstsp lemon juice
Black pepper
Wholewheat flour
Oil for frying

1. Put the chickpeas into a large bowl and mash well.

2. Add the onion, garlic, potato, shoyu, lemon juice and pepper. Mix together well.

3. With floured hands, shape heaped tablespoonfuls of the mixture into small burgers.

4. Coat each burger with flour and refrigerate for 1 hour.

5. Heat a little oil and gently fry the burgers on each side until golden brown.

TIME: Preparation takes 15 minutes, cooking takes about 15 minutes.

SERVING IDEA: Serve with a hot, spicy tomato sauce.

FREEZING: Cook and freeze for up to 2 months.

CHESTNUT HOT-POT

This enticing hot-pot is perfect served with a lightly cooked green vegetable.

SERVES 4-6

675g/1½ lbs potatoes
3 medium onions
225g/8oz brown lentils
225g/8oz chestnuts
Salt and pepper
1 dstsp yeast extract
430ml/¾ pint warm water
50g/2oz margarine

1. Peel and slice the potatoes and onions thinly.

2. Put layers of potatoes, onions, lentils and chestnuts into a greased pie dish ending with a layer of potatoes. Season well between each layer.

3. Dissolve the yeast extract in the warm water and pour over.

4. Dot with margarine and cover.

5. Bake at 190°C/375°F/Gas Mark 4 for an hour or until the potatoes are tender.

6. Turn up the oven to 200°C/400°F/Gas Mark 6, remove the lid from the casserole and return to the oven for 10-15 minutes until the potatoes are crispy and golden brown.

TIME: Preparation takes 20 minutes, cooking takes 1 hour 15 minutes.

VARIATION: Dried chestnuts may be used but need to be soaked overnight in stock or water.

GREEN LENTILS WITH FRESH GINGER AND SPICES

There's certainly no lack of taste in this spicy lentil mix.

SERVES 4

175g/6oz green or Continental lentils
Water or stock to cover
25g/1oz margarine or 1 tbsp soya or
    sunflower oil
1 medium onion, peeled and finely
    chopped
2.5cm/1" piece fresh root ginger, peeled
    and grated or finely chopped
1 tsp garam masala
1 tsp cumin seeds
1 tsp coriander seeds, crushed
1 tsp green cardamom pods, seeds
    removed and crushed
1 medium carrot, scrubbed and diced
400g/1 x 14oz can peeled Italian tomatoes
50g/2oz mushrooms, cleaned and finely
    chopped
1 tbsp shoyu sauce (Japanese soy sauce)
1 tbsp cider vinegar
Salt and freshly ground black pepper to
    taste
Freshly chopped parsley or coriander to
    garnish

1. Pick over the lentils and wash thoroughly.

2. Place in a large, thick-bottomed saucepan, cover with water or stock and bring to the boil. Turn off the heat, cover and leave to begin to swell.

3. Meanwhile, heat the margarine or oil in a separate saucepan and gently fry the onion, ginger and spices until they are well combined, softening and giving off a tempting aroma.

4. Add to the lentils, bring to the boil and start to add the other vegetables, allowing several minutes between each addition, beginning with the carrot followed by the tomatoes and lastly the chopped mushrooms.

5. Stir frequently to prevent sticking and check on liquid quantity regularly, adding more water or stock as necessary.

6. Just before the end of the cooking time – approximately 25 minutes depending on the age of the lentils – add the shoyu, cider vinegar and salt and pepper.

7. Cook for a few more minutes and serve hot garnished with slices of lemon and freshly chopped parsley or coriander.

TIME: Preparation takes about 25 minutes, cooking takes about 45 minutes.

SERVING IDEA: Serve with boiled wholegrain rice or jacket potatoes and salad made from beansprouts, red and green peppers and grated daikon.

VARIATION: Black olives can replace the chopped parsley or coriander.

LENTIL SAVOURY

This dish is quick and easy to prepare and very nutritious.

SERVES 4

175g/6oz lentils
½ tsp basil
½ tsp mixed herbs
2 medium onions, chopped
50g/2oz margarine
2 tbsps tomato purée
400g/1 x 14oz tin tomatoes
1 tsp brown sugar
Salt and black pepper .
175g/6oz sliced Cheddar cheese
140ml/¼ pint soured cream

1. Soak the lentils overnight.

2. Add the herbs and simmer with the lentils in the cooking water until tender.

3. Sauté the onion in the fat until soft. Add the lentils and all the other ingredients apart from cheese and cream.

4. Simmer for 15 minutes until thickened and pour into a greased ovenproof dish.

5. Cover with the cheese and cream and grill or bake at 180°C/375°F/Gas Mark 4 until the cheese has melted.

TIME: Preparation takes 15 minutes, cooking takes 35-45 minutes.

COOK'S TIP: The soured cream can be served separately if desired.

SERVING IDEA: Serve hot with a mixed salad.

FREEZING: This lentil savoury will freeze well but do not cover it with cream and cheese until you are reheating it.

PIPER'S PIE

Accompany this attractive dish with carrots
and sweetcorn for the perfect family meal.

SERVES 4

450g/1lb potatoes, peeled and diced
175g/6oz mung beans
225g/8oz leeks
1 onion, sliced
½ tsp dill
2.5cm/1" fresh ginger, chopped or finely
   grated
1 tbsp concentrated apple juice
1 tsp miso

1. Boil the potatoes and mash with a little butter and seasoning.

2. In a separate pan, cover the mung beans with water and boil for 15-20 minutes until soft.

3. Meanwhile, generously butter an ovenproof casserole dish and put in the leeks, onion, dill, ginger and concentrated apple juice. Mix well.

4. Drain the beans, reserving the stock, and add to the casserole dish.

5. Dissolve the miso in a little of the bean stock and mix into the casserole which should be moist but not too wet.

6. Cover and cook at 200°C/400°F/Gas Mark 6 for 30-45 minutes, stirring a couple of times during the cooking and adding a little more bean stock if necessary.

7. Remove from the oven and cover with a layer of mashed potatoes.

8. Return to the oven to brown or brown under the grill.

TIME: Preparation takes 20 minutes, cooking takes 50-60 minutes.

VARIATION: A small tin of sweetcorn may be added to the pie before covering with the mashed potatoes.

RED BEAN STEW WITH CHILLI SAUCE

For convenience and speed tinned kidney beans can be used in this recipe.

SERVES 4

175g/6oz dried red kidney beans, soaked
  overnight
2 tbsps oil
1 large onion, chopped
1 clove garlic, crushed
400g/1 x 14oz tin tomatoes
½ tsp dried oregano
½ tsp dried basil
½ tsp shoyu sauce (Japanese soy sauce)
450g/1lb potatoes, peeled and diced
Salt and pepper

Chilli Sauce
25g/1oz butter or margarine
1 small clove garlic, crushed
1 small onion, grated
¾ tsp chilli powder
1 tbsp cider vinegar
75ml/3fl.oz bean stock or water
A little salt
1 tsp tomato purée
1 tbsp fresh coriander, finely chopped
1 tsp natural yogurt

1. Drain the beans, put into a large pan and cover with water. Boil vigorously for 10-15 minutes, turn down the heat and cook for about an hour until the beans are tender but still whole.

2. Heat the oil and fry the onion and garlic until soft.

3. Add the tomatoes, oregano, basil, shoyu and potatoes, cover and cook for 20 minutes until the potatoes are softened. Season to taste.

4. Drain the beans, reserving a little stock, and add to the onion and tomato mixture.

5. Cook gently for 5-10 minutes.

6. In a separate pan, melt the butter or margarine and cook the garlic and onion until soft.

7. Add the chilli powder and cook for a further 1-2 minutes.

8. Add the vinegar, stock, salt, tomato purée and coriander and cook for 5 minutes.

9. Remove from the heat and leave to cool slightly before stirring in the yogurt.

10. Serve with the sauce handed round separately.

TIME: Preparation takes 20 minutes. Cooking time, including the beans, 1 hour 35 minutes.

BEANY LASAGNE

*This tasty lasagne is suitable for a family
meal or entertaining friends.*

SERVES 4-6

8 strips wholewheat lasagne
1 large onion, peeled and finely chopped
1 tbsp vegetable oil
1-2 cloves garlic, crushed
225g/8oz cooked aduki beans
1 green pepper, de-seeded and chopped
400g/1 x 14oz can chopped tomatoes
1 tbsp tomato puree
1 tsp dried basil
1 tsp dried oregano
Shoyu sauce (Japanese soy sauce) or salt
Freshly ground black pepper

Sauce
25g/1oz margarine or butter
25g/1oz plain wholewheat flour
400ml/¾ pint dairy or soya milk
50g/2oz Cheddar cheese, grated (optional)
Salt
Freshly ground black pepper

1. Cook the lasagne in a large pan of boiling, salted water for 8-10 minutes until "al-dente". Drain well and drape over a cooling rack or the sides of a colander to cool and prevent sticking together.

2. Soften the onion in a little oil, sprinkling with a little salt to draw out the juice. Add the crushed garlic.

3. Add the beans, green pepper, chopped tomatoes, tomato puree and herbs.

4. Simmer for about 10 minutes or until the vegetables are tender.

5. Add shoyu sauce and season to taste.

6. To make the sauce, combine the margarine, flour and cold milk. Gradually bring to the boil, stirring continuously.

7. When thickened, allow to simmer, partly covered, for approximately 6 minutes.

8. Stir the cheese into the sauce and season.

9. Layer the lasagne in a greased dish in the following order: half the bean mix, half the pasta, rest of the bean mix, rest of the pasta, and top with the cheese sauce.

10. Bake at 180°C/350°F/Gas Mark 4 for 35 minutes or until golden brown and bubbling.

11. Serve in the dish in which it has been cooked.

TIME: Preparation takes 20 minutes, cooking takes about 60 minutes.

SERVING IDEA: Serve with a green salad.

COOK'S TIP: Pre-cooked lasagne can be used but it is important to add an extra amount of liquid to the dish in order to allow the pasta to absorb enough fluid while cooking.

187

SWEET BEAN CURRY

This excellent curry will freeze well for up to six weeks.

SERVES 4

175g/6oz red kidney beans, soaked
   overnight
25g/1oz butter or margarine
1 onion, sliced
1 apple, cored and chopped
175g/6oz mushrooms, sliced
1 tbsp curry powder
25g/1oz unbleached flour
570ml/1 pint bean stock or bean stock
   and water
Salt to taste
1 tbsp lemon juice
1 tbsp chutney
50g/2oz sultanas
50g/2oz coconut cream, grated or
   chopped

---

1. Drain the beans, put into a large pan and cover with cold water.

2. Bring to the boil and boil vigorously for 10-15 minutes, turn down the heat and boil for about an hour until the beans are tender but still whole.

3. Melt the butter or margarine and cook the onion until it is very brown.

4. Add the apple and mushrooms and cook for 2-3 minutes.

5. Add the curry powder and flour and cook for a couple of minutes, stirring all the time.

6. Gradually add the bean stock and stir until smooth.

7. Add the seasoning, lemon juice, chutney, sultanas and beans and cook for 10-15 minutes.

8. Just before serving add the coconut cream and stir until dissolved.

TIME: Preparation takes 25 minutes. Cooking time, including the beans, 1 hour 25 minutes.

SERVING IDEA: Serve with boiled brown rice and fried plantains – peel, cut into 1.2cm slices and fry in hot oil until golden brown. If unavailable you can use unripe green bananas. Garnish the curry with quarters of hard-boiled eggs.

MUESLI DE-LUXE

*Dried mixed fruit and organic muesli base can
be purchased at most wholefood stores and health
food shops or you can mix your own if preferred.*

MAKES 1.6KG/3½ lbs

450g/1lb dried mixed fruit (apples, pears,
  apricots, prunes)
450g/1lb organic muesli base
  (wheatflakes, porridge oats, rye flakes,
  pearl barley flakes, jumbo oat flakes)
50g/2oz wheatgerm
100g/4oz sunflower seeds
175g/6oz sultanas
175g/6oz lexia raisins
100g/4oz hazel nuts
100g/4oz brazil nuts, halved

1. Chop the dried mixed fruit into small pieces with a pair of kitchen scissors.

2. Place in a mixing bowl with all the other ingredients.

3. Mix well.

4. Store in an airtight container in a cool place.

TIME: Preparation takes 10 minutes.

SERVING IDEA: Serve for breakfast with milk, soya milk, yogurt or fruit juice and add fresh fruit whenever possible or simmer with milk, water or fruit juice for 5 minutes and eat hot. Muesli can be used as a base for biscuits and a topping for fruit crumbles.

VARIATION: The nuts can be varied according to taste and pumpkin seeds can be added.

COOKING FOR SPECIAL OCCASIONS

How often have you heard the phrase 'Oh, it's nothing, I just threw it together at the last minute'? There are, however, few people who can say this in all truth. For the most part, a good host or hostess will have spent half the time on the planning, one quarter of the time on the shopping and the remaining time on the actual cooking. From a dinner party to a picnic, a buffet to a barbecue, the secret is forward planning.

Make lists – they are invaluable, not only for shopping but for all the steps you must take to the big event. There is nothing more frustrating than to be serving the starter only to realise you haven't put the vegetables on to cook. When selecting your menu, try to choose dishes that can be prepared in advance. You owe it to yourself to enjoy the occasion and your guests will not expect you to be slaving away in the kitchen for long periods before and during the meal. If you are not very experienced, try to choose two courses that do not require last minute attention: a pre-prepared soup and a cold dessert will give plenty of time to concentrate on the main course.

This chapter features a variety of dishes that are appropriate for occasions such as dinner parties, intimate meals and Christmas dinner. So no matter what the event you will never again have to worry about what to serve your guests.

CELERY STUFFED WITH SMOKED TOFU PATÉ

These tasty nibbles are perfect for drinks parties, picnics and buffets.

50g/2oz hard vegetarian margarine
1 medium onion, chopped
1 clove garlic, chopped
½ bunch watercress, roughly chopped
75g/3oz smoked tofu
50g/2oz Cheddar cheese, grated
1 head celery
A little parpika

1. Melt the margarine and fry the onion and garlic until soft.

2. Add the watercress and stir for 15 seconds until it becomes limp.

3. Place in a liquidiser with the rest of the ingredients, excluding the celery and paprika.

4. Liquidise until smooth, pushing down with a wooden spoon if necessary.

5. Leave to cool.

6. Clean the celery, stuff with the paté and sprinkle with a little paprika.

7. Refrigerate for at least 2 hours before serving.

TIME: Preparation and cooking takes about 15 minutes.

VARIATION: Serve with twist of lemon and very thin brown bread and butter.

FREEZING: This paté freezes well for up to 6 weeks. Thaw at room temperature for 2 hours or overnight in the refrigerator.

BRAZILIAN AVOCADOS

*The perfect way to impress your dinner guests
right from the first course.*

SERVES 4

2 large ripe avocados
A little lemon juice
Salt and pepper
50g/2oz finely chopped Brazil nuts
50g/2oz Cheddar cheese, grated
2 tbsps Parmesan cheese
2 level tbsps freshly chopped parsley
2 firm ripe tomatoes, skinned and finely
  chopped
Wholemeal breadcrumbs
25g/1oz melted butter
A little paprika

1. Halve the avocados and carefully remove the flesh from the skins. Brush the inside of the skins with a little of the lemon juice.

2. Dice the avocado and put into a bowl with a sprinkling of lemon juice and the seasoning.

3. Add the nuts, cheeses, parsley and tomato.

4. Mix gently.

5. Spoon the filling into the avocado shells, sprinkle with the breadcrumbs and drizzle the butter over the top.

6. Dust with the paprika and bake at 200°C/400°F/Gas Mark 6 for 15 minutes.

TIME: Preparation takes about 10 minutes, cooking takes 15 minutes.

COOK'S TIP: Do not prepare this dish too far in advance as the avocado may discolour.

SERVING IDEA: Serve with a little salad as a starter or with baked potatoes, vegetables and tossed salad for a main course.

197

INDONESIAN-STYLE STUFFED PEPPERS

*For this adaptable recipe you can substitute
pine nuts or peanuts if you don't have cashews.*

SERVES 8 AS A STARTER

30ml/2 tbsps olive oil
1 medium onion, peeled and chopped
1 clove garlic, crushed
2 tsps turmeric
1 tsp crushed coriander seed
2 tbsps dessicated coconut
100g/4oz mushrooms, chopped
75g/3oz bulgar wheat
50g/2oz raisins
25g/1oz creamed coconut
280ml/½ pint stock or water
200g/7oz tomatoes, skinned and chopped
50g/2oz cashew nuts
4 small green peppers, de-seeded and cut
   in half lenthways
2 tsps lemon juice
Stock for cooking

1. Heat the oil and fry the onion and garlic until lightly browned.

2. Add the turmeric, coriander and dessicated coconut and cook gently for about 2 minutes.

3. Add the mushrooms and bulgar wheat and cook for a further 2 minutes.

4. Add the rest of the ingredients except the nuts, lemon juice, peppers, and cooking stock, and simmer gently for 15-20 minutes until the bulgar wheat is cooked.

5. Toast the cashew nuts in a dry frying pan until golden brown.

6. Blanch the peppers in boiling water for 3 minutes.

7. Mix the nuts and lemon juice with the rest of the ingredients and fill the peppers with the mixture.

8. Place the filled peppers on the bottom of a large casserole dish and pour stock around the peppers.

9. Cook 180°C/350°F/Gas Mark 4 for 20 minutes.

10. Drain peppers and place on a hot plate to serve.

TIME: Preparation takes 20 minutes, cooking takes 45 minutes.

FREEZING: The cooked peppers will freeze well for up to 3 months.

COURGETTE AND PINE NUT LASAGNE WITH AUBERGINE SAUCE

*This unusual lasagne will leave your guests guessing as
to the delicious combination of ingredients.*

SERVES 4

12 strips of wholewheat lasagne
75g/3oz pine nuts
25g/1oz butter
675g/1½lbs courgettes, trimmed and
  sliced
275g/10oz ricotta cheese
½ tsp grated nutmeg
1 tbsp olive oil
1 large aubergine, sliced
140ml/5fl.oz water
2 tsps shoyu sauce (Japanese soy sauce)
75g/3oz Cheddar cheese, grated

1. Place the lasagne in a large roasting tin and completely cover with boiling water. Leave for 10 minutes and then drain.

2. Place the pine nuts in a dry pan and roast gently for 2 minutes. Set aside.

3. Melt the butter and cook the courgettes with a little water until just tender.

4. Combine the courgettes, pine nuts and ricotta cheese.

5. Add the nutmeg and mix together thoroughly.

6. In a separate pan, heat the olive oil and sauté the aubergine for 4 minutes.

7. Add the water and shoyu and simmer, covered, until soft.

8. Liquidise, adding a little extra water if necessary.

9. Place 4 strips of lasagne on the bottom of a greased 3 pint rectangular dish and top with half the courgette mixture.

10. Place 4 more strips of lasagne over the courgettes and add half the aubergine sauce followed by the rest of the courgettes.

11. Cover with the remaining lasagne and the rest of the sauce.

12. Sprinkle the grated cheese over the top and bake for 40 minutes at 190°C/ 375°F/Gas Mark 5, until the cheese is golden brown.

TIME: Preparation takes about 30 minutes, cooking takes 50 minutes.

SERVING IDEA: Serve with a crunchy mixed salad and Creamy Jacket Potatoes – bake the potatoes until soft, remove the potato from the skins and mash with a little milk, butter and seasoning. Cool a little and place the mixture in a piping bag with a large nozzle. Pipe the mixture back into the potato shells and re-heat when required. Note: you will need to cook a couple of extra potatoes in order to have plenty of filling when they are mashed.

201

ASPARAGUS AND OLIVE QUICHE

*An interesting combination which gives
a new twist to a classic dish.*

MAKES 2 x 10" QUICHES

2 x 25.4cm/10" part baked pastry shells
6 eggs
570ml/1 pint single cream
1 tsp salt
Pinch of nutmeg
Salt and pepper
2 tbsps flour
2 cans green asparagus tips
175g/6oz green olives
2 onions, finely chopped and sautéed in a
    little butter until soft
75g/3oz Cheddar cheese, grated
2 tbsps Parmesan cheese
50g/2oz butter

1. Whisk the eggs with the cream.

2. Add the salt, nutmeg and seasoning.

3. Mix a little of the mixture with the flour until smooth, then add to the cream mixture.

4. Arrange the asparagus tips, olives and onion in the pastry shells and pour the cream mixture over the top.

5. Sprinkle with the grated Cheddar and Parmesan.

6. Dot with the butter and bake at 190°C/375°F/Gas Mark 5 for 25 minutes.

7. Turn down the oven to 180°C/350°F/Gas Mark 4 for a further 15 minutes until the quiches are golden.

TIME: Preparation takes 20 minutes, cooking takes 40 minutes.

FREEZING: The quiches may be frozen but a slightly better result is obtained if you freeze the pastry shells and add the filling just before baking.

Sri Lankan Rice

*Serve this rice hot as an accompaniment
to vegetable curries or dhal.*

SERVES 12

3 tbsps sunflower oil
1 medium onion, finely chopped
2 cloves garlic, crushed
1 heaped tsp ground cumin
1 heaped tsp ground coriander
1 heaped tsp paprika
1 level dstsp turmeric
¼ tsp chilli or cayenne pepper
150g/5oz Basmati rice, washed and
  drained
325ml/12fl.oz skimmed milk
1 tsp salt
Ground pepper to taste
225g/8oz mange tout, topped, tailed and
  cut in half
100g/4oz mushrooms, washed and sliced
1 small tin (5oz) sweetcorn, drained
50g/2oz sultanas, washed and soaked

1. Heat the oil in a large non-stick pan.

2. Gently fry the onion and garlic for 4-5 minutes.

3. Add the cumin, coriander, paprika, turmeric and chilli, and fry for a further 3-4 minutes – do not allow the mixture to burn.

4. Add the washed rice and mix well with the onions and spices for about 2 minutes.

5. Add the milk, salt and pepper, stir gently, bring to the boil, cover and simmer until all the liquid is absorbed and the rice is cooked – approximately 15-20 minutes.

6. Whilst the rice is cooking, steam the mange tout, mushrooms, sweetcorn and sultanas and fold into the rice.

8. Cool and turn out onto a serving dish.

TIME: Preparation takes 15 minutes, cooking takes 25-30 minutes.

SERVING IDEA: Sprinkle with 2 tbsps of freshly chopped coriander
or parsley if not available.

VARIATION: Other lightly steamed vegetables may be used according to season and
personal taste – broccoli florets, diced carrots, peas and sliced green peppers.

FESTIVE ROAST

*Never again will Christmas dinner be a
problem with this festive roast.*

SERVES 8

---

2 tbsps sunflower oil
2 medium onions, finely chopped
2 cloves garlic, crushed
450g/1lb finely ground cashew nuts
225g/8oz wholemeal breadcrumbs
2 beaten eggs or 4 tbsps soya flour mixed
    with a little water
1 heaped tsp mixed herbs
2 tsps Marmite or yeast extract
280ml/½ pint boiling water
Salt and pepper

---

1. Heat the oil and fry the onion and garlic
until soft.

2. Place the onions and garlic into a large
bowl. Add all the other ingredients and
mix well.

3. Butter or line a 2lb loaf tin and spoon
in the mixture.

4. Cover with a double thickness of foil
and cook in the oven at 180°C/350°F/Gas
Mark 4 for about 1 hour 20 minutes until
firm.

5. Allow to cool for about 10 minutes in
the tin before turning out.

TIME: Preparation takes about 15 minutes, cooking takes about 1 hour 20 minutes.

FREEZING: An excellent dish to freeze cooked or uncooked, although a slightly better
    result is obtained if frozen uncooked and thawed overnight in the refrigerator.

SERVING IDEA: Serve with a wine sauce or gravy and decorate with sprigs of holly.

TOFU SPINACH FLAN

*Serve this tasty flan with a medley of
lightly cooked fresh vegetables.*

SERVES 4

Pastry
1 tsp brown sugar
2-3 tbsps water
2 tsps oil
100g/4oz wholemeal flour
½ tsp baking powder
Pinch of salt
50g/2oz Granose or other hard
   margarine

Filling
225g/8oz spinach
275g/10oz tofu
Juice of 1 lemon
2 tbsps shoyu sauce (Japanese soy sauce)
4 tbsps sunflower oil
140ml/¼ pint soya milk
Salt according to taste
175g/6oz onions, chopped

1. Dissolve the sugar in the water and mix in the oil. Keep cool.

2. Mix the flour, baking powder and salt together in a large bowl.

3. Rub in the margarine until the mixture resembles fine breadcrumbs.

4. Add the fluid mixture and mix into the flour, using more water if necessary. The dough should be of a wettish consistency.

5. Leave to rest under the upturned bowl for half an hour.

6. Preheat the oven to 190°C/375°F/Gas Mark 5.

7. Roll out the dough to line an 18-20cm/ 7-8" flan dish.

8. Pinch the base all over and bake blind for 5-6 minutes.

9. Wash the spinach, drain and cook in it's own juices in a covered pan until soft – about 5-8 minutes.

10. Drain the spinach, chop and set aside.

11. Crumble the tofu into a blender, add the lemon juice, shoyu, 2 tbsps of the oil, the soya milk and salt. Blend to a thick creamy consistency. Adjust the seasoning if necessary.

12. Chop the onions and fry them in the remaining oil until lightly browned.

13. Add the spinach and fold in the tofu cream.

14. Pour the mixture into the prepared flan shell and bake in the middle of the oven for 30 minutes or until set.

15. Allow to cool for about 10 minutes before serving.

TIME: Preparation takes 25 minutes, cooking takes 45 minutes.

WATCHPOINT: The filling may develop 'cracks' on cooling but this is normal.

CHRISTMAS PUDDING

A traditional end to a traditional meal.

SERVES 8

100g/4oz wholewheat self-raising flour
225g/8oz vegetarian suet
Grated rind of one small lemon
½ tsp grated nutmeg
100g/4oz sultanas
225g/8oz raisins
100g/4oz candied peel
25g/1oz chopped almonds
2 eggs, beaten
2 tbsps clear honey
140ml/¼ pint milk

---

1. Combine the flour and suet, add the lemon rind, nutmeg, fruit, peel and almonds.

2. Beat the eggs and whisk together with the honey.

3. Add to the dry ingredients with the milk and mix well.

4. Put into a greased pudding basin and cover with greaseproof paper.

5. Place the pudding basin in a saucepan with about 1" of boiling water and steam for 3 hours, topping up with more water as required.

6. Cool and wrap well in a clean tea towel. Store for between 4-6 weeks.

7. On the day on which the pudding is to be eaten, steam for a further 1½ hours before serving.

TIME: Preparation takes 40 minutes. Cooking takes 3 hours plus 1½ hours on the day of serving.

SERVING IDEA: Serve with rum butter, a white sauce or coconut cream.

CHRISTMAS CAKE

*This rich, moist fruit cake is made without sugar
or eggs and is suitable for vegans.*

100ml/4fl.oz clear honey
175ml/6fl.oz safflower or sunflower oil
75g/3oz soya flour
280ml/½ pint water
15ml/1 tbsp rum or 1 tsp rum essence
Grated rind and juice of 1 orange
Grated rind and juice of 1 lemon
50g/2oz flaked almonds
75g/3oz dried figs, chopped
75g/3oz dried dates, chopped
50g/2oz dried apricots, chopped
225g/8oz wholewheat self-raising flour
Pinch salt
2 level tsps mixed spice
225g/8oz currants
225g/8oz sultanas
225g/8oz raisins

1. Assemble all the ingredients and preheat the oven to 170°C/325°F/Gas Mark 3. Line a 23cm/9" square cake tin with greaseproof paper.

2. Cream the honey and the oil together.

3. Mix the soya flour with the water and gradually add to the oil and honey mixture, beating well.

4. Beat in the rum and the grated rind and juice of the orange and lemon. Add the almonds, figs, dates and apricots.

5. Mix the flour with the salt and spice and mix together the currants, sultanas and raisins.

6. Stir half the flour and half the currant mixture into the soya cream, then stir in the remainder. Spoon into the prepared tin.

7. Cover with two or three layers of brown paper and bake for 3¼ to 3½ hours, or until a skewer inserted into the centre comes out clean.

8. Cool for 10 minutes and turn out onto a wire rack to cool.

9. Keep in an airtight tin.

TIME: Preparation takes about 40 minutes, cooking takes 3¼ to 3½ hours.

COOK'S TIP: This cake will keep well but is best made three to four weeks before cutting and stored, wrapped in foil or greaseproof paper, in an airtight tin.

SERVING IDEA: Leave plain or decorate with glazed fruits. Try serving the Yorkshire way with chunks of sharp vegetarian cheese.

VARIATION: Other dried fruits may be used instead of figs, dates and apricots but make sure that the overall measurements stay the same.

HAWAIIAN PINEAPPLE PANCAKES

*You can try many different fruits as a
filling for these delicious pancakes.*

MAKES 12 PANCAKES

175g/6oz flour
Pinch salt
2 small eggs, beaten
450ml/¾ pint milk
1 tsp vegetable oil
2 tbsps cold water
Oil for frying
Filling
1 x 450g/15oz can pineapple
225g/8oz cottage cheese
25-50g/1-2oz sugar, finely ground

1. Sift the flour and salt into a bowl.

2. Make a well in the centre and add the beaten eggs.

3. Gradually beat in half the milk and mix until smooth.

4. Stir in the rest of the milk, the oil and the cold water.

5. Refrigerate for at least 1 hour.

6. Place a little oil into a 15cm/6" frying pan and heat until just smoking, pour in 2 tbsps of the batter and swirl round until the bottom is evenly coated.

7. Cook until the underside is golden, flip over and repeat.

8. Cool on a wire rack.

9. Repeat this process until all the batter has been used.

10. The pancakes can be frozen at this stage and filled just before cooking by interleaving them with greaseproof paper and wrapping well with foil.

11. To make the filling, drain the pineapple and chop finely. Sieve the cottage cheese.

12. Mix the pineapple, cheese and sugar together. Divide equally between the pancakes and roll up around the filling.

13. Place in a single layer in an ovenproof dish. Cover with foil and freeze.

14. To serve, remove the wrapping and thaw at room temperature for 2-3 hours.

15. Reheat at 200°C/400°F/Gas mark 6 for 20 minutes until heated through.

TIME: Preparation takes 10 minutes, cooking takes about 40 minutes.

SERVING IDEA: Serve the pancakes garnished with hot pineapple rings.

CAROB SUNDAE

A delightful treat which provides the perfect end to any meal.

SERVES 4

Carob Dessert
225ml/8fl.oz milk or soya milk
1 tsp pure vanilla essence
1 tbsp sunflower oil
2 tbsps honey
¼ tsp sea salt
1 tbsp cornflour
¼ tsp Caro (coffee substitute)
1 tbsp carob powder

Vanilla Custard
1 tbsp cornmeal flour
100ml/4fl.oz milk or soya milk
1 tbsp honey
½ tsp pure vanilla essence

Filling
1 large banana, chopped
1 punnet of strawberries, hulled, washed
   and halved.

1. Blend all the carob dessert ingredients together in a saucepan and cook until thick, stirring continuously.

2. Leave to cool.

3. Mix the cornmeal flour with a little of the milk to make a smooth paste and add the honey and vanilla essence.

4. Heat the remaining milk until nearly boiling and pour over the cornmeal mixture, stirring until smooth.

5. Return to the pan and re-heat gently until thick, stirring constantly.

6. Leave to cool.

7. Add half the carob dessert to the chopped banana and mix together carefully.

8. Fill sundae glasses with layers of carob dessert, banana mixture, strawberries, vanilla custard and finally the plain carob dessert.

9. Chill before serving.

TIME: Preparation takes about 20 minutes, cooking takes 10 minutes.

SERVING IDEA: Serve decorated with dessicated coconut.

VARIATION: Raspberries can be used if strawberries are not available.

DESSERTS

'The proof of the pudding is in the eating'.

Henry Glapthorne
The Hollander 1635

By far and away the easiest and healthiest dessert to serve is fresh fruit. A bowl filled with a wide selection of fruits in season provides a wonderful centrepiece for any dessert table. There are many occasions, however, when delicious home-made desserts cannot be beaten. Ice cream is one of the most popular and is well worth making in large quantities when fresh fruit is cheap and plentiful. There are also lots of alternatives to rich cholesterol-laded creams such as yogurt, and fromage frais.

If you are making a pie or pastry dish, it is just as easy to make two, three or even four and freeze them for a later date. Should unexpected guests turn up, everyday puddings can be transformed by the addition of a few chopped nuts and whipped cream piped around the dish. Serve light desserts at the end of a filling main meal and more substantial puddings such as cheesecake after a light meal or salad. If you are short of time don't forget that a mixed cheese platter is a very acceptable finale and you'll find a wide range of vegetarian cheeses are available at many supermarkets as well as specialist cheese shops.

FLAMBÉED CARAMEL CUSTARDS

The perfect dinner party dessert.

SERVES 6

Caramel
50g/2oz soft brown sugar
2 tbsps water

Custards
3 eggs
100g/4oz finely ground soft brown sugar
420ml/¾ pint milk
A pinch mixed spice
Thinly pared rind of 1 orange
140ml/¼ pint Spanish brandy

1. Melt the sugar in the water over a moderate heat and boil until it begins to turn golden brown.

2. Remove from the heat and divide the mixture to coat the base of 6 ramekin dishes.

3. Whisk the eggs and add the sugar.

4. Put the milk into a saucepan with the spice and orange rind and heat until simmering.

5. Add to the eggs and mix well.

6. Pour equal quantities of custard in the ramekin dishes and place them in a deep roasting tin.

7. Pour in enough water to come up to about two thirds of the sides of the ramekin dishes.

8. Bake at 150°C/300°F/Gas Mark 2 for about 1 hour or until the custard has set.

9. Turn out onto a hot serving dish.

10. Heat the brandy in a ladle or small pan and ignite for about 10 seconds.

11. Pour over the custards and serve immediately.

TIME: Preparation takes 5 minutes, cooking takes about 1 hour.

WINDWARD FRUIT BASKET

An impressive dessert which is surprisingly easy to prepare.

SERVES 4-6

1 large ripe melon
2 apples
Juice of 1 lime
2 mangoes
2 kiwi fruit
450g/1lb strawberries
225g/½lb raspberries
3 tbsps honey
2 tbsps dark rum
50g/2oz butter

1. Cut the top off the melon and scoop out the seeds.

2. Using a melon baller, scoop out balls of melon and place in a large bowl.

3. Remove the core from the apples, dice and toss in the lime juice.

4. Peel and chop the mangoes.

5. Peel and slice the kiwi fruit.

6. Combine all the fruits.

7. Heat the honey, rum and butter gently until the butter has melted.

8. Cool, and pour over the fruits.

9. Toss gently and fill the melon shell with the fruit mixture.

10. Place on a serving dish and serve immediately.

TIME: Preparation takes 20 minutes, cooking takes 2 minutes.

SERVING IDEA: For a special occasion, make holes around the top of the melon with a skewer and decorated with fresh flowers.

VARIATION: Use any fresh fruits in season, pears, peaches etc.

Low-Fat Brown Bread Ice Cream

This ice-cream is ideal for slimmers.

SERVES 4

35g/1½ oz brown breadcrumbs
35g/1½ oz brown sugar
3 eggs, separated
280ml/½ pint Greek yogurt
1 dstsp honey (optional)

1. Place the breadcrumbs on a baking tray and cover with the sugar.

2. Place in a moderately hot oven 190°C/375°F/Gas Mark 5 for 20 minutes or until they begin to brown and caramelise. Stir once or twice so they brown evenly. Leave aside.

3. Beat the egg whites until stiff.

4. In a separate bowl, mix the egg yolks into the yogurt and then fold in the egg whites. Add the honey if desired and fold in evenly.

5. Add the cold breadcrumbs and mix well.

6. Place in the freezer and when setting point is reached stir the sides to prevent ice crystals forming.

7. Return to the freezer and leave until set.

TIME: Preparation takes 20 minutes, cooking and freezing takes 20 minutes plus 4-5 hours or overnight.

COOK'S TIP: Remove from the freezer and place in the refrigerator about ¾ of an hour before serving.

VARIATION: Maple syrup may be used in place of honey.

COFFEE AND RAISIN ICE CREAM

Perfect for a sweet finale or just as a treat

MAKES 20fl.oz/1 pint

280ml/½ pint full cream milk
100g/4oz sugar
6 tsps coffee granules or powder
1 tsp cocoa powder
1 egg yolk
1 tsp vanilla essence
280ml/½ pint whipping or double cream
50g/2oz raisins

1. Heat the milk and sugar until almost boiling.

2. Add the coffee and cocoa, stir and leave to cool.

3. Beat the egg yolk with the vanilla essence until frothy.

4. Whip the cream until stiff.

5. Pour the cream and coffee mixture into the egg mixture and stir well.

6. Add the raisins and stir again.

7. Freeze until firm (3-4 hours), stirring several times during freezing.

8. Defrost for 10-15 minutes before serving.

TIME: Preparation takes 3-4 hours, including freezing.

SERVING IDEA: Serve with home-made cookies.

VARIATION: For a chocolate flavour use light carob powder in place of coffee.

CASHEW ICE CREAM

*For special occasions, just add 1 tbsp of rum for
an even more impressive ice-cream.*

SERVES 4

1 large very ripe banana, peeled and
   roughly chopped
100g/4oz finely ground cashew nuts
140ml/¼ pint concentrated soya milk
½ tsp vanilla essence
2 tsps clear honey
2 rings unsweetened tinned pineapple,
   diced

1. Put all the ingredients, apart from the pineapple, into a blender and blend until smooth.

2. Add the pineapple and blend briefly.

3. Put the mixture in a shallow container and freeze for 2 hours.

TIME: Preparation takes 10 minutes, freezing takes 2 hours.

SERVING IDEA: Serve with strawberries or fresh fruit salad.

APRICOT FOOL

*Serve Apricot Fool in individual serving glasses, and
decorate with curls of carob chocolate.*

SERVES 4

225g/8oz dried apricots
1 ripe banana
1 small carton plain strained yogurt
1 egg
Few squares carob chocolate

1. Soak the apricots in water for at least 1 hour. Cook until soft then purée.

2. Mash the banana and add to the apricot purée.

3. Fold the yogurt into the fruit mixture.

4. Separate the egg and stir the yolk into fruit mixture.

5. Whisk the egg white until stiff then fold into the fruit mixture.

TIME: Preparation takes 10 minutes. Soaking and cooking takes about 2 hours 40 minutes.

VARIATION: Decorate with toasted almonds.

LEMON TART

A classic dessert, loved by all age groups.

SERVES 6-8

100g/4oz vegetable fat
225g/8oz wholemeal flour
50g/2oz brown sugar
2 egg yolks
A little water

Filling
4 egg yolks
4 egg whites beaten
100g/4oz brown sugar
50g/2oz ground almonds
100g/4oz unsalted butter, softened
140ml/5fl.oz double cream, slightly
  whipped
2 lemons, rind and juice

1. Rub the fat into the flour until the mixture resembles fine breadcrumbs.

2. Mix in the sugar, add the egg yolks and a little water to mix.

3. Roll out to line a fairly deep flan tin.

4. Prick the bottom and bake blind in the oven for about 8 minutes at 210°C/425°F/Gas Mark 7.

5. Meanwhile, mix the egg yolks with the sugar and add the ground almonds, butter, whipped cream and lemon juice.

6. Beat until smooth and creamy and fold in the lemon rind and beaten egg white.

7. Pour into the pastry case and bake 180°C/350°F/Gas Mark 4 until slightly risen and golden brown.

8. Eat cold.

TIME: Preparation takes 25 minutes, cooking takes 48 minutes.

SERVING IDEA: Serve decorated with piped whipped cream.

WATCHPOINT: Do not overbeat the filling as it is liable to overflow during cooking.

ORANGE AND KIWI CHEESECAKE

Lemon could be used in place of orange if a tangy cheesecake is required.

SERVES 6-8

100g/4oz margarine
225g/8oz crushed wholemeal digestive
  biscuits

Topping
450g/1lb Quark or skimmed milk soft
  cheese
100g/4oz margarine
1 medium egg, beaten
Fruit and zest of 1 orange, chopped
25g/1oz ground almonds
¼ tsp almond essence
2 kiwi fruit

1. Make the base by melting the margarine and adding to the biscuit crumbs. Mix well and press into a dish or flan base.

2. Chill thoroughly.

3. Mix together the cheese, margarine, egg, chopped orange and zest, almonds, almond essence and one kiwi fruit, peeled and chopped.

4. Put onto base and smooth over the top.

5. Peel and slice the other kiwi-fruit and decorate the top of the cheesecake.

6. Chill for 2 hours.

TIME: Preparation takes 15 minutes. Chilling takes 2 hours.

SERVING IDEA: For a special occasion decorate with the kiwi fruit and halved and seeded black grapes.

CORN CAKE

This corn cake will freeze well.

MAKES 1 CAKE

675ml/23fl.oz milk
50g/2oz brown sugar
½ tsp vanilla essence
160g/5½ oz fine cornmeal
2 eggs
Pinch of salt
50g/2oz margarine

---

1. Line and grease a 17cm/7" loose bottomed cake tin.

2. Put the milk, sugar and vanilla essence into a saucepan and bring to the boil.

3. Stir in the cornmeal quickly to avoid forming lumps.

4. Remove the pan from the heat and allow to cool slightly.

5. Separate the eggs.

6. Beat the egg whites with a pinch of salt until it forms soft peaks.

7. Add the margarine and egg yolks, one at a time, to the cornmeal and beat well.

8. Stir in one spoonful of the egg white and then fold in the remainder carefully with a metal spoon.

9. Pour the mixture into a prepared tin and bake at 180°C/350°F/Gas Mark 4 for about 40 minutes.

10. Turn the cake onto a wire rack to cool.

TIME: Preparation takes 15 minutes, cooking takes 40 minutes.

SERVING IDEA: Decorate the top with fresh fruit and sprinkle nuts on the sides.

VARIATION: Use on a biscuit base to form a 'non-cheese cheesecake'.

CAROB APPLE CAKE

This cake is nicer if kept in an airtight tin for a day before serving.

MAKES 1 CAKE

150g/5oz soft margarine
100g/4oz light muscavado sugar
1 large egg, beaten
175g/6oz fine wholemeal flour
60g/2½ oz light carob powder
1½ tsps baking powder
1 tbsp Amontillado sherry
400g/14oz Bramley cooking apples,
    peeled and sliced

Topping
75g/3oz carob chips
Knob of butter
A little water

1. Cream the margarine and sugar together until fluffy.

2. Add half of the beaten egg and continue creaming.

3. Add the rest of the egg together with the sieved flour, carob and baking powder and sherry.

4. Place half of the mixture into a round 17.8cm/8" cake tin and cover with the sliced apples.

5. Add the other half of the mixture and smooth the top.

6. Bake at 160°C/325°F/Gas Mark 3 for 1¼ hours or until firm to the touch.

7. Melt the carob chips with the butter and water and drizzle over the top of the cake.

TIME: Preparation takes 25 minutes, cooking takes 1¼ hours.

SERVING IDEA: Serve hot with yogurt as a pudding or cold for afternoon tea.

De-Luxe Bread and Butter Pudding

Serve just as it is, hot from the oven.

SERVES 4

4 thin slices wholemeal bread
A little butter
Raspberry jam
2 eggs, beaten
450ml/¾ pint milk, warmed
2 tbsps single cream
3 tbsps light muscovado sugar
1 tsp vanilla essence
2 tbsps sultanas, soaked for 1 hour
1 tbsp dates
Grated nutmeg

1. Remove the crusts from the bread.

2. Sandwich the bread with the butter and jam and cut into small triangles.

3. Beat the eggs until fluffy.

4. Add the warmed milk, cream, sugar and vanilla.

5. Stir together well, making sure that the sugar has dissolved.

6. Arrange the bread triangles in a lightly buttered ovenproof dish so that they overlap and stand up slightly.

7. Scatter the dried fruits over the top.

8. Pour the egg, cream and milk mixture into the dish, ensuring that the bread triangles are saturated.

9. Grate a little nutmeg over the pudding and bake at 200°C/400°F/Gas Mark 6 for about 30 minutes.

TIME: Preparation takes 10 minutes, cooking takes 30 minutes.

VARIATION: Other flavoured jams may be used instead of raspberry jam.

CRANBERRY AND APPLE CRUMBLE

Serve hot with natural yogurt or serve cold with ice cream.

SERVES 4

675g/1½ lb Bramley or other cooking
   apples
50g/2oz raw cane sugar
175g/6oz fresh cranberries

Crumble
75g/3oz butter or margarine
50g/2oz sunflower seeds
75g/3oz raw cane or demerara sugar
150g/5oz wholewheat flour
50g/2oz Jumbo oats
50g/2oz porridge oats

1. Peel, core and dice the apples.

2. Place in a saucepan with the sugar and about 2 tbsps water.

3. Cook gently until just beginning to soften.

4. Add the cranberries and cook for a further minute. Remove from the heat.

5. Melt the butter or margarine in a small saucepan, add the sunflower seeds and fry very gently for a few minutes.

6. Meanwhile, mix together the other ingredients in a large bowl, rubbing in the raw cane sugar with the fingers if lumpy.

7. Pour the butter and sunflower seeds into this mixture and combine to form a loose crumble.

8. Place the fruit in a large, shallow oven-proof dish and sprinkle the crumble topping over.

9. Cook at 180°C/350°F/Gas Mark 4 for about 40 minutes or until the top is golden and crisp.

TIME: Preparation takes about 20 minutes, cooking takes 50 minutes.

RICE MERINGUE

*For convenience the rice pudding and apple purée can be
made in advance and assembled just before cooking the meringue.*

SERVES 4

25g/1oz short grain pudding rice
570ml/1 pint milk
Few drops almond essence
5 tbsps soft brown sugar
A little butter
2 large dessert apples
2 tbsps raspberry jam
2 egg whites

1. Wash the rice and put into a shallow, buttered ovenproof dish.

2. Add the milk, almond essence and 2 tbsps of soft brown sugar.

3. Dot with a little butter and bake for 2½ -3 hours at 170°C/325°F/Gas Mark 3 stirring two or three times during cooking.

4. Remove from the oven.

5. Meanwhile, peel and core the apples. Slice finely and put into a saucepan with 1 tbsp of water.

6. Cook for 5-10 minutes until softened.

7. Add a little of the sugar to sweeten.

8. Cover the rice pudding with the raspberry jam.

9. Spread the apple purée over the top.

10. Grind the remaining sugar finely and beat the egg whites until they are very stiff.

11. Fold the sugar into the egg whites and cover the pudding with the meringue mixture.

12. With the back of a spoon, pull the meringue into 'peaks'.

13. Bake at 170°C/325°F/Gas Mark 3 for 20-30 minutes until heated through and golden on top.

14. Serve immediately.

TIME: Preparation takes 20 minutes, overall cooking takes about 3½ hours.

VARIATION: Make in individual ovenproof dishes.

PEAR AND APRICOT SLICE

Serve as a dessert or for afternoon tea topped with thick Greek yogurt.

MAKES 8 SLICES

2 pears, approximately 350g/12oz
100g/4oz dried apricots, soaked
1 tbsp clear honey
½ tbsp pear and apple spread
1 tbsp sunflower oil
1 egg
100g/4oz fine wholemeal flour
1 tsp baking powder
Flaked almonds to decorate

1. Peel and chop the pears into small pieces.

2. Chop the apricots finely.

3. Mix together the honey, pear and apple spread, and stir into the pears and apricots.

4. Add the oil and egg and mix well.

5. Mix together the flour and baking powder and fold into the pear and apricot mixture.

6. Spread the mixture in a greased 15cm x 20cm/6" x 8" tin.

7. Sprinkle with the flaked almonds.

8. Bake at 190°C/375°F/Gas Mark 5 for about 25 minutes or until risen and golden.

9. Leave to cool and cut into 8 fingers.

TIME: Preparation takes about 15 minutes, cooking takes 25 minutes.

COOK'S TIP: Pear and Apple Spread is sugar free and can be bought at most health food stores. It is an ideal substitute for jam.

BAKED RASPBERRY APPLES

A lovely combination which is perfectly complemented by cream or yogurt.

SERVES 6

2 tbsps concentrated apple juice
4 tbsps water
2 tbsps honey
1 tsp mixed spice
3 very large eating apples
225g/8oz raspberries

1. Put the concentrated apple juice, water, honey and mixed spice into a large bowl and mix together well.

2. Wash the apples and, with a sharp knife, make deep zig-zag cuts around each apple.

3. Take one half of the apple in each hand and twist gently until the two halves come apart.

4. Remove the core and immerse each apple in the apple juice mixture.

5. Place the apples in an ovenproof dish and bake at 200°C/400°F/Gas Mark 6 for 20-25 minutes until just soft.

6. Remove from the oven and top with the raspberries.

7. Pour the remaining apple juice mixture over the raspberries and return to the oven, 150°C/300°F/Gas Mark 2 for 10 minutes.

8. Serve at once.

TIME: Preparation takes 10 minutes, cooking takes 30-35 minutes.

SERVING IDEA: Serve topped with a spoonful of Greek yogurt or whipped cream.

COOK'S TIP: Frozen raspberries may be used but make sure they are well thawed out.

FRUIT SALAD TRIFLE

*As this recipe makes two halves of sponge and only
one is needed for the trifle, the other half
can be frozen for use on a subsequent occasion.*

SERVES 6

Carob Sponge
100g/4oz soft margarine
75g/3oz light muscovado sugar, finely
    ground
2 eggs (size 3)
75g/3oz wholemeal flour, sieved
25g/1oz carob powder
1½ tsps baking powder

Trifle
6 tbsps apple juice
Apricot or banana liquer (optional)
2 crisps eating apples, cored and chopped
    but not skinned
1 large banana, sliced
2 oranges, peeled, segmented and roughly
    chopped
Half a pineapple, diced
50g/2oz dates, chopped
50g/2oz hazelnuts
100g/4oz whipping cream
100g/4oz Greek yogurt
Few grapes, halved and de-seeded

1. Cream the margarine and sugar together
until pale and fluffy.

2. Add the eggs, one at a time, then
carefully fold in the sieved flour, carob
powder and baking powder.

3. Turn into two greased 17.8cm/7"
sponge or flan tins and bake for 20
minutes at 180°C/350°F/Gas Mark 4 until
golden brown and risen.

4. Leave to cool.

5. Place one of the carob sponges into a
trifle bowl and saturate with the apple
juice. Leave for half an hour.

6. Add the liquer, fruits and nuts, making
sure they are equally distributed through
the bowl.

7. Whip the cream until stiff and fold in
the yogurt.

8. Spread over the trifle.

9. With the back of a fork, trace from the
rim of the bowl into the centre, making a
lined effect.

10. Chill before serving.

TIME: Preparation takes 30 minutes, cooking takes 30 minutes.

SERVING IDEA: Serve decorated with orange segments, pineapple cubes and carob chips.

CARIBBEAN PINEAPPLE

An impressive and delicious dessert which is easy to prepare.

SERVES 6-8

1 large fresh pineapple
150ml/5fl.oz double cream
1 quantity of Coffee and Raisin Ice-Cream
   (see index)
125ml/4fl.oz rum
2 tbsps chopped mixed nuts

1. Slice the top off the pineapple at the shoulder and scoop out the flesh from the top.

2. Using a sharp knife, cut just within the skin around the circumference until the bottom is almost reached.

3. Insert the blade 2.5cm/1" up from the base and cut round in both directions just enough to loosen the flesh. Do not cut the bottom off.

4. Insert a fork into the top of the pineapple flesh and twist to remove. Drain the cask and place in the freezer.

5. Remove the hard core from the pineapple and chop the flesh into tiny pieces, drain well.

6. Whip the cream until stiff.

7. In a large bowl, break up the ice-cream with a wooden spoon.

8. Add the cream and nuts and mix well.

9. Sprinkle this mixture with half of the rum.

10. Fill the frozen pineapple cask with the mixture, replace the top and wrap carefully in foil.

11. Return to the deep freeze until required. Any extra mixture can be frozen in a small bowl.

12. To serve, transfer the pineapple to the refrigerator three quarter of an hour before required.

13. Place a serving dish in the oven to become very hot.

14. Put the pineapple on hot dish, pour the rest of the rum onto the dish and a little on the sides of the cask and light it.

15. Scoop out a portion of the ice-cream into individual serving dishes and spoon over a little burnt rum.

TIME: Preparation takes 20 minutes.

VARIATION: Use plain vanilla ice-cream and add 1 tablespoonful of instant coffee powder and 50g/2oz of raisins to the whipped cream.

BANANA FLAVOURED APRICOTS WITH COCONUT CREAM

Make this dessert a day ahead and serve straight from the fridge.

SERVES 4

175g/6oz dried apricots
280ml/½ pint banana flavoured soya milk
  plus 3 extra tbsps
140ml/¼ pint water
100g/4oz creamed coconut, grated
Juice of ½ lemon

1. Chop the apricots finely and put into a bowl.

2. Pour the ½ pint soya milk over the top.

3. Heat the water in a pan and stir in the creamed coconut until it has dissolved. Allow to cool a little.

4. Put the creamed coconut, lemon juice and 3 tbsps soya milk into a blender and blend until smooth.

5. Cover the apricots and cream with cling film and refrigerate overnight.

TIME: Preparation takes 10 minutes, cooking takes 2 minutes. Refrigerate overnight.

SERVING IDEA: Serve in individual serving dishes topped with spoonfuls of the coconut cream.

VARIATION: Plain soya milk may be used if banana flavoured soya milk is not available.

MINTED GRAPES

A refreshing dessert to serve after a large meal.

SERVES 4

275g/10oz green grapes
A little Creme de Menthe
125ml/4fl.oz soured cream
Soft brown sugar

1. Halve and de-seed the grapes.

2. Divide the grapes equally between four serving glasses.

3. Sprinkle with a little Creme de Menthe.

4. Top with soured cream.

5. Sprinkle a little brown sugar over and serve at once.

TIME: Preparation takes 10 minutes.

SERVING IDEA: Serve garnished with mint leaves.

VARIATION: Use sherry in place of the Creme de Menthe and yogurt instead of soured cream.

GINGER LOG

Omit the sherry from this dish and it becomes the perfect kid's treat.

SERVES 6

1 x 200g/7oz packet ginger biscuits
2fl.oz sherry
280ml/½ pint double cream
225g/8oz tin pineapple chunks
Chopped nuts, toasted

1. Unwrap the ginger biscuits and set aside any broken ones.

2. Pour a little sherry into a small bowl.

3. Whip the cream until thick and divide into two.

4. Drain the pineapple chunks, divide into two and chop one half very finely.

5. Mix into half of the cream.

6. Briefly, dip each biscuit into the sherry and, using the cream and pineapple mixture, sandwich the ginger biscuits together to make a log.

7. Lay the log on a serving dish and cover with the other half of the whipped cream spreading evenly with a knife.

8. Using a fork, 'lift' the cream into peaks.

9. Refrigerate for at least 2 hours.

10. Sprinkle with chopped nuts and decorate with the remaining pineapple chunks.

TIME: Preparation takes 10 minutes. Refrigeration takes 2 hours.

SERVING IDEA: Cut diagonally to serve.

VARIATION: Sprinkle with toasted coconut instead of nuts.

CHERRY BERRY MEDLEY

A pretty combination, perfect for summer lunches.

SERVES 6

450ml/¾ pint water
100g/4oz soft brown sugar
1 tsp mixed spice
225g/8oz redcurrants
450g/1lb strawberries
225g/8oz raspberries
225g/8oz cherries, stoned

1. Put the water, sugar and spice into a pan.

2. Boil for 5 minutes.

3. Put the redcurrants into a heatproof bowl and pour over the boiling liquid.

4. Leave to cool.

5. When cold, add the strawberries, raspberries and cherries.

6. Stir well and refrigerate for at least 2 hours before serving.

TIME: Preparation takes 10 minutes, cooking takes 5 minutes. Cooling and refrigeration takes 2 hours 15 minutes.

SERVING IDEA: Serve with ice-cream and French wafer biscuits.

VARIATION: If using blackberries in place of raspberries, treat in the same way as the redcurrants.

Booksale

19/25 Union Street
Glasgow, G1 3RB
Tel No: 0141 221 7247
VAT No: 555 2619 34

25% off Clip Frames
permanently

DATE: 19/11/1999 TIME: 13:48
TILL: 0089   NO: 08962569
CASHIER: heather

DESCRIPTION	£
Brother Cadfael Omni	4.99 C
VEGITERIAN COOK BOOK	2.99 C
Step by Step Vegetab	1.99 C

3 PC. TOTAL	£9.97

DELTA	£9.97

VAT C 0.00% (£9.97): £0.00

Only 9 WEEKS
TO CHRISTMAS

25% off CLIP Frames
Permanently

DATE: 19/11/1999 TIME: 13:48
TILL: 0089   NO: 0896256 9
CASHIER: Heather

Only 9 WEEKS
TO CHRISTMAS

KOMPOT (DRIED FRUIT SALAD)

*This classic Middle Eastern dish is simple
to prepare and can be made well in advance.*

SERVES 6-8

225g/8oz dried prunes
225g/8oz dried apricots
100g/4oz dried figs
100g/4oz raisins
100g/4oz blanched almonds
50g/2oz pine kernels
1 tsp cinnamon
¼ tsp nutmeg
100g/4oz brown sugar
1 tbsp culinary rose water
Juice and zest of 1 orange

1. Stone the prunes and chop roughly.

2. Halve the apricots and quarter the figs.

3. Place them in a large bowl and add the rest of the ingredients.

4. Cover with cold water.

5. Stir well and keep in a cool place for 1-2 days, stirring a couple of times each day.

6. Before serving, mix again well.

TIME: Preparation takes 15 minutes. Standing time 1-2 days.

SERVING IDEA: Place the mixture in a glass serving dish, and serve with yogurt or cream.

COOK'S TIP: After 24 hours the liquid in which the Kompot is soaking will become very thick and syrupy. If you need to add more liquid, add a little orange juice.

VARIATION: Other dried fruits may be used but keep to the same quantities. Pistachio nuts can take the place of blanched almonds.

BAKING

There is something very satisfying about producing batches of home-made bread, biscuits and cakes even if they get eaten before they have time to cool down!

Wholefood cookery means using wholemeal, wholewheat and wheatmeal flours. 100 per cent wholewheat or wholemeal flours are suitable for making breads, pastry and heavier cakes, whereas 80-90 per cent flours have a finer texture and are suitable for pastries, sponges, scones and biscuits.

Most recipes using white flour can be easily adapted by replacing all or some of it with brown flour. To begin with it may be best trying half white flour and half brown as this will give an idea of the different tastes and textures you can achieve by altering the flours. If you like this mix then continue to use it or adapt the ratio of white to brown to suit your taste.

Fats are important in baking and the only restriction for vegetarians are lard and suet, both of which are obtained from animals. Vegetarian suet is readily available and lard is easily replaced with vegetable fats. Here vegetarians have a health advantage, as most fats and oils of vegetable origin are unsaturated, whereas those derived from animals are of the more unhealthy, saturated, nature.

Mrs. Murphy's Wholewheat Brown Bread

This is a very moist bread which will last for days.

MAKES 2 LOAVES

750g/1½ lbs wholewheat flour
1 cup white flour
1 cup porridge oats
1 cup bran
1 cup pinhead oatmeal
½ cup wheatgerm
½ tsp baking soda
½ tsp sea salt
1.2 ltrs/2 pints milk
2 eggs, beaten

1. Heat the oven to 180°C/350°F/ Gas Mark 4.

2. Mix all the dry ingredients together.

3. Mix the eggs and milk and add to the dry ingredients.

4. Spoon into 2 greased 1lb loaf tins and bake in the centre of the oven for 1¼ to 1½ hours.

5. Turn out to cool on a wire rack.

TIME: Preparation takes about 20 minutes, cooking takes 1¼ to 1½ hours.

VARIATION: A handful of caraway seeds can be added to the mixture and some sprinkled on the top before baking.

QUICK HOME-MADE BREAD

*The molasses in this recipe gives the
bread an attractive appearance.*

MAKES 3 LOAVES

1150ml/2 pints hand hot water
1 tbsp molasses
1 tbsp sunflower oil
1.5kg/3.3lbs 100% wholemeal flour
2 sachets 'Allison's Easy-Bake Yeast'
3 tsps sea salt

---

1. Set the oven to 220°C/425°F/
Gas Mark 7.

2. Oil three 900g/2lbs bread tins and place
them on top of a warm cooker.

3. Fill two 570ml/1 pint jugs with the hand
hot water.

4. Add the molasses and oil to one of the
jugs, mix and set aside.

5. Place the flour, yeast and salt into a
large bowl and mix together thoroughly.

6. Gradually pour the water and molasses
mixture into the flour, mixing in with your
hands.

7. Add the other jug of water bit by bit
until the dough is wettish but not sticky.
You may have some water left over.

8. Knead the dough about a dozen times.

9. Divide the dough between the three
tins and press down firmly.

10. Leave to rise on the top of the cooker
for 5-10 minutes or until the dough has
risen near to the top of the tins.

11. Bake in the preheated oven for 35-40
minutes.

TIME: Preparation takes 20 minutes, cooking takes 35-40 minutes.

FREEZING: This bread will freeze well.

RICH STOLLEN BREAD

*This makes an attractive centre-piece on the tea table,
particularly around Christmas time.*

MAKES 1 LOAF

250g/9oz strong unbleached white flour
Pinch of salt
12g/½ oz fresh yeast
12g/½ oz light muscovado sugar
87ml/3½ fl.oz milk, warmed
1 egg, beaten

Filling
1 egg
150g/5oz ground almonds
50g/2oz poppy seeds, plus extra for
   decoration
50g/2oz raisins, soaked overnight
50g/2oz currants
50g/2oz cherries, chopped
50g/2oz light muscovado sugar, finely
   ground
25g/1oz dates, chopped
Juice of half a lemon
Almond essence

50g/2oz margarine
1 egg, beaten to glaze

1. Place the flour and salt in a bowl.

2. Cream the yeast and sugar together,
add the milk and stir well.

3. Add the beaten egg and leave for a few
minutes in a warm place.

4. Add the mixture to the flour and mix.
Knead well for 5 minutes.

5. Put into a clean bowl, cover and leave
to prove in a warm place for 40 minutes.

6. To make the filling, beat the egg,
reserving a little, and add all the other
filling ingredients. Mix well – the mixture
should be fairly moist.

7. To assemble, knock back the dough
and roll out to a rectangle 30.5cm x
20.3cm/12" x 8".

8. Dot 25g/1oz of the margarine over two
thirds of the dough from the top. Fold
over from the bottom to one third up,
then fold from top to bottom. Seal edges
and make one quarter turn.

9. Roll out to a rectangle shape again and
repeat with the remainder of the
margarine. Fold over as before but do not
roll out.

10. Place in the refrigerator for about half
an hour. Remove and roll out a rectangle
as before.

11. Cover with the filling, leaving a tiny
margin around the edges. Roll up width-
ways to make a fat sausage shape and
tuck in the ends. Brush with beaten egg.

12. Mark out in 2.5cm/1" slices, snipping
either side with scissors.

13. Cover with the remaining almond
flakes and poppy seeds and leave to
prove for a further 15 minutes.

14. Bake at 200°C/400°F/Gas Mark 6 for
30 minutes.

TIME: Preparation takes 25 minutes, cooking takes 30 minutes.
Proving takes 1 hour 40 minutes.

GRANARY ROLLS

*For a crisp crust brush the rolls with salted water
and sprinkle with cracked wheat before baking.*

MAKES 10

12oz granary flour
1 tsp salt
25g/1oz vegetable fat
12g/½ oz fresh yeast or 2 tsps dried yeast
1 tsp brown sugar
225ml/8fl.oz warm water

1. Place the granary flour and salt in a mixing bowl and leave in a warm place.

2. Melt the vegetable fat in a pan and leave to cool.

3. Cream the yeast and sugar together with three-quarters of the warm water.

4. Make a well in the middle of the flour and pour in the yeast mixture.

5. Add the melted fat and mix to a pliable dough, adding the remaining water as necessary.

6. Knead lightly for a minute or two.

7. Cover with a clean tea towel and leave in a warm place until the dough has doubled in size.

8. Knead again for 3-5 minutes and shape into 10 smooth rolls.

9. Place well apart on a floured baking tray, cover and leave in a warm place until the rolls have doubled in size.

10. Bake in the centre of a preheated oven, 220°C/425°F/Gas Mark 7 for 15-20 minutes or until the rolls sound hollow when tapped underneath.

11. Cool on a wire rack.

TIME: Preparation and proving takes 1 hour, cooking takes 15-20 minutes.

FREEZING: The rolls will freeze well for up to 1 month. Allow to thaw for 1 hour at room temperature before use.

Scofa Bread

*The ideal chunky bread to serve warm with
a ploughman's lunch or lunchtime salad meals.*

MAKES 1 LOAF

550g/1¼lbs self-raising wholemeal flour
225g/8oz bran
1 tsp salt
100g/4oz vegetable fat
Just under 570ml/1 pint water
1 tbsp vegetable oil

---

1. Put the flour, bran and salt into a mixing bowl.

2. Rub in the fat and mix the water and oil together.

3. Make a well in the centre of the flour and pour in the water and oil.

4. Mix in the flour, drawing it into the liquid mixture gradually from the sides, until a dough is formed.

5. Shape into a 17.8cm/7" round and place on a greased baking tray.

6. With a sharp knife cut to within 1.2cm/½" of the bottom making four sections.

7. Bake just above the centre of the oven, 200°C/400°F/Gas Mark 6 for about 1 hour or until nicely browned and 'hollow' sounding when tapped with the back of your fingers.

8. Remove from the oven and wrap in a clean tea towel to cool.

TIME: Preparation takes 10 minutes, cooking takes 1 hour.

COOK'S TIP: Eat within a couple of days.

Yogurt Scones

Serve with jam and cream.

MAKES 10 SCONES

50g/2oz vegetable margarine or butter
200g/8oz wholemeal self-raising flour
25g/1oz demerara sugar
50g/1oz raisins
Plain yogurt to mix

---

1. Rub the fat into the flour and sugar.

2. Add the raisins and mix well.

3. Add enough yogurt to mix to a fairly stiff dough.

4. Turn the mixture out onto a floured board and knead lightly. Make two large circles of dough or cut into 2" rounds.

5. Bake in hot oven for 15-17 minutes at 210°C/425°F/Gas Mark 7.

6. Remove and cool on a wire rack.

TIME: Preparation takes 10 minutes, cooking takes 15-17 minutes.

VARIATION: Use chopped dried apricots instead of raisins.

OATLET COOKIES

*A delicious mix of oats, seeds and syrup
makes these cookies extra special.*

MAKES 10 COOKIES

100g/4oz porridge oats
100g/4oz plain flour
85g/3oz sunflower seeds
25g/1oz sesame seeds
½ tsp mixed spice
100g/4oz margarine
1 tbsp brown sugar
1 tsp golden syrup or molasses
½ tsp bread soda
1 tbsp boiling water
200g/8oz carob drops

1. Mix the oats, flour, sunflower seeds, sesame seeds and spice together.

2. Melt the margarine, sugar and golden syrup or molasses over a gentle heat.

3. Add the bread soda and water to the syrup mixture and stir well.

4. Pour over dry ingredients and mix.

5. Place spoonfuls of the mixture well apart onto a greased baking tray and bake for 10 minutes at 190°C/375°F/Gas Mark 5.

6. Allow to cool on the tray.

7. Melt the carob drops in a bowl over hot water and place teaspoonsful of the melted carob on top of the cookies. Leave to set. Store in an airtight tin.

TIME: Preparation takes 15 minutes, cooking takes 10 minutes.

VARIATION: Ground ginger can be used in place of the mixed spice.

COOK'S TIP: A block of carob may be used in place of the carob drops.

SUSAN'S OATIES

For a super taste add finely chopped nuts or desiccated coconut to this recipe.

MAKES ABOUT 20 BISCUITS

100g/4oz margarine
100g/4oz brown sugar
1 tsp molasses
1 tsp boiling water
1 tsp bicarbonate of soda
100g/4oz wholemeal flour
100g/4oz oats
½ tsp baking powder

1. Melt the margarine, sugar and molasses in a saucepan.

2. Add the boiling water and bicarbonate of soda.

3. Remove from the heat and stir in the flour, oats and baking powder.

4. Place teaspoons of the mixture onto greased baking sheets.

5. Bake at 160°C/325°F/Gas Mark 3 for 20 minutes.

6. Remove from the baking sheets and place on a wire tray to cool.

TIME: Preparation takes 10 minutes, cooking takes 20 minutes.

COOK'S TIP: Use 50g/2oz oats and 50g/2oz desiccated coconut, but reduce the amount of sugar.

Amaretti-Almond Macaroons

Serve these delicious macaroons with tea or coffee.

MAKES ABOUT 24

225g/8oz whole almonds
225g/8oz unrefined granulated sugar
2 egg whites
1 tsp almond essence

1. Blanch the almonds by plunging them into boiling water for 2 minutes.

2. Skin the almonds and spread them over a baking sheet.

3. Dry off in a warm oven for a few minutes without browning.

4. Grind the granulated sugar until it resembles fine caster sugar.

5. Grind the almonds.

6. Sieve the sugar and almonds together.

7. In a large bowl, beat the egg whites until stiff but not dry.

8. Gradually fold in the almond and sugar mixture and add the almond essence.

9. Pipe or spoon the mixture onto a floured baking sheet, alternatively put the mixture on to sheets of rice paper.

10. Leave for as long as possible to rest before baking.

11. Preheat the oven to 180°C/350°F/Gas Mark 4.

12. Bake for 15-20 minutes until golden brown.

13. Transfer the cooked macaroons to a cooling rack.

TIME: Preparation takes 15 minutes, cooking takes 15-20 minutes.

COOK'S TIP: The macaroons should be crisp on the outside but have a rather chewy centre. Longer cooking will crisp them all the way through if desired.

SHORTBREAD BISCUITS

*Sandwich these biscuits together with raspberry
jam for children's birthday parties.*

MAKES ABOUT 18

150g/5oz unbleached white flour
37g/2½ oz light muscovado sugar, finely
   ground
100g/4oz soft margarine
½ tsp vanilla essence

1. Sieve the flour and sugar together and
rub in the margarine.

2. Add the vanilla essence and bind the
mixture together.

3. Form into small balls and place on a
baking tray a few inches apart.

4. With the back of a fork, press the balls
down making a criss-cross pattern.

5. Bake at 190°/375°F/Gas Mark 4 for
about 10-15 minutes until golden brown in
colour.

6. Cool and store in an airtight container.

TIME: Preparation takes 10 minutes, cooking takes 10-15 minutes.

VARIATIONS: Add a tablespoon of currants to make fruit biscuits.
Omit the vanilla essence and substitute almond essence to make almond biscuits.

CRUNCH

*If kept for a couple of days the Crunch will
become deliciously soft and sticky.*

MAKES 24 SQUARES

225g/8oz butter or margarine
2 tbsps golden syrup
5 cups oats
1 cup soft brown sugar

1. Put the butter and syrup into a pan and melt gently over a low heat.

2. Place the oats into a large mixing bowl and mix in the sugar.

3. Pour the melted butter and syrup over the oats and mix well with a wooden spoon.

4. Put the mixture into a 30.5cm x 20.3cm/ 12" x 8" Swiss roll tin and flatten well with the back of a spoon.

5. Bake in the centre of a 180°C/350°F/ Gas Mark 4 oven for 30-35 minutes until golden brown on top.

6. Remove from the oven, allow to cool for 2-3 minutes and mark into squares.

7. Leave until nearly cold before removing.

8. Store in an airtight tin.

TIME: Preparation takes 10 minutes, cooking takes 30-35 minutes.

VARIATION: Use 3 cups of oats and 2 cups of unsweetened muesli.

CAROB BISCUIT CAKE

A very rich and delicious cake.

MAKES 16 SQUARES

225g/8oz digestive biscuits
100g/4oz margarine or butter
1 tbsp brown sugar
3 level tbsps carob powder
2 tbsps golden syrup
1 cup sultanas
225g/8oz carob bar

1. Crush the biscuits with a rolling pin and place in a mixing bowl.

2. Put the margarine, sugar, carob powder and syrup into a pan and melt over a low heat, stirring all the time.

3. Add to the biscuit crumbs together with the sultanas.

4. Mix very thoroughly.

5. Press the mixture into a 20.3cm/8" square container.

6. Break the carob bar into a heatproof bowl and place over a pan of simmering water until melted.

7. Cover the cake with the melted carob and mark it with the back of a fork.

8. Refrigerate until cold.

9. Cut into squares and store in an airtight tin.

TIME: Preparation takes 20-25 minutes plus chilling time.

CARROT CAKE WITH APRICOT FILLING

This cake will freeze well for up to 2 months.

MAKES 1 CAKE

100g/4oz dried apricots
175g/6oz butter or margarine
175g/6oz brown sugar
2 eggs, separated
200g/7oz plain flour
1 tsp baking powder
225g/8oz carrots (150g/5oz weight when peeled and finely grated)
50g/2oz sultanas
75g/3oz walnuts, finely chopped
2 tsps grated lemon rind
½ tsp ground cinnamon

1. Soak the apricots in water overnight, drain and purée until smooth.

2. Grease a 17.8cm/7" round spring mould tin or cake tin.

3. Beat the butter and sugar together until pale and creamy.

4. Whisk the egg yolks and beat into the butter and sugar.

5. Sieve the flour and baking powder and fold into the mixture.

6. Add the rest of the ingredients except the egg whites.

7. Whisk the egg whites until they form soft peaks, and fold into the mixture.

8. Place the mixture in the greased tin and cook at 180°C/350°F/Gas Mark 4 for 45-50 minutes.

9. Cool in the tin for 10 minutes and then turn out onto a wire rack.

10. When completely cooled, slice in half and spoon the puréed apricot mixture onto the bottom half. Place the other half on top.

TIME: Preparation takes 20 minutes, cooking takes 45-50 minutes.

VARIATION: Replace the apricots with dried pears.

VIENNA CAKE

A versatile cake which can be adapted to suit any occasion.

SERVES 8-10

225g/8oz butter or margarine
225g/8oz Barbados sugar
3 eggs, separated
3 tbsps milk
75g/3oz carob powder
225g/8oz wholemeal flour
175g/6oz carob bar

1. Place the butter and sugar in a mixing bowl and cream together.

2. Add the egg yolks and beat well.

3. Mix in the milk.

4. Combine the carob powder with the flour and fold into the creamed mixture, which will be very stiff at this point.

5. Beat the egg whites until they are stiff and fold gently into the mixture.

6. Put everything into a lined 17.8cm/7" cake tin and bake at 150°C/300°F/Gas mark 2 for 1½ hours until a skewer inserted into the centre comes out clean.

7. Turn out onto a wire rack to cool.

8. When the cake is completely cold, melt the carob bar in a bowl over a pan of simmering water.

9. Cover the cake with the melted carob, smoothing it with a knife dipped in boiling water.

10. Leave to harden before storing in an airtight tin.

TIME: Preparation takes 20 minutes, cooking takes 1½ hours.

SERVING IDEA: Serve with thickly whipped cream.

VARIATION: Instead of covering with carob, make into a gateau by filling with cream and topping with fruits. For a rich tea-time cake add 100g/4oz of chopped walnuts to the basic mixture.

RICH FRUIT CAKE WITH GUINNESS

A deliciously moist fruit cake which is easy to make.

MAKES 1 CAKE

225g/8oz soft margarine
225g/8oz dark brown sugar
4 medium eggs
275g/10oz wholemeal flour
1 dstsp mixed spice
500g/1lb 2oz mixed dried fruit
10 tbsps Guinness

1. Cream the margarine and sugar together.

2. Beat in the eggs one at a time.

3. Gradually stir in the flour and mixed spice.

4. Mix in the dried fruit.

5. Add 4 tbsps Guinness to mix.

6. Place the mixture into a 17.8cm/7" loose-bottomed cake tin and make a deep well in the centre, this allows the finished cake to have a flat top.

7. Cook for 1 hour at 170°C/325°F/Gas Mark 3 and then turn down to 150°C/300°F/Gas Mark 2 for a further 1½ hours.

8. Allow the cake to cool in the tin.

9. Remove and turn upside down. Prick the base of the cake all over with a skewer and slowly pour over the remaining 6 tbsps of Guinness.

10. Store in a cool place for at least a week before eating.

TIME: Preparation takes about 15 minutes, cooking takes 2½ hours.

SERVING IDEA: Use for birthdays and special occasions or serve with chunks of tasty cheese.

VARIATION: This mixture can be cooked in two 1lb loaf tins, reduce the final cooking time and cook until a skewer inserted into the cake comes out clean.

BANANA LOAF

*Eat on its own as a cake or slice thinly and
butter to serve for elevenses or afternoon tea.*

MAKES 1 LOAF

1 tea cup of porridge oats
1 tea cup of sugar
1 tea cup of mixed fruit
1 tea cup of Granose banana soya milk
1 breakfast cup of self-raising flour
Pinch of nutmeg

1. Begin preparing the cake the day before it is to be cooked. Place all the ingredients except the self-raising flour and nutmeg into a large bowl and stir well.

2. Cover and put into the refrigerator overnight.

3. The following day, line or grease a 1lb loaf tin.

4. Mix the self-raising flour and the nutmeg gently into the mixture and put into the loaf tin.

5. Bake at 180°C/350°F/Gas Mark 4 for an hour or until a skewer inserted into the loaf comes out clean.

TIME: Preparation takes 10 minutes, cooking takes 1 hour.

VARIATIONS: ½ a tsp of mixed spice may be used in place of the nutmeg. Ordinary milk or plain soya milk can be used instead of banana soya milk.

SERVING IDEA: Eat on its own as a cake or slice thinly and butter to serve for elevenses or afternoon tea.

COOK'S TIP: The loaf becomes more moist if left in an airtight tin for a day or two before eating.

PRUNE AND WALNUT LOAF

If you do not have prunes, dates taste just as good.

MAKES 1 LOAF

350g/12oz prunes
175ml/6fl.oz water
350g/12oz fine wholemeal flour
2 tsps baking powder
50g/2oz brown sugar
1 tsp mixed spice
100g/4oz walnuts, chopped
4 tbsps sunflower oil
1 egg
Orange juice
Whole walnuts to decorate

1. Simmer the prunes in the water until soft.

2. Allow to cool, retain the cooking liquid, remove the stones and chop finely.

3. Mix the flour, baking powder, sugar, spice and walnuts together.

4. In a separate bowl mix the prunes, cooking liquid, oil and egg.

5. Fold together the flour mixture and the prune mixture, adding orange juice to give a soft consistency.

6. Put into a greased and lined 900g/2lb loaf tin.

7. Decorate with walnuts.

8. Bake at 170°C/325°F/Gas Mark 3 for 1¼ hours.

TIME: Preparation takes 15 minutes, cooking takes 1¼ hours.

FREEZING: Freeze after cooking for up to 2 months.

FRUIT CAKE

This cake freezes well.

MAKES 1 CAKE

350g/12oz plain wholemeal flour
1 tsp mixed spice
1½ tsps bicarbonate of soda
175g/6oz margarine
175g/6oz demerara sugar
175g/6oz currants
75g/3oz sultanas
½ pint soya milk
1 tbsp lemon juice

1. Sift the flour, spice and bicarbonate of soda together into a large bowl.

2. Rub in the fat until the mixture resembles fine breadcrumbs.

3. Add the sugar, currants and sultanas.

4. Mix the milk and lemon juice together and add to the dry ingredients.

5. Mix well to form a dropping consistency.

6. Leave the mixture overnight.

7. Turn into a prepared 25cm x 12cm/10" x 5" tin.

8. Bake in the centre of the oven at 160°C/325°F/Gas Mark 3 for 2 hours.

TIME: Preparation takes 20 minutes, cooking takes 2 hours.

VARIATION: Use sour milk in place of the milk/lemon mixture.

INDEX